For Widows Only!

For Widows Only!

Annie Estlund

iUniverse, Inc.
New York Lincoln Shanghai

For Widows Only!

iUniverse, Inc.

For information address:
iUniverse, Inc.
2021 Pine Lake Road, Suite 100
Lincoln, NE 68512
www.iuniverse.com

ISBN: 0-595-29110-4

Printed in the United States of America

This book is

dedicated to the men

we loved, buried,

and mourn,

and to

us

Contents

Part II   *What Now? Living in the Present*

Part III   What Next? Embarking on the Future

Acknowledgments

My wonderful friend, Pauli Shelden Jensen Friedmann, has contributed monumentally to this project, from its conception four decades ago, through its various versions in the past few years, to its fruition. Through those years she has shared with me her most intimate concerns, her highest ups, her lowest downs, and her hard-won wisdom on the subject of widowhood. Without Pauli I doubt I would have written this book.

I feel indebted to all the widows who shared their experiences with me. My sister Joan, Eunie, Karen, Anna, Sue, Virginia, Ginny, Toni, Dale, Agnes, June, Thelma, Bonnie, Dianna, Caroline, and Jeanne were especially generous with their time and contributions over the years. In addition, countless others took the time to fill out survey forms, write me about their experiences, participate in *For Widows Only!* workshops, and visit with me at meetings and parties. Some women are identified by their first names; some by location; others remain anonymous. I tried very hard to honor everyone's wishes, but for any slip-ups in this regard I apologize in advance. Each of you added immeasurably to this book's value, by helping me to include a wide array of situations and variations in the experience of widowhood.

Way at the top of my list of supporters are my three incredible children: Cindy, Dave and Eric, along with their two spouses and five awesome grandchildren. They went out of their way to help me feel loved and needed. I also have been blessed by continuing support from Bruce's siblings as well as my own brothers and sisters. Too many friends to mention, mostly in Wisconsin and Florida, gave new meaning to the word "friendship." I can never thank them enough. They were attentive, concerned and always available when I needed them.

Last, but not least, many thanks to my patient and perceptive editor, Eric Estlund. His tireless edits and thoughtful suggestions polished my manuscript and made it far more professional. That he is also one of my three dear children has made his contribution especially precious to me. Any typos, misspellings, improper grammar or unwise word choices are strictly my own fault. I inadvertently slipped some pages past him, and with a little help from my spastic computer, I lost more than a few of his corrections along the way.

Prologue: About This Book (You will want to start here.)

ALONG THE ROAD

I walked a mile with Pleasure
She chattered all the way,
But left me none the wiser
For all she had to say.

I walked a mile with Sorrow,
And ne'er a word said she,
But, oh, the things I learned from her
When Sorrow walked with me!

—Robert Browning Hamilton

Welcome, friend. Come walk along with us. I have invited several widows, from a wide range of ages, backgrounds and experiences, to join us on this journey through grief. We want to take your hand and help guide you through the worst of widowhood. Maybe we can help a little. Please let us try.

For Widows Only! is the book I searched for and couldn't find as a new widow. I was looking for "nuts and bolts" advice, but I also desperately needed comfort, encouragement and understanding from an ordinary widow (or many) like myself. Lynn Caine's *Widow* and *Being a Widow* were pretty good, especially for young mothers, and they remain available even though they are decades old. Aside from those, I was surprised to find how few widowhood books were on the market and that most of those were written either by celebrities or by professionals who had studied widowhood but not experienced it. Many books dealing with grief in general were written by men, and others treated grief as a one size fits all malady. Sometimes I found only a hole on the bookstore shelf where widowhood books should have been. For all the obvious need, there seemed surprisingly little help available.

This also is the book I had begun writing decades before my husband died. I became a sympathetic student of the mourning process as a young mother, when my best friend from Cottey College days, Pauli Shelden Jensen, lost her young husband to cancer when she was just 29. She was left with three babies, the youngest born the week her husband underwent surgery disclosing the extent of his malignancy. Having three little ones of my own at that time brought home the horror of her situation.

A few months after Will's death, Pauli and I began recording her thoughts and gathering piles of research material on the subject. We interviewed other widows, formulated an overall theme and outlined chapters. But due to the demands of our six young children and the many miles that stretched between us, that project withered on the vine. Papers languished, yellowed and became havens for silverfish in our garages, as the realities of daily life consumed us. Pauli put some of our ideas to use, forming a local support group for widows and widowers in Minneapolis. But following her move to Phoenix, our dream collapsed. Perhaps if we had had e-mail available then, we might have finished that book.

Over the years we often talked about how we really should resuscitate "the book." Then, several years ago, "it" happened to me; I was suddenly a widow. I was completely thrown. All I thought I knew about the subject seemed remote and unreal. I quickly learned that in widowhood, as in most life changes, experience is the best, but most painful, teacher. Only someone who has been through such intense grief can fully appreciate the pain. That stunning lesson is worthy of capital letters: IT'S ENTIRELY DIFFERENT BEING A NEW WIDOW THAN KNOWING ONE.

No woman can sufficiently prepare for the role of widow and thereby escape pain. In my research I ran into several counselors who had worked with individual widowed clients and as grief support group leaders prior to becoming widowed themselves. They were stunned to find themselves just as helplessly shaken as their clients. It's not that we don't hurt for our friends, clients, and loved ones when they suffer losses. We do; we even share some of their agony. However, once we experience the loss personally, we realize that the pain is magnified a hundred-fold and lasts far longer for widows themselves than for their sympathetic friends and counselors.

Six months after my husband died, I awoke with a start, sat up on the edge of my bed, sucked in a deep breath and decided it was time to write that long overdue book for widows. I had just awakened—again—with a jolt that left my pulse racing, my palms sweating and my heart pounding. I seemed intent on reliving the death scene, over and over again. Why? Would that never end? Was that natural? Would anything ever seem normal again? I had bushels of questions. What I needed was a book that would be like a sympathetic widowed friend to keep by my side, one that would try to anticipate and answer my questions and assure me that my scary feelings were natural, predictable and temporary. I needed the book that I had wanted to write years earlier. Pauli was delighted with my plan to take on this project; she agreed to listen, edit, advise and support my effort, from her home in California, which she indeed has.

From the first day of my nightmare, I had poured my pain into a journal as therapy. Those words had been meant "for my eyes only," but I soon realized many entries included the kind of intimate sharing I had been seeking from an author. I needed to know that she had suffered many of the fears and insecurities I felt, so it made sense that you readers might also need that. I include some of those entries, mostly at the beginnings of chapters. Because most widows cling to a few poignant or pithy sayings, keeping them stuck to the refrigerator or tucked into a wallet for when they need a "lifeline," I include many of my favorites here.

Some editors suggested I expand my target audience to include all men and women who suffer grief of any kind. While I am sympathetic to other people and their feelings, I know of several such books that try to be all things for all people. I read one, and scanned others, and found they were little help to me. In fact, I felt insulted to read that loss of a long-time pet or being jilted by a boyfriend caused the same kind of grief as loss of a spouse to death. The process of recovery may follow similar patterns, but the visceral experience isn't similar in any way. Although widowers, divorced spouses and others might glean helpful ideas from the following pages, from start to finish I speak directly to widows about widowhood. I wanted the kind of intimacy that comes from having shared very like experiences. Besides, it seems to me that with about 12 million widows in the US alone, and with hundreds of thousands of new ones each year, there certainly are enough of us to justify a book of our very own. *In fact, for this book I consider a "widow" any woman whose mate has died.* That includes "significant others" and those who are separated or divorced but still feel "connected." This definition expands the numbers substantially.

I knew I couldn't hope to understand every widow's situation. We widows share a major life experience, but we each arrived here by a different route. My hair stands on end at the thought of being widowed at 29 with three babies, as Pauli was. That could have happened to me, or worse. I had my youngest child when I was only 24. Could I possibly have survived alone? Pauli and others like her have made it, but not without ten trips through hell. Another friend, 82 years old, recently lost her husband. She has even more maturity to draw on than I had, but it would be a stretch for her to anticipate decades of world travel or entering the dating scene, as I could. Our individual situations dictate our reactions and our recovery.

In order to make *For Widows Only!* pertinent to as many readers as possible, I surveyed and/or interviewed more than 80 widows. They ranged in age from their 20s to their 90s, financial situations ranged from poverty to prosperity, and they had been widowed from one week to more than 50 years. Many were jolted into widowhood without warning or preparation, as I was; others had months or years of waiting. Some of these women sent pages and pages of memories and advice; others answered my questionnaire with *yes* or *no* answers.

Although each widow and each situation is different, in many ways we are the same. We walk the same road. I feel an immediate bond with almost every widow I meet. I know much of what she is feeling—or has felt—and she knows that I know. Our gazes connect and speak volumes without words. We widows are soul sisters, all 12 million of us.

On some days as a recent widow, I considered myself one of the luckier widows (or is "lucky widow" an oxymoron?) I had 35 good years of marriage and 55 years of maturity, and yet I was young enough to see—on good days—that life held some promise for me. On other days I floundered at the bottom of a pit and wondered how I would ever crawl out. Except for when I was mired in depression I tried to write, good days and bad. Please try to keep that in mind as you read. The path of grief is dynamic, with ups and downs, oases and pitfalls, twists and turns. I may have been "up" while writing what you are reading while you are "down," or vice versa. Writing about grieving while still grieving is tricky. Try to remember we each are changing and growing as we move through this book.

If you are still raw with grief and find certain chapters too forthright or cavalier, skip them. Concentrate on those parts that help you wherever you are in your recovery, and save others for another time. Be charitable with any whose views seem insensitive. We each are different from each other, and we each are different at different stages of recovery. You and your views will undoubtedly change, too, as you continue to recover.

I have always loved giving advice, and I do a bit of that, based primarily on my experience and that of widows with whom I talked. I have tried, though, not to set myself up as an authority on anything more than my own widowhood experience. This is not an academic or clinical treatise; I have no alphabet soup after my name, unless you count the BS for my Bachelor of Science degree in Journalism (which I finally attained when I was 45 years old). In this book I am just Annie Estlund, Widow. I can't promise to give you ten magic words of wisdom for skimming through the terrible stages of widowhood. I wish I could. I only can offer my reflections, those of other widows and some hints from experts, in the hope you'll sift through and find what you need at the moment. I have tried to share my silly mistakes along with my gratifying successes. Along the way I remind you of advice that has become "common knowledge," because remembering that advice helped me and it just might help you.

In my first days as a widow, a friend reminded me of the millions of women who had gone through the same trauma as mine or worse. I doubted it then; my grief felt unique. Before long, though, I realized it was true. I had just been initiated into a huge sisterhood of widows who truly understood. So have you. Maybe our experiences will help you see that we all walk pretty much the same path, AND we survive. Most of us thought we never would, but we have. Believe me, so will you.

PART I

What Happened? From Reeling to Healing

Dame Fortune is a fickle gipsy,
And always blind, and often tipsy,
Sometimes for years and years together,
She'll bless you with the sunniest weather,
Bestowing honor, pudding, pence,
You can't imagine why or whence;
Then in a moment—Presto, pass!—
Your joys are withered like the grass.

—"The Haunted Tree"
by Winthrop Mackworth Praed

1

The First Few Days:
Functioning in Shock

*We are healed of a suffering
only by experiencing it to the full.*

—Marcel Proust

Annie's Journal (11 hours)
*Dear Bruce: I am supposed to be napping. I tried pulling the blanket up to shut out
the light or, more honestly, to shut out reality, but…I know I need sleep. We…I…we
slept less than four hours and then…But how can I sleep when I'm so confused?
Should I have known how sick you were? Did you know? I still can't believe this. I
wish I could turn off everything: all noise, all thoughts, all memories of last night. Better yet, I'd like to start last night over at, say, 11 o'clock or so. This time you can bet
I'd change the ending!*

I will probably always remember Friday, July 5, 1991, as "the last day of the
best of my life." It wasn't a memorable day of blissful intimacy or magic
moments. It was a routine day of work at home, catching up after the holiday.
Bruce puttered about in the woods while I slaved at my laptop, finishing the first
of a series of articles about an upcoming House and Garden Walk. The day was
remarkably normal.

We went to bed after the 10 o'clock news and weather. Before falling asleep
we snuggled a bit and visited about our day, as had been our habit for 35 years. I
remember thinking Bruce smelled like a guy who had worked hard on a hot day,
even after his shower, and it smelled healthy to me. We talked about our day-old
grandson, a Fourth of July baby to carry on the Estlund name. We also talked
about the peculiar, flu-like symptoms—heartburn, diarrhea and chills—we had
both experienced two nights earlier. The symptoms had subsided by morning,

but we still wondered what had caused them. Very odd, we thought. On that note we went to sleep.

About 1:00 a.m. I woke up, suffering from heartburn and nausea again. As I got up to get something for it, Bruce asked what was wrong. He had been awake and felt sick too. We thought we might have contracted a strange virus or mild food poisoning, possibly even hepatitis, from a restaurant. Although I felt wretched, I worried about Bruce. He seemed sicker than I, and he seemed a little frightened. But he refused to let me call our doctor. We both took some "pink stuff," as we had before, and agreed to try to sleep a few hours. I vowed I would call the doctor first thing in the morning. Something definitely was not right.

Two hours later I woke up to what I initially thought was Bruce snoring. But it was an eerie, gurgling sound. I tried to rouse him, but he didn't respond. Then it hit me...he was dying! I remember wailing, "Oh, no! Oh, my God!" I grabbed the phone and punched in 9-1-1. While still trying to awaken Bruce, I gave the dispatcher details on his condition and directions to the house, begging them to hurry. She seemed so calm. Didn't she realize how urgent this was? I recall wishing we lived closer to town. It would take them at least fifteen minutes, no matter how fast they drove, to reach our home on the lake.

Desperate, I blew into his slack, wet mouth...one, two, three, four. Nothing. What was I forgetting? What was I doing wrong? He was cold, limp, heavy in a dead-weight way. His eyes were sightless. My mind raced back to CPR training sessions, and I tried talking myself through the process. But panic overruled my thoughts. Although it didn't seem to be working, I kept trying, along with emitting groans of denial and screaming urgent pleas for him not to die and leave me alone.

After a few minutes I grabbed the phone and tried to awaken the neighbors to come and help. No answer, so I rushed back to make another effort at CPR. I knew my friends were at home, so after a few minutes I redialed and let it ring for what seemed like forever, until it finally penetrated their visiting son's sleep. I screamed at him to come as fast as he could to help. It seemed to take another forever for Scott to run—barefoot—through the woods to our house.

When he took over I grabbed Manda, our stunned little fluff of a dog, and ran outside to flag down the arriving rescue squad. I sensed it already was too late, but I knew Scott was trying his damnedest. Now that the pros were arriving, I let myself think, "Maybe..."

We agonized quietly while the paramedics worked. I knew we had both done all we could. I had done what I had always imagined doing if such an unlikely thing ever happened. But my efforts were supposed to help. I paced the floor and pleaded urgently, "No, no. Please don't let him die."

I neither cried nor screamed when they told me he was gone. I just nodded and clung to Manda. I doubt I could have cried tears even if I had fallen apart at the seams, though. The trauma had sapped my body of its moisture. My throat was so dry I could hardly talk; my tongue felt like a dry chunk of wood. And I felt so cold. Water didn't begin to quench my thirst and a wool sweater didn't ease my chills.

I answered the paramedic's questions as best I could. But my answers didn't make sense. Nothing made sense. We both had symptoms. Was it a virulent illness? Would I be next? They didn't know, but they didn't leave. They also assured me that my efforts to save Bruce probably would have been adequate, if it hadn't already been too late when I woke up.

I felt confused, isolated. All this was the real thing—not a dress rehearsal. I couldn't believe it. I wanted to rewind the film that was ending so tragically. I wanted the control I have as a writer when things go awry…to edit, delete or rewrite until the story would fall back in line with my plans. I kept thinking…Wait a minute! Maybe this is a dream. This can't really be happening! But it was. Undaunted by my protests, time marched on. Bruce had died suddenly, of cardiac arrhythmia, without pain and without any history of heart disease. He was 60.

I was a widow. I was 55.

◆   ◆   ◆

I confess that I had wondered how I would "do" if something like this happened. Hadn't you? We had even talked about it. Bruce used to say I would handle it like a trooper, but he would be a "basket case" if I went first. I am not sure he was right about either of us. And I am not sure whether my occasional practice sessions helped me or not. I know I moved through the first hours, even days, like a well-programmed robot. It's natural for wives to wonder about widowhood, I think, especially as we move up in years. Most of us marry men older than ourselves and, as the media keep reminding us, men have shorter life expectancy by 6.8 years. Where the prospect of premature death looms for the middle-aged man, widowhood looms for the woman. Did you know the median age for new widows is just 56? I was almost 56. I sure didn't feel "median," or even average. I felt way too young to be a widow. By age 65 almost half of America's women are widows. No wonder we wonder.

But all the wondering in the world doesn't prepare us for the stunning psychological impact, especially if the death is sudden, without warning. It's amazing we can function at all.

Our reactions vary as much as we do. During those first days of shock, my mind was alternately useless and razor-sharp. I might not remember how to spell my own name one minute, but I spewed forth what seemed like "great truths" at other times. *Life goes on, but not forever.* This "flash of brilliance" struck me within hours of Bruce's death. I thought then that it was both original and profound. Now I realize it is simply stark truth. Another, of which I was particularly proud at the time, formed in reaction to my first time of being present at the time of death. What surprised me, even while trying desperately to revive my husband, was that death for him was not like "switching off a light," as I had often imagined. It took some time, and it involved stages of the body shutting down. I thought then: *Death may sometimes be beautiful, but dying isn't.* The sobering experience of witnessing sudden and unexpected death will likely influence the rest of my life. I hope it will mean a healthier respect for life. I know now that because life is so short and so fragile, we dare not waste much of it worrying about death. We must, instead, spend every minute of our precious life living.

Although it sounds painfully obvious now, another of my "profound thoughts" involved how permanent death is. Watch out, here comes another adage: *Life is short, but death is forever.* I later discovered that, among others, Moliere (1622-1673) had stolen this idea from me centuries before I was born. "We die only once, and for such a long time," he said. Perhaps it was my newspaper background that led me to synopsize life and death in these terse headline-like phrases. Other widows noted different reactions in their earliest hours of shock. Anna, a young mother of four girls when she was left alone, told me she stayed in bed and cried for a week, letting others tend her family and all the details. Diane, on the other hand, said she became the Master Sergeant, making lists and barking orders at family helpers.

Looking back, I see some of my first hours and days of widowhood with stark clarity, my memory recording every feeling, and nuance of this terrible time. Other times simply dissolved into a fuzzy blur. I'm surprised to recall how many things did get done, mostly by friends and relatives who came to help. I recall that a pattern of responsibility evolved quickly. It has always been the same, after other family deaths. Someone would answer the phone; someone would answer the door; someone would record each message, gift of food, flowers or thoughtfulness. They would then ask whether I cared to respond in person. I usually agreed to, although those first days I always cried when someone said something nice about Bruce or about old memories. I guess I needed to cry, and their kindness helped me do that.

Other widows I know chose solitude, isolating themselves from all the activity that springs up in the face of tragedy. A few widows mentioned that they were so cushioned by shock (or tranquilizers) they hardly realized the impact of what had happened. A few widows told me they became hysterical, completely unable to function. There is no right or wrong way. One just reacts automatically.

Unfortunately, or fortunately, when most of us would like to just crawl in a hole and hide, there are urgent tasks to be done…arrangements to be made, friends and relatives to be notified, housing to be found and readied for guests, myriad details to be decided. Priorities shift; major adjustments must be made to previous plans. I was in the midst of a feature writing assignment with a deadline looming. I was absolutely sure no one else could do that for me, but they had to. What had seemed a "must-do" yesterday became a "can't possibly do" today. Everything that had seemed essential faded to insignificance in the space of a single heartbeat, or rather, the lack of one.

—ADVICE AND CAUTIONS—

In spite of my conviction that most of you will read this book *after* those first horribly chaotic days, some of you may be clinging to it in search of help to get you through this confusion. Below I offer some generic advice, based on my 20/20 hindsight. Don't feel guilty if you didn't do all of these things. Please use whatever helps you and ignore the rest.

- *Grit your teeth; get through this period as graciously as possible.* Try to remember that the days are still only 24 hours long, although they may seem much longer. When you are in shock life may shift down to s-l-o-w m-o-t-i-o-n; clocks seem to nearly stop. The moment of death becomes your benchmark…this happened two hours after, that happened two weeks before, etc. At first you measure forward in minutes, each of which seems to stretch on forever. Then it becomes hours, and then days, but time references are skewed. Try to get these minutes, hours and days behind you with as little anxiety as possible. If you aren't feeling alert enough to take control, content yourself with going through the motions. Do what those around you say you "should" be doing, or do nothing until you get a grasp. Your mission is to emerge on the other side of this period whole, with enough energy to face your new life alone.

- *If your husband made a will, locate it and notify your lawyer.* He or she will set up a meeting to discuss provisions of the will and advise you about essential legal steps to take. If there was no will, get advice from a professional you trust as to whether you will need a lawyer. Many estates are so simple, with jointly held property, that they require minimal legal work.

- *As soon as possible, begin a journal of your thoughts and feelings.* You needn't show it to anyone, but recording your response helps bring your grief into focus, making it easier to deal with. Re-reading your earliest entries also will help you see your progress when you may think you're not making any. You may choose, as I did, to address some entries to your husband. I found that after 35 years of sharing problems, I often was incapable of handling this—the worst of all problems—alone. My private journal also became a safe place for me to vent anger.

- *Don't make funeral arrangements without a cool advisor present.* Horror tales abound of widows persuaded to spend next year's food budget on fancy services, caskets or burial markers by disreputable funeral directors. With my friend Debby by my side, I resisted sales pitches and made arrangements I knew were compatible with Bruce's wishes and with his life, much to the young funeral director's dismay. You can, too. If you don't already know what he wanted, consider his character, his social status, his reactions to other people's funerals, and—above all—your financial wherewithal.

- *Order enough death certificates.* What is enough? Depending on the complexity of your husband's estate, you will probably need between 10 and 50. Everyone's situation is different, but you will need one each time you apply to have property or an account changed to your name. It's safe to say you will need more than you think you will, so get extras now if you can. It can be much more expensive to order additional copies later. My daughter advised me to get 30. I ended up with a few left over because several were returned for reuse. In most states you can order these through your funeral home or your county health department.

- *Don't run away from your sadness.* It will follow you around, nip at your heels, haunt you and sock it to you later if you don't allow yourself to feel it fully at this time. But…

- *Don't worry if you don't cry right away.* Everyone's grief timetable is different, depending on the circumstances of the death, on your situation and on your personality. No one's is in a predictable straight line. Tears are therapeutic, though, so in a later chapter I'll offer suggestions for how to nudge them a bit if you feel you've gone too long without crying.

- *Talk openly about your feelings.* It will act as a catharsis for you and for those around you. *TIP:* To avoid future regrets, try to use discretion in revealing negative feelings or facts about your deceased spouse at this time. Although it's natural to have such feelings, others may not understand that. It serves no use to damage your loved one's image in the eyes of those who idolized him, especially when they are personally suffering from the loss. I wished I could go back and retrieve a few silly remarks I made, to share privately with a veteran widow someday. She would know they were only fleeting thoughts spun off a jumbled mind.

- *Accept help from those who offer it.* You are not your usual capable self, so lean on others. A couple of close friends guided me through the first hours and started notifying people. My widowed sister, Joan, arrived in four hours and ten minutes of her phone call (it's a four-hour trip). She knew how badly I would need her before my children could arrive. When my daughter Cindy, who happens to teach law, arrived that night, she became my guardian on business matters and my gentle caretaker for the first week. After she left, I clung to Debby, my next-door neighbor, and later in Florida to Nancy. I leaned hard on each one, but they absorbed my weight and kept me upright. If you see "leaning" as a sign of weakness, you're right. Face it, you are weak right now. You'll have to put on a brave front often enough, but don't wear yourself out by trying to be stoic when you need sympathy and understanding. Lean when you can; let yourself heal. With a broken leg you lean on crutches; with a broken heart you lean on friends. I worried that I was offending my friends by leaning on them, but I have since learned they actually appreciate the opportunity to help in any way they can. I have had the chance to let newer widows lean on me now, and I can say it is a great help to me to feel useful.

- *Be cautious about driving.* From my own and friends' experiences, I advise that, if your husband's death was a shock, *don't drive for at least a week*, longer if you can avoid it. Your mind has had a terrible jolt and it needs to recuperate before it can be trusted to react reliably. I witnessed this phenomenon years earlier with a widowed friend, but I was amazed when my (usually competent) self also became incapable of the careful attention driving requires. If you don't have the luxury of being chauffeured about, put a note on your steering wheel: *"Concentrate on driving—and nothing else—when driving!"*

There are close to 12 million widows in this country according to a 2000 US Census Bureau report, and it's estimated there are about 175,000 new ones each year. Nationwide, 45 percent of all older single women are reportedly widows. I think I speak for all of them when I say, "Eventually it gets better." It won't go away like chicken pox or measles, and you'll never forget your husband, but you will feel stronger and better able to cope as time passes.

Try to remember that, and when you need someone to listen, seek out another widow. She will understand. While I'm pontificating, let me suggest a few other words of encouragement:

- You *will* survive, though not without suffering.

- You *will* grow as a person, though not without an occasional slip into child-hood.

- You *will* make a life for yourself, though it won't be the same as before.

I am now certain of those things, from what I know of other widows and from signs I have seen along my own path. So, don't be afraid of the grief process ahead of you. Millions are going through it at the same time as you, and many millions have gone through it before and survived. As much as it hurts, and as unique as you feel, you are beginning a very natural process as old as humanity itself. As a carrot to lead you on, some widows say—after several years—that their new selves and new lives are *in some ways* better than their old ones. That may sound like blasphemy when you're hurting so, but it is meant to be HOPE when that's what you need the most.

—AT LEAST...—

For all my disbelief and horror those first dark hours, I had little glimpses of comfort and consolation. I think most widows do. The circumstances could have been worse, and/or I could have been less prepared to handle them. I guess we all grab at what straws are left us, what I call the "at leasts." "At least he knew no pain." "At least he didn't suffer a long, drawn-out cancer." "At least we had 35 years together." "At least we enjoyed five years of retirement." "At least he knew about his new grandson." "At least we were home, not driving to or from Florida," etc., etc. Your "at leasts" won't be the same, but I am sure you will have some. They help cushion the blow.

Much of what I have felt since that awful moment, when the paramedics confirmed what I already knew, probably isn't too different from what you felt, regardless of how your mate died. However, reactions to death of a spouse can vary widely because of individual circumstances. I had often heard it was easier with a lingering death, because you could talk about it, prepare and say good-byes. Several friends mentioned this to be so and said they had done much of their grieving before the death. However, several younger women at a widow's support group said they had no chance to discuss the subject openly because their men remained in denial, unable to face their approaching death.

My Bruce hated hospitals, and he was terrified of debilitating illness. He would have agonized and suffered every minute of a lengthy illness, resisting any efforts to prolong or ease his life. And, if he had been able to face his impending death, he probably would have insisted on total seclusion for the two of us, reject-ing efforts by friends or relatives to help in any way. As bad as your husband's death may have been for you, or the two of you, it can almost always have been worse. Realizing that helps.

As those early minutes reluctantly stretched into hours, and eventually days, it became obvious I had even more things for which I should be grateful. Everyone has positive life experiences or memories to cling to, even in the face of widow-hood. It can be hard to appreciate them when life seems so bleak, but at the risk of sounding trite, I strongly urge you to count your blessings when you can. It may help to do so in your journal so you can refer to them whenever you are blue.

—COUNTING BLESSINGS—

Following is a list of the blessings I remember clinging to. Maybe you can relate to a few, or they will trigger other ones for you.

- *The circumstances of Bruce's death were relatively straightforward.* Not all of you were so lucky, I know. His heart quit beating of its own accord. I keep won-dering how we could have anticipated it and/or prevented it, of course. But with heart disease claiming so many men—and women—in their middle years, little explanation is called for. No scandal, no violence, no undue media attention, for example. How much worse it must be for those of you who lost your husband to murder, suicide, AIDS, fire, crime, terrorism, war, drowning or drunk driving, for example. My heart goes out to you. But I urge you to think how it might have been worse. I often reminded myself of a Wisconsin woman whose entire family was wiped out in a car accident one Thanksgiving morning. Thinking of her helped put my situation into a more acceptable per-spective.

- *Bruce had arranged to provide for me and to make the economic adjustment relatively simple.* I am NOT the "rich widow" he so often joked about leaving, but with care (and a reasonable return on investments) I can keep the bills paid, maybe even travel a bit. How terrifying it must be to be left with debts, inadequate funds or totally tangled records. It's one more awful thing to worry about when you already feel like someone has cut your feet out from under you. Most widows agree that financial troubles make the grieving process much more difficult.

- *Throughout our marriage I handled finances, insurance, taxes and my own IRA investments.* We had discussed joint investments and company benefits, but Bruce was in charge of those; I had charge of the rest. Frankly, I often hated having all that responsibility, but I am thankful now that the financial nuts and bolts of running a household were second nature to me. I have several widowed friends who had never written a check before their husbands died. I would hate to have had to learn about our finances—from the bottom line up—as a stunned new widow.

- *Our marriage was better and more loving than most.* Our 35 year marriage wasn't as "perfect" as the inscriptions on our wedding bands promised, but no one's is. I wish we had worked even harder to make ours even better, of course. We all go through some remorse about that. But it must be especially hard to grieve if you know that you had been a thoughtless nag, or that your mate had always been hateful or abusive. I suppose the death could provide a measure of relief in such a case, but I'm a firm believer that good memories give you strength. So be thankful if you were happy.

- *Our three grown children are bright, happy, healthy and loving.* That is not to say we haven't had our difficulties. We have. But, generally, we are closer than most families, I think. Our three arrived to help as soon as they could, under incredibly difficult circumstances, and their support continues to be immeasurable. My grandchildren are wonderful and serve as constant reminders that life goes on. Little ones have a way of reaching into your heart and making you smile when you thought you never would again. Being without children, and/or grandchildren has to be harder. And, maybe even worse, are those widows whose children provide more conflict than sympathy, adding unneeded additional stress. If such is the case for you, you may need professional help to maintain your sanity at this time.

- *I read that my presence at the time of death will help me cope.* "They" say my presence, and especially my involvement in trying to save Bruce, will help me accept the reality of his death. It is somewhat easier, they say, than for the wife who learns remotely of her husband's death. Reality for her sinks in more slowly. I was there. It was real, no doubt about that. My presence meant recurring nightmares and a struggle getting to where I could picture Bruce ever having been alive and well. But, in the long run I should be better off, "they say."

- *We maintained a large network of friends over the years*—mostly couples, but some women alone and a few single men. I can't think of anything that helped me more those early days than my wonderful friends. I had heard widows say that, but I never fully understood the support friends could provide until mine had a chance to show me…starting at first light that morning. Some were called and came to help; the lingering rescue squad in our drive drew others. Gradually, others heard and came. Our children, our siblings and other relatives set in motion plans to come as soon as they could. And the telephone began to ring.

Thank heavens for "the bubble." The public phase of mourning was about to begin.

—THE INSULATING BUBBLE—

My sister Joan tried to help prepare me for this horrible time after she was widowed four years earlier. She said, "I hope this never happens to you, Ann. But if it does, I want you to know that you will be shielded from the worst of it. A protective bubble forms around you that allows you to function normally, make appropriate decisions, deal with people and do whatever you must do…all while you're completely numb with shock."

She was right, of course. I think almost every widow will agree, especially every one for whom the death was unexpected. The effects of shock take over within seconds and ease us through the worst time of our lives. One woman calls it "grief's blessed anesthesia." Another friend says she was "flying on automatic pilot." Karen said, after six years, "I'm amazed my early days of widowhood are so difficult to retrieve! I guess the 'cotton batting' of numbness was more profound than I had thought." Some women report that they feel God was carrying them or that their husbands were right beside them. A doctor or psychiatrist could probably explain it physiologically; others attribute it to a higher state of mind than we yet understand. I think most widows, whatever their predilection, can relate to my sister's "bubble" analogy.

From inside this bubble I could see what happened and hear what others said, and I could contribute, if necessary, but nothing really touched me. What continually amazes me, though, is that I made decisions—pretty good decisions—during those days when I was just pretending to be a real human being. Maybe some of my decisions will help you make some of yours, or help you to appreciate the ones you have already made.

—EARLY DECISIONS—

- *My first decision was to make no other major decisions for the first year or two.* I had two homes and three cars, more than I needed and more than my shrunken budget would sustain. During the first year I sold one of the cars, but I knew intuitively I could not make a sound decision about anything more important than that until life had had a chance to sort itself out. This is good advice for you, too.

- *I decided quickly, because one must, to follow through with Bruce's oft-repeated wishes to be cremated.* I also decided to scatter his ashes in Lake Michigan in front of our summer home. I had been uncomfortable with his plan; sometimes I thought I might disregard it when the time came. But when it came, I knew I could only live with myself if I respected his wishes. After the fact, I'm glad I did.

- *I decided to confront demons instead of letting them control me.* In spite of being known as an inveterate worrier, I decided to "conquer molehills." For example I slept, or tried to, the first night in our king-size bed, where I had just hours earlier tried to revive Bruce. I knew if I didn't do it while I was still numb with shock, I would have a hard time doing it at all. I also quickly decided to spend time alone after my daughter left, instead of looking for someone to stay with me. I had watched a widowed friend become so spooked that she was, five years later, unable to spend evenings alone in her own house. Having forced myself to face these issues early, they have never been problems for me. I have no "bugaboos," things I can't do, places I can't go. I figured life was going to be tough enough alone, without building obstacles for myself. On that issue I think I was right. Do TRY to keep from psyching yourself into a corner. Face what you can as soon as you can, while you are cushioned from reality.

- *I decided quickly to follow through with plans the two of us had made.* In three months I would drive to Florida and spend the cold months there. That astounded some of my Wisconsin friends. I felt comfortable with the plan then, and I know now it was right for me. That seemed far less traumatic than facing my first winter alone isolated in the north woods. Of course I knew I had lots of dependable friends in Florida, as well as Wisconsin, which was a big factor in my decision.

I think you will agree that my brain functioned fairly well on the intellectual level. On the emotional level I was in a state of suspended animation. A young widow-friend, Diane, described this stage another way. "It was like a gatekeeper had closed the gate on the feeling part of my brain and permitted just tidbits of reality to seep in, one tiny electric jolt at a time, to prevent circuit overload. How you can be alert and yet so numb, I don't know." What an amazing service one's mind provides (or one's spirit, or God). You remain alert enough to register the events for future reference, to make necessary arrangements and decisions, but you don't feel the most intense suffering until you can better handle it.

Looking back I think, "Wow! How did I do so much while I was functioning like a robot?"

So many details had to be taken care of in those first awful days. We all have to provide needed information for death notices, for example. For me, that included notifying the local newspaper and three newspapers where Bruce had worked in our early years. Because he had a high profile job in Milwaukee (AVP of Public Relations for Wisconsin Bell, later a part of Ameritech) the daily papers there wanted information for obituaries.

Along with photos and biographical information, it was necessary to provide suggestions for memorial gifts. I requested that instead of flowers, people send money to a heart research fund, so people would know the cause of death, or to the Milwaukee Press Club Foundation, because Bruce and the Press Club were important to each other for years. Even now I can't think how I could improve on that decision. Other widows have started scholarship funds, purchased major artwork for their community or suggested contributions to their favorite fund raising project. It takes some thought, but you can let others help if the answer isn't readily apparent to you.

Decisions have to be made about a memorial service, so that information can be included in death notices. I quickly decided to have the service in Sturgeon Bay, near our Door County home, although we had lived there only two years full-time. That decision was testimony to the warm welcome our neighbors and the community gave us when we moved there. Or maybe it was just easier for me.

How did I manage to do whatever needed to be done, while feeling like a dead stick? The same way anyone else does, I imagine. I plowed along like a windup doll and I delegated. I had always disliked asking others to help me, but for a new widow it is not only necessary, it also is *de rigueur*. Pauli suggests new widows try to be prepared to delegate. "Make a list," she said, "or have someone else make one, of things that need to be done. As people ask what they can do, tell them.

They really want to help, but they don't know how without some guidance." That is wonderful advice.

I could never thank my friends, neighbors and relatives enough for all they did for me, especially in those awful early morning hours. I think, especially, of nearby neighbors and friends who rushed to my aid; of longtime friends of his, mine and ours, who themselves felt crushed by Bruce's death, but who had to comfort me and make dreadful telephone calls to others. I cringed as calls went out to our children, to my sisters and brothers, to Bruce's siblings and his mother, to key people in key groups so they could spread the word. I ached for the callers when they did it. I still ache for them and hope I never have to do that for someone I know and love. But if asked, I will, because I know it has to be done, and unless the widow (or whomever) is Superwoman, she cannot do it. At least I know I couldn't.

It surprised me that although the bubble protected me from some of the pain of my own grief, temporarily, it didn't protect me from knowing what other people were going through. Many people admired and loved Bruce. I don't imagine one ever knows how many do until death intervenes. In addition to family, there were those he had worked with, volunteered with, fought social battles with, gone to school with, served on committees and boards with, socialized with, told jokes with, car pooled with, golfed or played tennis with and on and on and on. I hurt to the core every time I knew someone else was being told. I kept wondering, irrationally, if we could keep it a secret so these people could avoid the agony of knowing. For days I felt I was carrying all his friends and relatives around in my arms, trying to ease the pain for them. Maybe my preoccupation with their grief was a way of postponing my own.

All of them, even Bruce's mother and siblings, seemed more worried about me than about themselves. They were probably right to be. The reality had not set in for me, although I thought it had.

—THE MEMORIAL SERVICE—

Several members of a widow's support group I visited bemoaned the fact they hadn't been thinking clearly enough to plan a truly meaningful service. Most of those widows were younger than I, in their 30s and 40s. I can only guess that their shock was even worse than mine, suddenly faced with the terror of life alone before they had even contemplated such an event. They also may have dependent children, which greatly magnifies a widow's problems. In addition, their personal experience with other funerals or services may have been limited. Having attended many, I fell into a known routine. My children were old enough and functioning well enough to contribute ideas for the memorial service. I helped some, incorporating ideas that had taken root in my brain over the years. By middle age, most of us have unconsciously registered positive and negative aspects of services we have attended.

Because Bruce wasn't a churchgoer and because his body was cremated, I chose to have the service at a local funeral home/mortuary. I asked a liberal-minded minister with a philosophical bent to preside. He agreed and spent a few hours getting to know Bruce through the kids and me. We liked and connected with him immediately, making the prospect of the service somewhat less formidable. I kept thinking how Bruce would have enjoyed this brilliant and witty man. I think he might have pulled Bruce back to churchgoing as he did me. You, of course, must make your choices based on your situation. I would hope you are free to make choices that will add to your comfort at this time and later.

We chose to keep the service as personal as possible. Our three children each participated in a way we thought helped capture some of their father's more memorable qualities. Bruce excelled in art, writing and singing, having sung professionally as a young man. He was featured vocalist on several RCA Victor recordings with Lawrence Ducho's Midwest polka band, touring with them and with "Hot Lips" Henry Busse (a nationally known big band) before his stint in Korea. Our son David, a rare talent on the guitar, spent hours transposing "Believe Me Beloved One," from one of the recordings into a classical guitar piece. It was beautiful, touching and appropriate.

Eric, our amateur thespian, read a simple but tender poem Bruce had written twenty-some years earlier about his four valentines, the three kids and me. If there was a dry eye left after that, it gave way when daughter Cindy, who has a lovely voice, tearfully sang one of our family's favorite sing-along songs, "Michael, Row the Boat Ashore." The service you design will serve its purpose best if you can make it meaningful and personal for all those who cared for your spouse.

I am confident I picked the four men Bruce would have chosen to deliver testimonies, or eulogies. Each spoke eloquently of Bruce's uncompromising sense of ethics, his compassion, his many talents, his wit and humor. I wish I had thought to record their kind words. You might wish to do that, if it isn't too late. It's quite wonderful to see your husband through the eyes of others who had known him well.

Although several widows told me they were in such a fog they can't remember the service at all, I remember ours keenly and I probably will forever. I remember saying later, "If a memorial service ever could be beautiful, this one was...at least for me." On the chance that you will remember it, try to make it one you can remember warmly instead of with regrets. Keep in mind that it should be appropriate for the deceased, as well. Pauli and Will were very involved in their church and choir, so she planned a church funeral with choir music. My sister's husband played blues and jazz with a small combo, so she asked the rest of the combo to play a New Orleans-style funeral dirge at the church funeral. It was gripping. I will never forget it.

Many question the value of a service at all. I thought I agreed with those who say funerals, especially traditional ones with open caskets, are "barbaric." But just a generation or two ago, the family dressed the deceased for viewing and prepared him or her for burial. They laid the body out in the front parlor and family members—young and old—sat with it in an around-the-clock vigil, or death watch.

In comparison, today's funereal traditions are impersonal in most cultures, relegating the widow and family to roles as hosts for those who come to pay their respects. Perhaps grief would be better served if we still had more intimate involvement with the deceased.

But, having said all that, I must admit our service for Bruce did wonders for me and helped enormously as I struggled through the next months. The outpouring of love and respect for our family and for Bruce was my life preserver. I retrieved the memory of it often and clung tightly to it whenever I felt swamped by my future alone.

I used to be aghast at funerals where widows seemed downright jolly, enjoying seeing old friends and long-lost relatives. I swore I would never be like that! I would "grieve properly" when, or if, my time came. Well, let me tell you, there are lots of lonely nights for that. It was absolutely wonderful seeing every person who came to the service and to the house later. They gave me the support they knew I badly needed. Thank heavens I didn't spend the day hiding from them, "grieving properly." That was my take on the subject, of course. You may react differently, which is your right. Do what feels best for you.

Ginny noted that offers of help flow freely at a funeral, but often fall through. She said, "Many teachers, scout leaders and neighbor men told me they would take my boys camping, fishing, etc., when their father died. I believe they meant it at the time. But once people see you are 'still standing,' their good intentions fade away." I'm sure that's very true. I know I didn't need anywhere nearly as much help as she did, having two young boys at home. But it's good to keep in mind that we all tend to make promises we fail to keep, especially when we're emotionally stricken. I know I have, so I tried to remember that. I tried to appreciate their thoughts and intentions without dwelling on whether they would fulfill their promises. It was fairly easy for me that day, because for all my tears I was anesthetized by their outpouring of love, like I was on "happy gas."

Our service was followed by a magnificent meal, coordinated and provided by the world's greatest neighbors and sisters of my new PEO chapter (a women's philanthropic educational organization). It is especially good to provide such a meal if several people have come from out of town for the service. It has the added benefit of giving you more time to visit, reminisce and play with memories. With luck you will have contributions of food and volunteers to serve it. Otherwise have it catered, if you can, or keep it nice and simple. The food is secondary to the cathartic interaction between family and friends.

One of my neighbors volunteered to stay at the house during the service, to discourage thieves. It's hard to imagine, but it's true that professional criminals often note wedding and funeral times, expecting the house to be empty and "available" to them. It's something to consider if you have not yet had your service.

If the service is over, but you regret that it wasn't more personal, consider doing something meaningful with the family the next time you're together. Plant a tree in his name, each saying a piece about him first. Decide together to donate money to some worthy cause in his honor. Create a scholarship or "chair" in his honor if your pockets are deep, or pool small contributions to make one gift in his name to his favorite theater group, concert series or charity. Such a project helps provide more satisfying closure. Such a memorial, especially if it is visible and touchable, can provide a link to the deceased. Just don't go overboard and focus all your energies on a shrine, in an effort to keep him "alive." You can honor his life, but you shouldn't cling to it.

I will continue to pass on lots of advice, some good, maybe some not as good. Keep in mind, above all else: *Each widow should do whatever feels right for her, not what some self-righteous author tells her to do.* If you choose (or chose) to wrap yourself in a cocoon of privacy, and you feel right about that, so be it. It is, or was, right for you. You will have no regrets. If you choose to take umbrage at thoughtless words, or closet yourself away from all visitors, or postpone the memorial service for months, that may be your best way of dealing with such harsh reality.

—CALLS, CARDS AND VISITS—

I learned a lot in a hurry about the value of traditions surrounding death. For example, I learned about the value of sympathy cards. I could kick myself for the ones I haven't sent in years past because I didn't think they would help anything, or I didn't know what to say. Cards do help, don't they? Whether from business associates I had never met or friends I had lost track of, I still treasure every one. It didn't matter to me what anyone wrote; it seemed like exactly the right thing to say. I have reread them since, knowing I was in a fog when they arrived. Even now I wonder that hundreds of people could think of something so appropriate to say at a time like that.

Not every widow feels that way. Some become offended by almost anything people say to them in person or on paper, because their emotions are so ragged and raw. Often it's a case of feeling life has been unfair to you and no one can possibly understand. It's true that some people can say the stupidest, most offensive things in their efforts to cheer the bereaved. A young widow who has just lost her hopes and dreams, and maybe her only means of support, doesn't want to hear that she is "still young and will find someone else." Most widows don't want to hear "It's for the best," or "You'll get over it." If some made such remarks to you, try to understand. Remember how you felt in such stressful situations, not knowing what to say but wanting to cheer up the bereaved. Stewing over such things saps your much-needed energy.

I hate to think of the times I did not call or visit someone who was mourning the loss of a loved one for fear I would "disturb them." Truthfully, I know now I was just taking the easy way out. Realizing that gave me more reason to appreciate those who made the effort on my behalf. Even though sometimes it seemed the phone or doorbell would never stop ringing, I felt buoyed by knowing people cared. I usually spoke with them in person. I think I hugged everyone who came within hugging distance those first weeks. I know I needed hugging and I think they did too. Sometimes I couldn't find the strength to respond personally, but I still felt hugged by their call. I certainly never felt offended or that they had "disturbed" me. I will try to remember that in the future and contact bereaved friends.

This might be a good place to back off and tell you that all was not as sweet and smooth as I make it sound. From reading so far, you might think I was a paragon, always upbeat and grateful for small favors those first days. I recall a few times I did think, "This isn't as bad as I thought it would be," or "I'm really doing great!" Then, without warning, *Wham! Bam!* I felt like hell, in spite of my protective bubble. There were times I thought I would never laugh again, or ever be strong enough to survive grieving, or have enough money to feed myself, or have any friends left because most of ours were couples. My head ached, my eyes burned, my heart felt leaden. My stomach rebelled at the thought of food; sleep became a rare commodity and the future loomed like a massive pit full of insurmountable problems. If I occasionally sound upbeat, it's because I am most able to write on the better days. Whenever I could I tried to appreciate what I had left. But I do remember plenty of the other times.

The only consistency those early days was my inconsistency. My feelings were unpredictable and as exaggerated as a roller coaster ride. A friend, Claudia, warned me: "Expect the unexpected." I didn't know what she meant, but I do now. Your appetite may fluctuate, from having none to feeling ravenous and pigging out. You may have insomnia for a week, and then fall asleep hourly during the day. You may become exhausted by the simplest tasks and be bursting with energy when it's time to rest. You may go weeks unable to cry and then break into tears while studying a soup label in the grocery store.

On the other hand, you may have none of the expected symptoms, keeping all the pain suppressed…for awhile.

Dear Bruce (6 days): As I lie in the dark, my mind darts erratically from scenes of you dying beside me, of shell-shocked friends at the service, of the uneventful evening before, alone, together, before… "You are doing wonderfully well," people keep saying. But I know what I am doing is doing wonderfully well at acting like I am doing wonderfully well.

2

The Beginnings of Grief: A Necessary but Painful Process

Music I heard with you was more than music,
and bread that I broke with you was more than bread.
Now that I am without you, all is desolate;
All that was once so beautiful is dead.

—Conrad Aiken

Annie's Journal (7 days)
I am being weaned into aloneness. First there were the crowds. Then most left, but there was still some of Bruce's family, my family and our family. One by one they are all leaving now. Then there will be just me...alone. This little log cottage is going to seem very big, very empty and much too quiet, by Monday night. I wonder how I'll handle that?

Most widows initially are granted some respite from isolation, as I was, with family and friends hovering around. I knew that, although I would rather have crawled in a hole, I had better make the most of that time. I forced myself to stay involved and visit. I recall thinking that if Bruce were there, he'd have us laughing. He'd have called it "a time to sit around telling lies." I spent a lot of my time behind the kitchen counter, tucked safely inside my bubble, watching and listening.

I remembered other family gatherings over the years, when our kids were young, family dinners, weddings, and other funerals. Most were good times—poker games, charades, family cookouts and holiday dinners, sing-alongs, good-natured teasing, practical jokes, and late-night discussions when we solved world problems. But there were serious times and unhappy times, too: personality clashes, tragedies to share and endure, individual hard times when we tried to help and support each other. Through thick and thin we were family—pretty typical family. How can a widow survive her trauma without being warmly embraced by family?

—FAMILY SUPPORT—

I assumed every widow's extended family surrounded her, as they did me and as they did every other widow I knew personally. Unfortunately, that isn't always the case. Some people have no family; some become estranged from theirs; others are kept apart by illness, great distance or other circumstances. And some family members shun death—or keep it at arms length—even when they should be comforting a relative. I know some people for whom the threat of participating in the mourning process is so great they become physically ill, and hence unable to participate.

So it's possible you faced much of this early period without traditional family support. And there is always the chance you chose to be alone. Either way, I can only send a long-distance hug and tell you to hang in there. Without the buffer of close relatives and friends, and without conversation and activity to provide some semblance of normality, you may face the grating pain of reality sooner and it probably will be much harder.

If you are alone but wish you weren't, don't be afraid to call someone and tell them. Most people will feel flattered that you would think enough of them to call. Anyone, but especially another widow, will understand if you need company at this time.

Within a few days of the service, everyone had left my house except our children. That was a blessed time for me. The kids and I sorted out our feelings, unearthed old memories and leveled with each other in a way only possible when emotions are unsettled. Bruce had been terrific, just like everyone said, but he wasn't a saint. No one is. We knew that, and we needed to talk about it after the euphoric days following the service. We needed to flesh out the picture of this man we loved, to make the loss more real, perhaps. For me, the "children" became adults that week. High time at that, as they were in their early to mid-thirties. Grown children can be a widow's strongest allies. Young children can be helpful, too, in different ways…from asking tough questions in wide-eyed innocence, to keeping you busy even when you don't feel like it. I hope you'll remember to tell them how much you appreciate their support. I hope I did, too.

Each of the children selected a few of Bruce's things to take with them, at my urging. But I came close to making a mistake common to new widows; I felt generous to a fault and wanted to give away more than was sensible. WARNING: Keep a cool head, especially when giving away items you may need later, items of value or gifts of money from which you may later need the income.

On the last day our little family would be together, the minister helped us through a simple ceremony on the rocky shore that would complete Bruce's wishes. He helped us see this as an ending of the life we had known with Bruce and a beginning of a new life, where he would live in our memories. My son Dave and I rowed out into Lake Michigan where I performed one of the hardest tasks I've ever done. I committed Bruce's ashes to their final resting-place, to become part of the eternal sea. I said, "Good-bye, my love," and we rowed back to shore where my three children and I hugged and wept quietly.

None of you will have had exactly that experience, but each of you probably faced the finality of the death with some moment of ceremony. Perhaps it was when the casket closed, when they lowered it into the ground, when you accepted the folded American flag or when you received the urn of ashes. Whatever the ritual, it probably meant "this is real," "he'll never be back." That's not to say that subconsciously you won't continue to deny the fact; you probably will. Denial is an integral part of grief. But your conscious mind will know that life with your husband is over. For me, it happened that Friday noon on Lake Michigan in our canoe.

After a quiet lunch it was time for the boys to leave. Ric was overdue for a play rehearsal in southern Wisconsin and Dave was eager to get back to Meg, two-year-old Corey and week-old Marshall in California. In a month the family would move to Rhode Island, where Dave would begin teaching philosophy at Brown University. He had brought a charming hospital photo of the newborn with Meg and him, taken two days before Marshall's Grandpa Bruce had died. The picture was a center of interest on my refrigerator all week, as we reflected on this new life and the promise of the future. Isn't it interesting how often a new baby enters a family about the same time someone else dies?

—THE OUTSIDE WORLD—

Although my daughter Cindy was anxious to rejoin Sam and their two kids, who had left earlier in the week, she agreed to stay another few days to help me begin converting "our joint interests" into "my interests." She and I dashed into town, trying unsuccessfully to avoid seeing people I knew. We went through the contents of the safe deposit box, signed papers and had them notarized, ordered thank-you notes from the printer. We did a few other errands, bought some provisions and headed back out to the lake. That little excursion broke the ice for me…my first trip out into the larger world, with Cindy at my side. It would be a while, I knew, before I'd feel up to doing it alone, but it would be eased somewhat by that trip. During those first days I learned I wasn't as "Gloria-Steinem-independent" as everyone seemed to think I was.

Cindy also made initial contacts with the company benefits office about death benefits, life insurance proceeds, survivor's health insurance, etc. and she set up appointments for me to meet with my investment counselors and my Wisconsin lawyer. I'm not sure how I'd have managed to get those balls rolling alone. Allow someone, or ask someone, to help so the process doesn't overwhelm you. Most people appreciate the chance to help a new widow. It's best to get personal recommendations if you don't have a financial counselor and/or lawyer. There are unscrupulous people in all professions, and "the helpless widow" is especially vulnerable to such people.

Cindy and I spent a quiet evening visiting, then I headed for bed early, desperately needing a good night of sleep. At 4:10 a.m. I woke up with a start, just as I had every night for a week. I suppose we all do that, at least those of us who witnessed an unexpected death. I had to relive the terror and rehash every minute detail of that first half-hour or so as if my mind were a VCR stuck on "play." It was terrifying; I became afraid to doze off. Was it only seven days ago, I thought? It seemed more like seven weeks; the days moved along like cold molasses. I pondered all kinds of questions. Would I ever feel comfortable sleeping in this bed where he died? Would I ever sleep through the night again? Would I ever think clearly again? Would I ever feel normal again? Would I ever laugh freely again? Would I survive those first nights of being totally alone? The answer to these questions, I know now, is "yes." Although "normality" appears in spurts at first, those spurts become longer and more frequent as the months go by. I can see that one day they will run together and I will resemble a regular person again.

It was about then, after one week, that I adopted a philosophical attitude that has helped me a great deal. *You have to go through grief to get beyond it.* I realize that's a seemingly obvious statement, but picturing grief as a process with a beginning, a middle and, especially, an end, made it seem more doable to me than picturing it as an endless state in which I could imagine spending the rest of my life. You can't ignore it, steer around it or try to race through it. You simply have to slog through the process, taking as long as it takes. I tried to picture my grief as a continuum, a straight line stretching from its beginning to the promise of its end. I tried then to picture how far along I was on this line, and to think of each dismal day as one more out of the way, never to be seen again; one day that would bring me closer to the end of grief.

—BUSINESS MATTERS—

The next day my little girl (34 at that time), who used to argue with me about the merits of orderliness in her room, quickly organized a filing system for me to use while settling Bruce's affairs. She tabbed folders for "Autos," "Homes/Mortgage," "Funeral," "Death Certificates," "Veteran, SS Benefits," "Company Benefits," "Will and Copies," "Insurance," "Wisconsin/Florida Lawyers," "Federal Estate Tax," "Recent/Current Income Tax Info," "Investment Summaries," and "Miscellaneous." We searched and found necessary papers to file in them, then assembled them neatly into Bruce's locking brief case. That way we knew I could find things I'd need when working with lawyers, my tax accountant, my investment counselor and others. This also gave them the impression I had control of things, although I can assure you I didn't.

Tailor any such system to your own needs, of course, but I can't stress enough the value of having some kind of a system. My mind balked at handling details right away, but I could stick papers into appropriate files for looking at later. Then when a lawyer called to ask for the title or registration for Bruce's car, for example, I didn't have to search for it. I knew I'd find it in the "Auto" file. That was about the limit of my business abilities during this initial period of shock.

If your husband had been ill, be sure to make a file folder for "Medical Bills/Insurance Claims." Keep them all together until they are paid in full, either by your insurance or by you. And don't forget to take all allowable deductions for those expenses on your income tax return for the year you actually pay them. I suggest adding another file, "Family Documents," to include Social Security numbers for you, your husband and children; birth certificates; marriage certificate; military discharge papers. You can order copies of missing certificates from the clerk of court of the county in which you were born, married or had children. If you don't have his discharge papers, contact your local Veterans' Affairs office for a request form and instructions for filing. The Social Security Administration can help you find those numbers and replace lost cards.

Where's the will? Was there one? Look in your bank safety deposit box, among his business papers, every desk drawer at home or at his office and/or call your husband's lawyer, if he had one. He or she should have a copy. A will is nothing more than a document that designates heirs and a "personal representative" to settle the estate, pay outstanding debts, and distribute remaining assets. It must, however, conform to rules of your state. If your husband had no will, or you can't find it, the state will determine how his estate will be divided. That may not be in your best interest, so—if you possibly can—hire a good lawyer to represent you.

Looking back, I see I was lucky to be in the capable hands of trustworthy bankers, lawyers and financial counselors, and to have an uncomplicated estate. Even with property in two states, there was no need to go through probate. We held all property jointly; and Bruce had established a bank trust that was named beneficiary of the insurance proceeds. I had always been directly involved in business matters, so I knew where everything was or who to call. It's a good thing, because my mind was so flabby and dulled by the trauma that "thinking" often was impossible. I doubt I could have recognized even a blatant effort to misdirect my funds or to cheat me. I blindly trusted our advisors to help me through this, and they did. I wonder if I would have even noticed or reacted to any shenanigans if they had pulled them. Who knows? I hope you were—or will be—as lucky.

If you don't have dependable professionals to rely on, seek suggestions from people you know and trust. If you cannot afford professional help, there are sources of free advice. These often are listed in your telephone book's "community pages," or you can find referral numbers for many of the professions listed in the yellow pages. Otherwise, help can be found by calling your librarian, your local college extension office or the senior citizen center. Trying to muscle through this stage without guidance can magnify feelings of inadequacy. Be gentle with yourself.

—HANDLING EARLY FINANCES—

There is an old saying, "No one's so poor as the new widow." It's true that financial uncertainty is a root cause of our early fears, regardless of our actual income. You'll feel better once you start dealing with the situation, though, instead of just worrying about it. Here is a list of suggestions, lifesavers to help you stay afloat financially until you learn to swim in your strange new pool. If (1) you have always taken care of the family's finances, (2) you know you have plenty of money for the years ahead, (3) you know exactly what you have and where, and (4) you know that all your bills are up to date, you may wish to give the list a quick glance and skip ahead in your reading.

- *Do a quick accounting of cash on hand, including checking and savings account(s).* You probably can access any accounts in your own name and in joint accounts, unless they required both signatures. Some authorities advise a new widow to immediately remove contents of a jointly held safety deposit box and all money from joint checking and savings accounts, in case the court seals them upon notice of the husband's death. That practice has generally gone the same way as a formal "reading of the will," more likely to be seen in juicy fiction than in real life. My lawyer said this somewhat archaic practice is no longer done in most states, under normal circumstances of a death, but check with your lawyer or bank customer service desk about your situation and act accordingly.

- *Estimate how much money you will need during these first weeks.* Remember to include the following: the cost of food and beverages for family or friends who will stay with you; provisions for out-of-towners after the memorial service or funeral (unless that's being handled by someone else); immediate family and household expenses; undertaking services, cremation expenses and/or the cost of funeral or service; newspaper obituaries. You may be able to stall some payments until more assets are accessible.

- *Check your tax calendar for approaching deadlines.* Do you—or did he—have quarterly federal or state income tax due? Is the deadline near for annual taxes? Do you need to file sales tax forms for rentals or for your business? Do you owe withholding or unemployment tax for employees? *Do not fail to file by the deadlines,* even if you must request an extension to get your facts, figures and thoughts together. Unless you have done this before and feel perfectly comfortable doing it at this time, seek professional help. With enough patience to wait "on hold," most questions can be answered by phone from the IRS or State Department of Revenue.

- *Check status of all essential insurance payments.* Be sure premiums are paid on time for homeowner's, auto, health or life insurance for you and your dependents. There usually is a "grace period" on insurance premiums, but don't assume that without checking. If you're late or beyond the grace period, your coverage may be canceled. Reinstating a policy can be difficult or expensive.

- *Check to see if you have other essential unpaid bills.* If at all possible, pay bills the day they arrive so they don't build up such a stack that you can't face them. At the very least, make a file for current bills—and use it—so they don't become lost in the midst of your confusion. The consequences would only add to your problems. Ask a relative or friend to help if this problem begins to swamp you.

- *Make arrangements to free up funds if they'll soon be needed.* Your banker, financial consultant, accountant or lawyer may be able to help. After the dust has settled, give yourself time to grieve and regain your senses. But as soon as you can add and subtract, determine whether you will have adequate funds to live on in the years ahead. If not, you must consider your only two options: adding to income or subtracting from expenses. Until you do this, you will waste a lot of your limited energy projecting how bad things might get. Better you spend that energy solving the problem…if you find you have one.

Within the first several weeks, you will need to take care of some or all of the following, depending on your situation.

- *Make arrangements to change the name on each of your bank accounts.* Visit the customer service desk of your local bank(s) and explain your situation. Be sure to take death certificates with you. Ask if you should have an additional person able to sign checks and access your safety deposit box, if you have one. You probably can continue to use checks imprinted with both names until new ones are printed. If not, the bank will provide you with temporary checks to tide you over. Don't hesitate to ask "dumb" questions about anything financial. Customer service representatives are trained to know many of the answers, and they can point you in the right direction if you stump them. If the estate will go through probate, and you are the appointed representative, ask them about establishing a separate account for estate business.

> **What is probate? Maybe you know. I wasn't sure. Probate is no more than a court-supervised procedure for validating a will (if there is one), paying debts, and distributing property of a deceased person.**

- *File forms to collect insurance proceeds, death benefit, spousal pension, etc.* This may require little more than a phone call to your husband's company benefits office. Or, it may mean a lot of digging, phoning and writing. Don't panic; ask someone to help. If you aren't sure about the existence of life insurance policies, send an inquiry and a self-addressed, stamped envelope to: American Council of Life Insurance, Policy Search, 1001 Pennsylvania Avenue, Washington, DC 20004. This service is free. If the death was due to an accident, check for possible extra insurance coverage provided with bank accounts, credit cards, automobile clubs, professional associations, etc. Call each for instructions on how to collect.

- *Respond quickly to requests for signatures, certificates and notarization.* It's hard enough to do these jobs individually, but it's sheer agony if those requests start growing into Alpine-sized stacks. Every time you look at them you'll suffer. I had "Do Immediately" and "Do Soon" files that haunted me for weeks until I finally got angry at myself and plowed through them.

—FACING TOO MUCH ALONENESS—

Eventually it happens to each of us. We're left alone to face our bleak futures. Jeanne, a Wisconsin friend, says she held up well the first two weeks. Then her daughter left. "As I got in my car to drive home from the airport," she said, "I battled intense feelings of aloneness. So I spent a few minutes doing what I had done at other critical times in my life. I spoke to God. My prayer was simple and to the point. 'I can't do it alone; I need your help.' This might not work for everyone," she said, "but it had worked for me before and I knew it would again."

For me, day ten arrived and my daughter departed. I stood on the porch and blinked away tears as good friends pulled out of the driveway to take her to the airport. From there she would fly home to Austin, Texas. It could have been Mars. With her went much of my fragile confidence. I remember that I gulped audibly. I didn't feel threatened, exactly; in some ways I almost looked forward to being alone to grieve. I had barely flirted with the job while being gracious to friends and relatives, and I knew it awaited my attention. As I had often heard, and quoted to other widows, "Grieving is work…and it must be done."

I have never heard such deafening quiet as when I walked back into my house alone that day. Silence enveloped me, made my ears ring. I sank into a corner of the sofa and waited…to cry hysterically, I guess. Nothing happened. The nineteenth century mantel clock ticked steadily, our old refrigerator stuttered along uncertainly and Manda, my sad little puppy dog, curled up next to me…comforting and seeking comfort. Minutes ticked by while I surveyed this once-familiar room. Everything looked a bit alien; like seeing it in an old photo or through the eyes of a stranger.

I had this sudden need to change something. I had always thought the room had too much furniture for its size; now it was painfully obvious. I couldn't stand it. I jumped up, hoisted the love-seat on end and wriggled it out through the door to the garage. Next, out went an oversized ottoman, my bulky hand-hooked hearth rug and a large antique basket of magazines. Then I rearranged the rest of the furniture and sat down to survey my work.

"Ahhh." I felt elated. I could do whatever I wanted with the house. I didn't have to ask permission or wait to see if Bruce approved. Without thinking, I reached over and picked up the TV-remote, what we had called the "clicker." As is the case in most homes, the clicker had always been "his" property. From now on it was mine; I could choose the channel now…my personal favorite usually being Channel OFF.

What a shock! I was not only stunned to realize that I was fully in charge, but that I…oh, no…I enjoyed it! Wham! Zonk! Guilt landed like a left hook to my solar plexus. How could I possibly enjoy being alone? What was I, some kind of monster? I had loved Bruce for 36 years.

Then I remembered hearing, years earlier, from Virginia Graham about her experiences as a widow. She attracted attention on talk shows because she dared to suggest in her book that there were some consolations for being alone, and that it was both natural and acceptable to appreciate them. Few, if any, widows would choose their lot, she admitted. She knew we'd prefer having our husbands back, warts and all. (Isn't that the truth?) But she said these little consolations help make life more palatable as we learn to live alone.

I had often wondered about that, but I guess I had just found out she was right. Whew! That meant I must not be crazy. But I felt embarrassed and guilty. I swore I would never tell anyone else about this little private elation. Most people would probably think I was an insensitive lout. But, I share my guilty secret with you, dear reader: there are a few advantages to living alone, and it's okay to recognize, even enjoy them. They may help ease you through the nastier parts of this process.

—WHEN YOU NEED TO BE ALONE—

My feelings plummeted quickly after my brief flirtation with the joys of independence, but I had little chance to wallow in self-pity. Nearby friends became vigilant, stopping by and calling regularly. They watched me like hawks watch mice. How was I doing? Had I been crying? Was I okay? Was I eating properly? I could tell they didn't want me to feel alone and sad. Little did they know I was beginning to worry because I wasn't weeping uncontrollably. I decided I needed a way to signal them when I wished to spend some time alone. I told them I would close the lower portion of my front mini-blinds if I preferred they not come to my door just then. I could sit on the sofa and cry my heart out without threat of rescue. I didn't do that at first, because tears wouldn't come, but I did several times later. And, the signal worked.

If you feel "smothered" by friends or family, you might try a signal of your own. Or if they try to keep you from grieving, let them know you understand that they mean well, but that if you didn't feel sad much of the time, something would be wrong with you or with your feelings about your former mate. If some try to keep discussions free of words like death, died, or dead, or they shrink from speaking your late husband's name, try to explain that it's helpful for you to discuss him and his death openly. They may not enjoy it at first, but doing so will be cathartic and educational for them as well as you.

Sometimes I needed time alone to think. I have always been more a thinker than an emoter, so I did a lot more thinking than crying right from the start. I'm not bragging; I can almost guarantee that shedding gallons of tears is more therapeutic than thinking. I just have trouble doing it.

Some among you may have way more "aloneness" than you can tolerate at first. Karen said, "Prior to Gene's death, my house had been filled with family and friends. Suddenly there was only emptiness and loss. The worst part was that I had not only lost my husband of 28 years, I had lost my caregiver role, which gave me some comfort during his illness." Dale and Thelma agreed with her that losing their nursing roles added to their emptiness.

Others of you undoubtedly are even more starved for time alone than I was. Pauli, whose children were mere babies when she was widowed, remembers how they kept her occupied. "I was so busy I had no time to think," she says. "Sometimes that helped; sometimes not." Ginny agreed, although her boys were preteens. "I was so busy working and escorting the boys to lessons, scouting events and games," she said, "that I had no time to dwell on being alone."

We have all seen stories of the early struggles of the many young mothers widowed in the World Trade Center tragedy. Although they had each other to commiserate with, each one faced aloneness and her own frantic busyness, trying to compensate for the loss of her children's father. Their earliest pain dealt with the public and gruesome nature of their spouses' death, watched by everyone the world over. That piled on top of all the "normal" expected reactions to widowhood. Most of those widowed were young women and, we hope, adaptable. I often wondered if it helped or hurt individual widows to have to share their personal tragedy with a nation of mourners. Perhaps some of each.

Some of my sister's painful reality was postponed, as she lived with our brother and his wife for six months while her home was repaired and remodeled after the fire that killed her husband. "That was helpful," she said. "I had hours alone while they went off to work, but I had company in the evenings if I wanted it. When my house was ready for me, though, I was ready for it. I needed to live alone, to take command of my life again."

I don't recall much of interest about my first night in the house alone. I probably slept like the proverbial log, since I didn't even confide in my journal. I know I sighed with relief when it was over and I was proud as a peacock to have triumphed over potential hobgoblins. I had taken the first step toward getting control of my life. I would not always be dependent on others; I would become self-reliant, and real soon. I was sure of it.

I recognize that feeling now as the first sign of a stage of grief I have never read about. Most of us have heard about Shock, Denial, Anger, Anxiety, Guilt, Depression, Acceptance, Bargaining and others. But has anyone ever read about the stage called "Cockiness?" I will deal with it more in chapter four, but suffice it to say I went through the stage of cockiness as surely as I went through those other expected stages, and more than once.

However, little incidents kept interfering with my well-laid plans to barge ahead unscathed. I would spot Bruce's red toothbrush in his vanity drawer. Manda would sniff all over the house looking for her master and then curl up in his chair with mournful eyes, pleading with me for an answer. The mailman would deliver another especially touching sympathy card or note. A letter would arrive addressed to Bruce. Or, worse, I'd get a telephone call for him.

What can you say when someone asks if they may speak to your recently deceased husband? You might try, as I did at first, to sidestep the issue by being assertive. "No, you may not," I would say. It never worked for me, and I would have to tell them why. When I felt cocky and sassy one day I thought of saying, "If you manage to speak with him, please ask him to call home. I would like to know where the monkey wrench is." Another time, when I had finally worked up some anger at Bruce for dying, a call nearly prompted me to say, "You're not the only one who wants to talk to him. I have a thing or two I would like to say to him myself!" But, of course, my better judgment prevailed and I didn't. For the life of me, I have been unable to come up with an easy, polite, satisfying answer to this question. I could find nothing better to say than, "I'm sorry. Mr. Estlund died several weeks ago (or whenever)." Brutal honesty seems to be the only way. I thought of leaving off the "I'm sorry," to be more assertive, but I was sorry...sorry that he died and sorry that I had to tell the caller.

—WHAT WILL YOUR MAJOR PROBLEM BE?—

I soon realized I probably wasn't going to be the weepy widow who is unable to face life alone. I decided I would not seek solace in pills or liquor. It also seemed unlikely that I would become hopelessly despondent, suffering the quiet agony of dark depression for extended periods. Would I emerge unscathed from this disaster? There are those who do—or, who seem to. It seems they barely miss a beat as they get on with their lives. But none of us really knows how another widow is handling her grief. For me, the wound felt deep and I knew it wouldn't heal without first festering; it would express itself somehow. For weeks I wondered how.

Then I realized I was routinely having those panicky "jolts" just as sleep settled around me, followed by a rerun of the death scene. I worried about this problem and felt hurt when some friends smiled funny at me whenever I mentioned it. Finally, through my haze of numbness, I realized that what I often said to them was, "Every night I wake up with an awful jerk!" Now I can see that it sounded funny. At the time, I didn't. It isn't unusual for people to occasionally suffer a muscle spasm or electrical jolt that releases tension just before falling asleep. What I experienced was far more severe. Each woke me up like a lightning strike and left my heart pounding, my palms sweating and my mind spinning. I was convinced I would have died had I not waked up in time. This happened nearly every night at first, often more than once, causing severe sleep deprivation.

Stress and anxiety, of which I had always had my fair share, were taking their toll. A prescription antihistamine, sugar, caffeine and other stimulants exacerbated the problem. Add to those an intense subconscious fear caused by my own lifelong irregular heartbeat. Irregular heartbeat equals arrhythmia. Bruce died—in his sleep—of arrhythmia. It apparently hadn't taken my subconscious long to add up those facts and develop "somniphobia"; the fear of sleep. Panic attacks, or anxiety attacks, which I discuss more fully in a later chapter, are common for new widows. I assume these were similar to that, maybe mini-anxiety attacks.

After Cindy left me alone, I also became terrified that another trauma would happen, either to me or to one of my children. I fretted most about myself, irrationally thinking that people who had mourned the loss of Bruce couldn't survive if anything happened to me. In retrospect I see that is terribly egocentric, but I have also been assured that it is quite common. Widows often feel preoccupied with their own and their loved ones' well-being, and the wish to protect others from additional pain.

I also realized every muscle in my body felt taut and ached from tension. Suddenly it dawned on me. I was suffering the same symptoms I had all my life, overall muscle pain and anxiety, but now I felt them much more intensely. It was clear to me that problems from my past were going to be *problems* during my recovery. I wondered if that is always true. If a woman has frequently suffered depression, will she find depression her biggest burden in grief? If she has tried to solve her problems with pills or whisky, will she do that even more when she becomes widowed? And if she has easily succumbed to tears throughout her life, will copious tears prove to be her nemesis? Will other widows revert to old habits of their own, such as excessive TV watching, over-surfing the Internet, over-eating or over-work? I suspect so.

We don't become different people when our husbands die, although we often feel like strangers to ourselves. But at first I think we may become exaggerated composites of our previous foibles. Once I recognized that, I tried to deal proactively with my stress and anxiety. I had regular massages with a massage therapist, I learned to meditate, I watched my eating habits more carefully and I tried to get more vigorous exercise. Each of these efforts helped some. I also taught myself how to short-circuit irrational fears before they could scare me into an anxiety attack.

Being a very analytical person, I followed my line of reasoning further. If I was destined to experience my usual responses, but just more so, what else could I expect? In order to predict how I would respond to grief, I dissected my "normal" personality with pad and pencil. I do not believe in astrology, as such, but I am amused by how clearly I seem to fit the usual profile of a Virgo. "They" say we are pretty hyper, impatient, doing everything fast; keeping busy; trying to use every moment productively; striving endlessly for perfection, punishing ourselves when we fall short; internalizing our stress, often suffering abdominal problems as a result. Embarrassing, but true. That's pretty much me in a nutshell. This gave me a list of behaviors to watch out for. For example, it helped me to realize that since the first days of this mourning process, I have had to slow myself down. I become too anxious to get beyond the pain, to feel "normal" again, without doing the required work of healing.

When I first analyzed myself, I had to acknowledge that I had returned to smoking a pack of cigarettes and drinking four or five ounces of vodka every day. Not excessive amounts, I guess, but I disliked both habits immensely and—more to the point—I disliked myself for indulging in them. I also worried that I would gradually lean more heavily on those false crutches and find myself in a heap on the floor. I had often said I would have no trouble quitting either habit if I were alone, which seems an obvious attempt to avoid personal blame. Well, here I was. I was not only alone, but I suspected those two bad habits, which Bruce shared, were at least partially responsible for why I was. So I put on my agenda: "Quit smoking and drinking as soon as you can." Four months into widowhood I felt I could and I did. Doing so helped my health and boosted my confidence.

I listed a few of my other known problems: disorganization, forgetfulness, tactlessness. I could see that those problems, too, had intensified during grief. I also worried about my tendency to deny reality whenever it was unpleasant.

Although we all do that to some extent, I was a master at it. That was a characteristic I knew I had to work on.

However, the news wasn't all bad. I had some strong points, too. I normally feel optimistic, so that should help, I thought. And, it has. Almost from the beginning, I have believed that someday I would feel happy and productive again. I will never forget Bruce, of course. I just expect that eventually I will move on to a different, but satisfying, life.

I have always dabbled in the various fine arts. I can draw, paint and write—not perfectly, but better than some. So I thought those skills might help me fill my hours and find satisfaction. There, too, I was right; they have. I have even found their pursuit to be therapeutic.

I have a fairly good sense of humor, although it rarely surfaced those first few weeks. The first time it did, I was shocked. I said something clever and followed it with a cheerful laugh, only to shrink back, startled and embarrassed. Those around me understood that I had reacted normally. I felt demented, laughing when my husband had just died. As time marched on that sense of humor revived a bit and helped me occasionally to find life more bearable. A good hearty laugh seems to help almost as much as a good hearty cry.

I usually find it easy to speak openly with people, so I have developed several friendships where I feel free to "unload." Friendships like that can be pure gold to a new widow.

"So, okay, Annie," I remember thinking. "You're going to suffer more than usual from your personality weaknesses, but you have strengths you can maximize, too." I concluded that with effort I might avoid some of the pitfalls of grief by weaving myself a security net of those positive attributes.

This isn't a textbook, loaded with quizzes and homework, but you might begin to help yourself by doing a similar exercise to mine. List attributes, characteristics and habits you consider negative, or that have caused you problems in the past. You won't have to show this to anyone, so be totally honest. Underline, or star any of those you fear might be especially treacherous to you now. Next, list your strengths, those you expect to help you survive and make a worthwhile life for yourself. If you can't think of any positives, you may be in depression, about which I'll say more later. Ask a close relative or friend for suggestions. Outsiders often can see our strengths when we can't.

Once you've committed your lists to paper, search them for danger signs. Are you drinking too much? Are you suffering from insomnia? Do you have too many long crying spells? Are you sinking into despair? You might avoid a major problem by being aware of its potential and seeking help before it paralyzes you.

Review your lists often: Are you at least trying to use your strengths and control your weaknesses?

You may not feel up to doing this exercise at this moment, especially if it is very early in your mourning or if you are at the stage of depression. If it doesn't feel right to you now, put it aside with a mental note to try it on a better day.

I often had to do just that while writing the earliest draft of this book. The first chapters were especially grueling, pulling me back to those first days of fear, anguish and exhaustion. The task of digging through and reliving those terrible times often reduced me to tears. More often, though, I felt swamped with sleepiness. Type A people usually don't nap, but I would crawl into a cocoon of sleep two or three times a day when I was writing "tough stuff." When it became too much for me to handle, I tried to wait patiently until I had moved beyond the problem. Sometimes that was a few hours; other times it was weeks.

We all have ups and downs, highs and lows, smart days and dumb days as we plod along the path of grief. As I say, when I'm feeling smart, "Do what you can when you can; don't push or pull when you need, instead, to rest by the side of the path."

—SPECIAL ADVICE FOR SURVIVORS OF A MAJOR TRAGEDY—

We all suffered a severe blow with the tragedies of September 11, 2001. When the World Trade Centers fell, so did much of our sense of security, our innocence and our optimism. It seems to me that the tragedy hit particularly hard for those who happened to see it happen live, but we all felt a personal loss quite unlike anything in our past. I have had a special pain in my heart for the many sudden widows. What a special terror each of them must have known.

Shortly after the event, Richard K. Harding, M.D., a child and adolescent psychiatrist who serves as president of the American Psychiatric Association, published a list of ways we all can cope with such a major tragedy. Although I certainly hope we'll not have anything of the magnitude of 9-11-01, the suggestions apply for tragedies of any sort. In the interest of space, I condensed and simplified the list.

"...Grief and loss are normal and universal human reactions, and each of us will cope with the loss in our own way and in our own time. While psychiatry as a medical specialty has no unique knowledge of how a country can recover from the trauma over the coming months, we offer these suggestions for individuals and communities:"

- *Talk about your feelings of fear, anger and grief.*

- *Talk with children about the disaster and assure them they are safe and protected.*

- *Limit television watching about the event. Help children gain mastery over situations they can control, such as homework or sports.*

- *Talk with others about hate and prejudice.*

- *Participate in ceremonies to remember and honor the dead and wounded.*

- *Contribute in some way to the rescue work and to the victims.*

- *Write sympathy and support notes to affected individuals and groups.*

- *Give blood when it is needed.*

- *Draw strength from your spiritual or religious beliefs and traditions.*

- *Resume a normal routine as quickly as possible. Be informed of events, but avoid gruesome detail.*

- *Understand that the strong feelings of grief can resurface sporadically even months after the events, and that such feelings are normal. If grief, loss and fear become chronic and impair your daily activities and relationships, consult your doctor or mental health professional.*

This tragedy will pass; buildings will be repaired and rebuilt; life will go on, and our nation will remain strong. But, as with a death in the family, life will never be quite the same. Grief, whether it is national, regional, local or personal, must be acknowledged and experienced before it can subside. We must feel it and know it intimately. We must cry if we can.

Dear Bruce (3 weeks): I couldn't cry again today. I know I need to, but I can't. I wish I could press the right button, just make it happen. How can I miss you so much, feel so sad, and not be able to cry?

3

Tasks That Must Be Done: How to Do Them or Let Others Help

A man's dying is more the survivor's affair than his own.

—Thomas Mann

Annie's Journal (6 weeks)
Dear Journal: Oh please, no sweet condolence letters in my mail today. Or notices of thoughtful memorial gifts. Or touching phone calls. Or, even a sympathetic look from a neighbor. Just for today, let me pretend to be normal. I need a break. Maybe I could pretend Bruce is just out of town. I could clean the house, fix myself up and cook a nice meal as though to welcome him home. Let me enjoy one "normal" day, so I won't forget what normal is.

My plea for a "normal" day went unanswered for many weeks. Meanwhile, however, I tried to act normal and take care of myriad duties related to Bruce's death.

It was only after I interviewed other widows that I realized how lucky I was to have sufficient time to do these things. Many widows my age or younger have demanding jobs or volunteer positions, or they care for one or more of the couple's parents, or they care for grandchildren so their offspring can work. Younger widows, and there are more of them than I ever would have believed, may have dependent children as well as essential full-time jobs. Add those chores we all have—house, yard, meals, laundry, etc.,—and one wonders how widows, stymied by shock and confusion, ever plow through the tedious chores involved with their husband's demise. Except for an occasional writing assignment with a tight deadline, my career was self-driven and could be postponed when necessary. In that way I was lucky.

—THE DREADED THANK-YOU NOTES—

One of the first difficult duties of a new widow is sending thank-you notes. The prospect causes almost universal dread. It's not that we resent the job or feel that it is unnecessary, but that it requires the most personal kind of effort. We appreciate so intensely the outpouring of support, whether it is in the shape of kindness, money or food, that thanking the givers properly is difficult. We know our words will be inadequate, no matter how hard we try. We know the chore also will make us feel sad, as we recall better days. To do the job properly, we must consider each of the givers and their relationship with us during better times. This task looms larger than life when we're still numb from the death. I recall my mother putting the job aside for months, which I couldn't understand at the time. A good friend of mine simply could not do hers alone, so I helped her. Others I talked with turned the entire job over to their children or friends. Some let the job slide endlessly, still feeling guilty about it years later.

I knew I wanted to do my thank-you notes myself, and within a reasonable time. But how? My list seemed to grow unmercifully. There were all those who contributed food for the service and for out-of-town guests, those who sent flowers, those who donated money for unspecified use or for a memorial fund. A single group gift could mean ten or more thank-you notes. If we also had to thank those who sent thoughtful cards and letters, I probably would still be at the job.

Weeks later I realized that I dreaded hearing the mailman drive up to my box. I knew there would be updates of memorial contributions and maybe belated notes from friends who had just heard the news. I fretted about neglecting my responses, but that did nothing to solve the problem. I tried sporadically to tackle what seemed a gargantuan task, to no avail. I either dissolved in tears or I felt overcome with sleepiness. Even the seemingly impersonal donation from a business group mostly unknown to me revived some memory of better times. I clearly wasn't ready for the task.

After a few more weeks I confronted the problem again and then I found it possible to design a solution. Every morning after my walk, breakfast and a shower, I put on an audio tape of new age keyboard music that always lifted my spirits. I opened the patio door, so I also could hear the lake sloshing. I found my favorite pen, poured myself a cup of tea and sat down at my dining room table. Here was my secret key: instead of sitting down to write 200-plus notes, I sat down to write five—and no more—each day. Although it would take several weeks, I knew it eventually would be done, by me and without too much pain. I usually picked an especially difficult one for my fifth note. Knowing it was my last for the day helped me speed through it. I also resolved that my message needn't be "special," "unique" or "absolutely perfect." People only wanted acknowledgment of their contribution and to know I was okay. Instead of searching endlessly for exactly the right words or waiting for something original to pop into my head, I simply thanked them and said I was doing as well as could be expected.

I still groaned whenever the list expanded, but I dutifully kept plugging along. Soon I had mastered the routine and found I could do ten, which was still a tolerable task but it speeded up the process and encouraged me. When I finally caught up and sealed that last envelope, I sighed with profound relief, and chalked up that task as the first of what became a long line of little successes.

You don't have to use my exact method for writing thank-you notes, but if the job looms larger than life for you, perhaps you can break the job up into more manageable chunks. Find your own mix of peaceful sounds and non-threatening setting to make the job easier. Try to remember that thanking those who contributed to your husband's memory is not just a gracious and courteous task; it also serves as a catharsis and healer for you. You may find, as I did, that like so many chores in life the anticipation is much worse than the task itself.

It was a year or so later that I learned one also should write a note to each person who calls on the bereaved at home. Woops. That was one list I hadn't thought to keep; without a list I was lost. Undependable in the best of times, my poor memory was "out to lunch" those early weeks of mourning. Instead of trying unsuccessfully to remember everyone, I pretended I didn't know of my obligation. I don't recommend that, especially if you appreciated those visits as much as I did. I felt special and cared for, that such busy people took the time to come and express their support. The "also-widowed" among them helped me to survive; they all gave me strength. I later noted my thanks on holiday cards to those I could remember, somewhat assuaging my guilt.

—DISPOSING OF HIS BELONGINGS—

Another task, equally daunting, is disposing of your husband's belongings. I can still summon up a fair-sized headache thinking about it. Because of our "double life," Wisconsin and Florida, I got socked with the chore twice. The Florida project turned out to be especially horrendous, because moths and spiders had invaded my outdoor owner's closet during the summer. They ruined some of our clothes and good linens, and they made it necessary either to wash or dry-clean every item worth saving. The air turned blue that day as I unleashed utter frustration on my poor defenseless late husband for…for what I didn't know, but I tried it all: for buying cheap tape for sealing the boxes, for not spraying the closet with insecticide first, for wanting to buy the condo in the first place, and, of course, for dying and leaving me to clean it up alone! I think it was at that point that the absurdity of my tantrum reached my consciousness. I apologized to him and got on with the task.

No one can tell you when to dispose of belongings. Some of us need to wait until we feel stronger. Several young women told of hugging the clothes and smelling their husband's unique smell on them. Pauli said, "I would wrap my pillow in one of Will's flannel shirts, and hug it and cry. Sometimes I would scream into it so as not to wake up the children."

As with other chores, I didn't want to postpone it so long that it became an insurmountable project, so I picked a day in advance, put it on my calendar and then performed like a robot set on automatic. "Don't think too much," I chided myself. "Just do what has to be done." I put my feelings on the shelf for a few hours and dove into the task maniacally, pretending the items belonged to a total stranger.

What to do with these things? I gave to each of the children what they most needed or wanted, and sent the rest to a church rummage sale and to the Salvation Army. It helped me to know needy people would eventually appreciate them. After loading the last box into the trunk of a friend's car, I sighed in relief and gave in to my sadness. Then I murmured a few reassuring words to Bruce (who seemed to have been hovering over my shoulder while I worked.). "I'm not throwing you out, dear; I'm just trying to face my new life alone."

I held onto a few things that were either too personal for anyone else to use or too valuable to be discarded. Among the former were well-smoked pipes, the bowls still caked. Bruce smoked a pipe for nearly 30 years, and it was as much a part of his visage as his thinning blond hair. They continued to comfort me when I would see them in the back of the kitchen drawer. It's okay, and maybe therapeutic, to keep a few special reminders of him around the house. We do have to get on with our new lives, but we don't have to forget our former mates. It's hard to predict what items will be so meaningful to each of us. I can't describe the lump in my throat when I saw his bifocals on the dresser the morning after he died. I had never considered eyeglasses to be intimate items, but it was as though a part of him had stayed behind when they removed his body. I was unable to part with them for years.

I kept some things for purely practical reasons. I adopted his tools as my tools. His lawn care equipment became mine, too, like it or not. I saved his guitar, tennis racket, ping pong paddle, bicycle and helmet, canoe, cross country ski and fishing equipment for the kids and other guests to use when they came to visit. I took his laptop computer, identical to my own, as my Florida computer so I would no longer have to tote one back and forth. You undoubtedly will decide to keep some items, as well. But do try not to be silly about it; most of it needs to go on to a new life with someone else.

I confess I kept one thing that I couldn't justify: Bruce's 1977 red MGB convertible. It was in nearly mint condition; because the former owner, a fireman, had lavished it with the same attention he paid his fire truck. During its decade with us, Bruce had poured money and love into it to the point we all laughed about "her" being my rival for his affection. I know he felt happy either tinkering with her or driving her. One of my most treasured photos, taken just two weeks before he died, is of him proudly returning from a spin in the little red car with our "almost three-year-old" grandson, Luke.

For weeks after Bruce died, I found that every time I walked outside through the garage, I gently patted the MGB's fender. I wondered why. Did I unconsciously think of her as his surrogate and need to reassure him that I would be all right? Did I pat "him" to reassure myself? Or did I simply need to reassure the previously pampered car that I would continue to take good care of her? Whatever the reason, it was embarrassing. Doing such silly things seems to go with the widowhood territory.

I was strongly attached to the car, although I only could drive it on warm, dependably sunny days. My wrists were too weak to lock the top in the up position by myself in case of a sudden shower. In case you don't know, warm, dependably sunny days are NOT the rule on Wisconsin's Lake Michigan shoreline, even in the summer. Realizing that, I made a totally impractical move and paid to ship her to Florida, thinking I would drive her more often there. After I got it there, I realized that dependably sunny and "warm" Florida days were usually sunny and hot, too sunny and hot to have the top down OR up, without air conditioning. Eventually I wised up, bit the bullet and sold her to a friend who needed something to pamper.

Most upsetting of all was Bruce's wedding band. My grandfather, a dentist for 65 years, crafted our matching rings of dental gold. His generosity overcame his practicality, though, and he made the mixture so rich with gold that they scuffed easily. Bruce and I had them engraved inside: "Perfect 4/14/56," convinced that our match was indeed perfect.

—OUR PERFECT MATCH—

Everyone has a story about their romance. I only repeat a summary of mine to explain some of my reactions to Bruce's death, and hoping the telling may jog forth memories of your own. Family friends who published a weekly newspaper in my hometown of Lancaster, Wisconsin, hired Bruce as their 1955 summer journalism intern. One July night, without even noticing that he was as "available" as I was, they just happened to invite both of us for a cookout. Likely story! Fortuitous or not, it proved to be a wildly successful match, as we learned that we shared an incredible number of interests and principles. Both journalism students, we belonged to the same church, we were liberal Democrats, we descended from Scandinavian and German stock, we each had two brothers and two sisters, we both spouted rigidly high standards of ethics and, amazingly, we shared the same birth date: September 3. Bruce was five years older than I was, although he took great pleasure in assuring people the reverse was true.

In 35 pretty good—but not perfect—years of marriage we learned that we both also were stubborn, competitive, assertive Type A's, who always knew we were right. It was a challenge, as are the best of marriages. This mélange of thoughts popped into my head whenever I'd spot his wedding band in my jewel box. After nine months, I added my own. Together they symbolize our life together, solid as gold and only slightly dulled by 35 years of scrapes and scratches.

For all my sentimentality, I've tried to heed the advice of professionals by not keeping a shrine to him. I agree with them that it's unhealthy to focus too long on the past. We need to look forward and keep our memories of the past where they belong…in our memory.

—ABSORBING HIS DUTIES—

During our 35 years of sharing a household, we spent considerable time struggling to find an equitable division of labor. A routine finally became clear and workable with Bruce's early retirement and our move to the small cottage. We shared cooking and cleaning duties; he took responsibility for the cars, garage and all outside work (although I helped) and I took responsibility for interior maintenance, finances and most shopping (although he helped). This gave us both enough time to write, read and have fun.

One of my hardest practical adjustments to widowhood was the realization that I had only me, myself and I to do all the work inside and out. Bruce had just finished landscaping our lot with low-maintenance plantings and gravel-mulch in front. Thank heavens. Even at that I was unable to match his devotion to keeping it meticulously neat. Except when he was in the middle of writing a novel, he worked outside an average of eight hours a day, admittedly doing some things that didn't need doing. I knew it would be a problem for me when I saw how the fresh gravel walk and driveway had been scuffed up by guests who visited after the memorial service…and it was still that way a week later. I hadn't appreciated how quickly and easily Bruce had taken care of such things.

I also had not appreciated how many little, hardly worth mentioning, projects he had done without a word. I suspect most widows find this to be true. Within the first months I realized that he had easily taken care of such things as gluing loose chairs, installing book shelves, unscrewing too-tight jar lids, emptying mouse traps, programming the VCR and remotes, carrying trash to the roadside, replacing starters in fluorescent lights, helping to flip mattresses, cleaning out the fireplace, painting "the hard parts" when we painted a room, moving the stove and refrigerator for cleaning behind, etc.

At least in retirement, Bruce never postponed a project. If I mentioned it, it was as good as done. I had to be careful not to mention a chore I hadn't thought through. He might have a room painted before I even realized that what I really wanted was to have it wallpapered. When I was alone, I could complain about projects like that until the cows came home, and nothing got done unless I did it or hired it done. Few of us can afford calling in a professional every time we face a stuck jar lid or a burned-out light bulb, so we do what we must do. We grit our teeth, arm ourselves with the proper tools and tackle the projects ourselves. The tricky part for me was accepting this reality graciously instead of resentfully.

No, it's not "fair" that he died and left us with all this extra work. But stewing about it doesn't change a thing, it only makes the job seem harder than it is and makes life even more miserable. We might as well do it and smile.

—FINDING OTHER HELPERS—

I soon realized I wasn't Superwoman, though; I couldn't do everything two people had done by myself. For some things I needed help. I stretched my budget to find room for occasional help with yard work and home repairs. Our neighborhood's young handyman pitched in to keep the rain gutters clear, to deliver and stack firewood, to prune trees and shrubs, to haul away rubbish, to move heavy lawn furniture in for the winter and out in the spring. He also fixed things. He was a lifesaver. If you need and can afford help, try to find someone who can help you keep from becoming swamped and resentful.

I also acquired an accountant/financial advisor to help with taxes and investments. I had always done the former and Bruce the latter, but everything became more complex when I was alone, and I knew I needed professional guidance. I also had heard from another widow that the IRS was quick to audit new widows' income taxes the first year or so, "knowing it would be their final chance to extricate funds from the deceased." Although the accusation may be totally unfair and inaccurate, I felt better with my taxes in the hands of a pro. One major plus to this arrangement was that the man I selected had a knack for explaining all things financial to me without causing my eyes to glaze over. I learned a great deal from him and I continue to play a more active role in my investment portfolio. Without his tutoring I would feel daunted, because without either a salary or a pension, my income rests largely on those investment choices and the vagaries of the national economy.

For as long as I could afford it, I allowed myself the luxury of bi-weekly cleaning help, justifying it as mental health support. I knew I would resent having to take up his load of the cleaning as well as all the rest. I know many of you don't have the option of hiring help, but there are other methods to help you adjust to your increased work load. Whether your husband was enlightened and shared household chores, or was an oblivious couch potato who deigned to carry out the trash, you will miss him every day. You can't avoid that. It's not fair, or healthy, however, to resent him endlessly for leaving you with his chores. Try to prevent this by using one of more of the following solutions:

- Simplify your life, so there's less work to be done.

- Learn to accept somewhat lower standards.

- Hire whatever help you can afford.

- Learn efficiency techniques, to do more work in less time.

- Spend a little more of your day picking up the slack.

—NOTIFYING INTERESTED PARTIES—

One task I found tedious and annoying was the necessity of notifying so many interested parties of my husband's death. Maybe your lawyer, financial advisor or accountant can help with this, but if my case was at all typical, most of it still falls in your lap. Reading through the following may help you get rid of these chores more quickly. Learn if you can from my successes and mistakes.

Whether your property was in your husband's name, or in your two names, it probably became yours when he died. A lawyer can help you sort this out, depending on the laws of your state and on provisions of a will, if your husband left one. You must, however, change names on all licenses, files and legal records. That is rarely done automatically. This requires that you provide official written notification, usually verified by a notary public and/or accompanied by a copy of the death certificate.

No one can say, without knowing your personal circumstances, just whom you need to notify. Here is a list to consider:

- **Your home(s).** Call the clerk of court in your county courthouse to determine procedure for changing names on the deed(s). Also notify your mortgage holder(s).

- **Credit Life policy on your home(s).** If you had credit life insurance on your mortgage, notify the company immediately of the death; they should pay any outstanding mortgage balance.

- **Title(s) for your car(s), boat(s), trailer(s).** Call the branch office of your state department of transportation and ask how to proceed.

- **Internal Revenue Service.** If possible, hire professional help for filing taxes for the year of your husband's death. It isn't necessary to notify the IRS of his death before filing, but do so at the time you file taxes.

- **State Department of Revenue.** Hire help, or call for explicit directions when first filing state taxes as a widow. There is no need to notify them of the death before filing, but do so then.

- **Insurance Companies.** Request that companies transfer policies on real estate and cars into your name alone. Be sure your health is insured, if possible. If your husband was covered by a company policy, check to seek if the plan continues to protect you. Bruce's company covered me at no cost for a few months and then permitted me to convert to a policy with the same group, for which I shared the cost. If you have insurance on your life, which named your deceased spouse as beneficiary, notify them in writing of the change to new beneficiary(s).

- **Medical Bills/Insurance.** If you have bills from your husband's illness, keep them in a folder and pair them with insurance statements of what was paid by them. Note your check number on any bills you pay. Be sure to check limitations on filing dates, being sure any legitimate claims are filed on time. This can be a real headache, so find a willing helper if you find the job overwhelming.

- **Property tax.** Contact your county treasurer or tax assessor for clarification if you are in doubt as to what and when to pay for property taxes.

- **Investments.** Transfer investments to your name. If held by a single brokerage firm, call your broker or counselor there for the procedure. If your investments are held individually, you must write each firm asking them to change to your name, being sure to enclose a copy of the death certificate.

- **Credit cards.** If you have established credit in your own name and have your own cards, notify your husband's card carriers of his death. If you have always used jointly held cards, and you have no impressive salary to show, I recommend you postpone notification until you have had several months to establish that you are able as a widow to support the payments. Use his cards and make regular payments *on time*, even if you could pay cash for your purchases. It's important to establish your credit while you can. Otherwise they may cancel your accounts upon learning of his death. Most firms are not impressed that the wife has paid the couple's bills, nor are they swayed by her listed assets. They want to see regular income or salary. It's infuriating how picky they can be, when we all know they send cards out willy-nilly to college students with no credit history and even less sense of responsibility. *Cancel and destroy all cards not in use.*

- **Utilities and other creditors.** Notify each creditor when you first pay bills alone that your husband his died. If they need you to do more, they will notify you. I got a surprise "refund of capital" from our electric cooperative after reporting Bruce's death.

- **Social Security/Veterans Affairs.** Notify the Social Security Administration's local office and, if he was a veteran, the Department of Veterans Affairs local office. Benefits may not be paid if you don't apply for them. Social Security advisors can tell you of immediate or future benefits as the surviving spouse, as well as accumulated credits in your personal account. As a widow you are eligible for full benefits (yours or his) at age 65, or reduced benefits as early as age 60. (My 60th birthday was eagerly anticipated!) For most of us, early benefits make sense. A disabled widow can get benefits at 50 to 60 years of age. A widow of any age can get SS benefits if she takes care of a dependent or disabled child who gets benefits. Unmarried children under 18, or up to 19 if they are in elementary or secondary school full time, can get benefits. You probably also qualify for a special one-time SS funeral benefit (only $255 at the time of Bruce's death). The Veterans Affairs officer will help you determine if you have benefits coming from them.

- **Miscellaneous.** As time goes on, you need to notify others: associations to which he belonged, periodicals to which he subscribed, charities to which he contributed, etc. Sometimes a notice brings sweet results. I notified the frequent flyer offices of our favorite airlines, and learned that upon presentation of the death certificate, Bruce's mileage credits were transferable to my account, providing me with an additional free ticket to visit grandchildren.

I felt sluggish and dim-witted most of the time those first weeks, from shock, and also from a potent antihistamine I needed to take. I relied heavily on my lawyers, my stockbroker and Wisconsin Bell's benefits office to keep me apprised of what needed to be done. They, and my daughter, led me by the hand through this maze of paperwork. I hope you have people around you can count on. If not, ask friends you trust for professional referrals.

If you feel overwhelmed just from reading about all the details you must take care of, call a widow friend who seems to have put her life back together. Ask if she will be your mentor on this new job for which you have had no training or experience. Because she will understand your situation better than anyone else, she probably can help you grapple with the process. If you don't have access to a widow, ask a relative or friend who seems to be good with handling details. The list is long and inclusive, but it doesn't all have to be done in one day or even one month. Much of it may not pertain to you in any case, so try not to sag from the weight of it until you know how much there really is on your shoulders.

Dear Bruce (9 weeks): The title to "your" MGB arrived today, in my name. When I first saw documents reflecting the change of ownership to Ann T. Estlund, I felt a brief flutter of pride. I hadn't owned much in my name before. But now it's like I am watching you fading out of an old photo. You fade out and I fade in…as a viable person for the first time? I don't like that any better. I'd rather have you back.

4

Stages of Grief: The Work We Must Do

I never knew a man trubbled with melankolly,
who had plenty to do, and did it.

—Josh Billings

If you want to be happy, be.

—Tolstoi

Easy for you to say.

—Annie Estlund

Annie's Journal (14 months)
Dear Journal: I don't know what's wrong with me. I can't work; I can't play; I can't laugh; I can't cry. I feel irrelevant, insignificant, about as interesting as a rock in a pile of gravel or a grain of sand on a deserted beach. I don't even feel like writing today; I think I'll crawl back into bed. Maybe I will feel worthwhile one of these days.

Everyone agrees that grief is a process with various stages. All grief manuals I've seen include a list of the Stages of Grief, but no two agree as to exactly what they are. Most include most of these: **Shock, Denial, Anxiety, Anger, Guilt, Depression and Acceptance.** Some others include **Bargaining, Isolation, Disorientation or Confusion;** some add **Numbness.** Although I certainly experienced each of those latter ones, I considered them reactions to shock. I add **Cockiness,** based on my experience, but that might qualify as a symptom of

56

denial. **Relief** seldom makes any list, but that's a very real stage many women go through, whether it's because of the death ending a stressful relationship or because of the death ending a spouse's long and painful illness.

Some authors and grief specialists organize the stages into phases. I might as well join the crowd. I felt my grief process most closely followed a four-phase plan, with **Shock** (numbness, disbelief, disorientation, confusion); **Denial** (cockiness, frenetic activity, guilt, disorganization, withdrawal); **Confrontation** (intense grief, anger, sadness, anxiety, depression, bargaining); **Acceptance** (gradual decline of grief, recovery of stability, social re-entry, self growth). Elisabeth Kubler-Ross, in her famous book, *On Death and Dying*, names five stages: **Denial and Isolation, Anger, Bargaining, Depression, and Acceptance.** A funeral home pamphlet I picked up made the division into Four phases: **Numbness, Intense Turmoil** (fear, anger); **Deep Depression**; and **Decline of Grief/Acceptance**.

Regardless of whose list you feel best fits your grief, it's important to know that not all widows experience all stages. In addition, we experience the ones we do in our own order, to our own degree and according to our own timetable. There are no firm rules, no rigid deadlines. You may not even recognize what stage you are experiencing until it has passed.

Pauli told me, "My grief lasted until I moved to Phoenix six years after Will died. But don't put that in your book or it will scare the heck out of every new widow!" She later gave permission, saying it might help some women. "My grief became a crutch," she said. "It prolonged the healing process but it was a safe place to be." I have spoken with other widows who claim still to be grieving after ten, twenty years, although they say it has gotten easier, more manageable. After studying their claims, I think it's more accurate to say they still miss their husbands after that length of time. A few have fallen into a rut of grieving and will need help emerging, but most I've met continue to plod forward with admirable courage.

Grief books within easy reach of my computer state these estimates on how long grief can be expected to last: "18 months to 2 years," "2 to 3 years," "6 months to 18 months," "one year or more." A highly publicized study a few years ago proclaimed, "…it has now been learned that the process can take from four to seven years." That one scared the very devil out of me; I knew I could not handle the intense stress that long. What I know now is that for most hours of most days of those later years, life ranges from "tolerable" to "pleasant." When I slipped back into grief after a few years, the intensity was nothing like it had been those first weeks *and* I knew it was temporary. Don't be dismayed by numbers people throw at you. You may continue to have grief symptoms after a year or two, because grief lingers beneath the surface and bursts forth occasionally. You will, however, notice that you have more and longer periods of happiness, fun and peace as time goes on. Those women who are incapacitated for years should seek professional help so they can find a way to enjoy the remainder of their lives.

My first question of "recovered" widows was always, "How long did your grief last?" I couldn't understand why they wouldn't give me a definite answer, like "One year, two weeks and twelve hours." Now I realize there is no answer. I repeat: *Grief is not a disease you get over; it is a condition that you learn to live with and accept gradually. It gets easier, but it never magically disappears.*

—FACTORS THAT INFLUENCE GRIEF—

Psychologists have studied grief and dissected it, finding certain similarities among those who grieve, but the process defies simplistic description. One thing is certain though, and Karen (who lost a son and a mother to suicide and a daughter and a husband to cancer) puts it well. "I came to believe during the first year after [her son] David's death, that grief is something you do, not something that happens to you." Experts agree; grief is a job that must be done. You can temporarily ignore it, but it won't go away without being dealt with.

A woman's sense of independence may influence how she mourns. Many women lose their identities when they lose their mates. I don't pretend to know whether a wife is happier with an independent identity or thinking of herself primarily as her husband's wife. However, I'm fairly sure the woman with a secure sense of self will handle widowhood more easily. If your only identity was "the wife of...," his death may mean the death of a part of your "self," intensifying the loss.

I was quasi-independent, having established myself as an occasionally successful writer in the outside world and as half of a fairly egalitarian partnership in the home. None of this came easily, but I think those years that I spent building my self-esteem and that we spent adjusting to a changing social environment eased my adaptation to life alone. On the other hand, the wife who chose to run the entire show at home, with little help from her spouse, will notice less change in her daily routine than those who came to rely on enlightened mates. The essential factor in handling grief seems to be self-esteem. There is little doubt that women who believe themselves competent will survive and grow from the experience. Those who question their competence also may survive and grow, come to think of it, but the process may take longer and be considerably more painful.

It's impossible to predict how you or any other woman will handle this worst of all crises. Virginia, a Wisconsin friend widowed ten years before I was, described her early feelings as absolute chaos. "His life…our future…my world, severed, irretrievable! Nothing had logical sequencing anymore. I look back on that time and see myself as a child lost in the woods, afraid of the dark and stumbling every step of the way. I would start things and couldn't finish them. I cried daily." I suspect this woman, who was trained as a social worker/counselor, might have expected her background to protect her from the worst of grief. I probably would have expected that, had I been her. Unfortunately, the blow of widowhood is so stunning that it floors the best of us and surprises even the best prepared.

I have special affection and concern for young widowed mothers. Talking with them breaks my heart. As we know, one of the biggest tragedies of the 9/11 terrorist attacks was the lingering grief for the families of about 3,000 people who died there. Most of those who died were young men, from upwardly mobile brokers and businessmen, to heroic fire and police personnel, to blue collar maintenance workers. Most left behind young wives, several of them pregnant at the time, and dependent children. These widows, and young widows anywhere, have all the problems the rest of us have plus those that are unique to their situation. They must continue to cope with the needs of their children, even when they would rather crawl in a hole or sleep for a week.

While most housework is instinctive, child-rearing seldom is. One would hope each young widow has a lot of helpers standing in the wings, in case she becomes depressed and can't handle her responsibilities. A few young mothers said they simply didn't have time to wallow in depression, which I am sure is true. Most who looked back after a few years, admitted that they had gone through their own private hells trying to keep it all together while they—and their children—grieved the loss.

It's difficult enough having to assume the father's half of the parenting role while grieving, but the job is often complicated by the children's grief. They may experience intense fears, worrying their mothers also will leave them; or deep feelings of guilt, thinking they might have caused their fathers' death. This presents their mothers with urgent problems just when their own resources are challenged with mere survival. Shortly after I was widowed I met a young widow who looked like a teenager with her ponytail and frayed blue jeans, camped out on the floor of a Boston area bookstore. Just a few weeks into her trauma she was reading every book on the shelf about how to handle her children's grief. I so wished I had some magic formula for her, but I didn't.

If you are a young mother, I hope you will tap every outside source you can, be that self-help books, other single parents, a support group or professional counseling, to help you and your children through these first years. In a later chapter I offer hints on child-rearing that might help. It's important that this sensitive period be handled properly. Don't expect to be able to carry the entire load alone all the time; ask for and accept offers of help.

Many widows of all ages say their faith pulled them through the rough times. If you have an unshakable faith in God, and/or you are part of a close religious community, calling on these resources may greatly ease your mourning process. Some get strength from others who share their beliefs; others find the strength within themselves by tapping into their own spiritual nature. If you're lucky, you have some of each to rely on. Your cultural heritage also may play a role. In some cultures, death triggers extensive displays of public anguish, with wrenching moans, loud cries and breast-beating. Other cultures expect stoicism; public weeping is discouraged. Some ethnic groups ritualize the grief process, providing widows the comfort of a timetable to follow.

In addition to social and cultural traits, personality differences affect how we handle grief. Some women cry easily; others find it nearly impossible. Some become depressed easily; others manage to remain placid in the face of great sadness. Some women deal easily with anger; others feel threatened by it. To these characteristics, and circumstances of the death, you can add a variety of demographics to explain differences in grief patterns. Age (his and yours), status of health, number and ages of children, locale, financial status, and level of education all influence the response of a new widow. It's easy to see why no one can predict a pattern or span of time for grieving.

Each widow must learn to "go with the flow," to grieve at her own pace, in her own way, because her situation is truly unique. It is helpful, however, to learn about each generally acknowledged stage of grief so you will better understand what is happening as you experience unfamiliar or scary feelings. It helps to know that your erratic emotions, craziness and "abnormal" behaviors are perfectly natural.

—SHOCK/NUMBNESS—

Nearly all women, when faced with the unexpected death of their husbands, go into immediate shock or numbness. I likened my feelings of shock to being inside a protective bubble. I tumbled through this unbelievable nightmare as an interested observer, communicating with others, doing things without knowing I was doing them. Others describe that state of numbness as feeling like robots, as being set on automatic pilot or as being invisible.

Several women said they weren't aware of being in shock at the time; they hurt so much they thought there was no protective anesthesia whatsoever. It was only as that shock faded away, sometimes months later, that they realized it had been partially cushioning the blow.

I'm sure I was in clinical shock at first, which undoubtedly explains why the paramedics stayed with me for three hours. I had chills and complete dryness of the mouth and throat. I imagine my blood pressure was dangerously low, since it is sometimes 90 over 58 when I'm just resting. You probably felt similar symptoms, or even worse.

As shock and numbness dissipate gradually, weaning us into reality in little, more manageable, spurts, we may suddenly have a rude awakening. One day we realize that we feel even more keenly anxious and fearful than before. Although the impact is startling and frightening at the time, it may help to consider that your initial hours and days may have been intolerable and dangerous to your health had shock not cushioned the blow. Those wives who expect the death, or find it a blessing, are sometimes spared the brunt of the initial reaction, although most experience a delayed reaction several months later.

Some widows report periods of disorientation, when they lose their bearings and think they are going crazy. I called my more dramatic episodes "anxiety attacks," so I discuss them later, under ANXIETY. Whatever you label this disorientation, it is a terrifying feeling of losing control, as though you are hurtling through space. With minor incidents I regained my grip on reality by pinching myself, biting my lip, stretching, running in place or taking long, deep breaths. Of course, if you're sitting in church or walking down the detergent aisle at the store when it happens, even those actions might get some attention. Don't worry about it; keep reminding yourself that your fear of "losing it" or going crazy is natural, and it's temporary. Almost every widow has at least a few such episodes and lives to talk about them. So will you.

I recall several periods those first months when familiar settings seemed unfamiliar, best friends seemed like strangers, and I felt out of sync with the rest of the world. Within the first few weeks I had to go to Waukesha, where Bruce and I had lived for 26 years, to meet with my lawyer and friend, Casey. I couldn't trust myself to drive the 3 hours, so a friend had to drive me there. I was really out of it that day. I remember slinking along Main Street, as though I had never seen it before, paralyzed with fear that I would meet someone I knew. I feared that I wouldn't know their names or, worse, that they wouldn't know about Bruce.

What would I say? How should I act? It didn't happen; we left town without incident. A lesson: Much of what we worry about doesn't happen.

A month later ten people I knew quite well came to my house for the dessert course of a progressive dinner. I should have canceled out as a hostess, but I thought I was fine...until we sat at the table. I looked around and panicked; my heart raced and I felt lightheaded. What was I supposed to do, entertain them or tell funny jokes? Make small talk to put them at ease? I couldn't think of a thing to say. I wanted to run to the bedroom for a good cry; I could just barely make myself sit still and pick at my cherry pie. I have often thought how much more pleasant their dessert would have been if they had drawn one of the more "normal" houses. It was a relief to all of us when it became time for everyone to leave.

After that I made it a point to share these confused moments with friends. I learned to accept them as temporary and I expected my friends to as well. They seemed to understand, although they may have discussed my strange behavior among themselves. If your disorientation and confusion persist or take a turn to more serious aberrations, seek help. Put yourself in the capable hands of a recovered widow you trust, a professionally-guided widow support group, your doctor or a psychologist, depending on your resources and the severity of your problem. Remember: The only cause for embarrassment is to neglect real problems, or to fail to seek help when it's needed.

—DENIAL—

Denial is a complicated stage. In its most blatant form, it is easy to recognize. If you refused to listen when told of your husband's death, or you have continued to drive to meet the 6:10 bus every night, or you still set his place at the table a year later, you may be deep into denial. Many widows told me they converse with their spouses daily. One 90ish lady in Milwaukee placed a fresh rose by her husband's portrait every day for more than 20 years, and set a place for him next to her at the breakfast table, "...so we can talk," she said. I thought it was very sweet, but probably not particularly helpful to her recovery.

How can we recognize more subtle signs? We may say "we" and "us" most of the time, instead of "I" and "me." Some of that is inevitable because old habits die hard, but too much for too long can mean lingering denial. We may forget to buy or cook smaller amounts of food. We forget to take out the trash or get the car's oil changed. It is with some chagrin that I admit I forgot to claim my bags at two airports and a bus station during that first disoriented year. I had never had to worry about the baggage. We postpone even simple decisions; we make no changes to the house. Those first weeks, or months, I think we each expect him back at any moment.

That's not all bad, unless it continues too long. Without denial to protect us for awhile, we likely would suffer too much reality too fast. The result could be disaster, with us all really going over the edge, instead of just feeling like we were. Denial acts like a cushion, softening the blow until we can better handle it. Even after years some widows slip into brief episodes of denial as respite from the stress of reality, little moments of "R&R."

At nine months I felt like "Ms. Super-Griever of the Year." I was marching through this process in the best way anyone ever had. However, a prominent Harvard doctor-friend told me that he recommends that every widowed patient, without exception, have at least two sessions with a professional counselor or psychologist. I took his advice.

My counselor was great, very perceptive. He agreed that I was doing well, saying to me, "You seem to be doing amazingly well…(pause)…intellectually." He paused again while I digested that, then added, "But in your heart you haven't begun to let go. You are in deep denial; you haven't absorbed that your husband is gone and that he'll never be back." I couldn't believe my ears. He said I was a failure at this, the Big Daddy of All Tests! I had lots more work to do, and I thought it was all over. That was a comeuppance, a real blow to my ego, but he was right. Those sessions with him helped pull me down to earth, and his suggested homework helped peel away more of my cocky veneer. It wasn't an instant cure, but his insight surely helped expedite the grieving process for me.

Having said that, and having read seven grief books, I still couldn't tell for sure whether I was still in denial after many months or had finally moved on. It seems easier to spot denial in others than in ourselves. That's why I checked in with my counselor again, at the end of two years. I wasn't "cured" at that time, but I had fought my way out of denial.

—ANGER—

"How could I possibly be angry with poor Bruce, for heaven's sake? None of this is his fault." I remember saying that many times, I wrote it in my journal and I believed it with all my heart. The experts were crazy if they thought I would ever feel anything but sadness or remorse about my husband's premature death. Many women mentioned they had had this same feeling. One, Toni, said she sailed through early grief, keeping herself too busy to think, feeling sorry but not angry. "Then one day," she said, "I was driving home from Dallas, and sleet began to make the road icier and icier. Suddenly I felt a great swell of anger and I lashed out at my husband with a string of epithets, which I won't repeat. 'How dare you die and leave me alone to deal with so much,' I wailed."

I know how she felt. As I mentioned earlier, just weeks after disposing of Bruce's belongings in Wisconsin, I discovered moths and spiders had wreaked havoc with linens and clothing we had stored in Florida for the summer. This meant every item had to be discarded or thoroughly cleaned. I remember suffering nobly through most of the task. However, when I found our box of photos and memorabilia ruined, I blew like a great whale that had been under water too long. My long-suppressed anger gathered force and spewed out in most unladylike fashion, directed mostly at Bruce. Once through that litany I railed at the moths and spiders, at Florida's summer heat, at the sealing tape that failed, at the bug spray that wouldn't kill a fly if it were drowning in it. I knew, though, my underlying anger was at being left alone to deal with that and many other crises. It wasn't fair, and somehow I had been led to believe life should be fair.

I can laugh about my temper tantrum now, and I apologized to my visiting sister, who got the full brunt of my explosion. I almost lost it like that a few other times, like when I had persistent car trouble in a strange town, and when I got pinned against the bedroom wall by my half-flipped queen-size mattress, and when I pulled out one fireplace log and the whole neatly stacked cord of wood collapsed on my feet.

Once I learned how to get angry, and that it was socially acceptable behavior for widows, my rage didn't want to quit. Even more distressing was that it didn't stay focused on Bruce, where at least it wouldn't hurt anyone but me. It kept popping up all over the place. Apparently I had been stashing away resentments and hostilities for years in the name of keeping peace. Those refused to stay buried with my new short fuse. I either worked a barbed comment into a conversation, or I picked a fight about an entirely different subject.

When my anger really got sharpened, it cut a wider swath, hitting political and social issues in general, and those who disagreed with me in particular. I had, maybe I still have, "hot buttons," triggers that set me off like fireworks gone haywire. How I survived the presidential campaign in my second year of widowhood with any friends at all, I don't know. And the medical profession! I couldn't think of enough bad things to say about it. I finally recognized that related directly to Bruce's death. "If they're so darned smart," I subconsciously thought, "why didn't one of them find his problem and treat it?" In short, often I felt like actor Peter Finch in the movie *Network*, when he hollered to the world: "I'm mad as Hell, and I'm not going to take it anymore."

I'll be the first to admit my anger exceeded what most of you probably felt. I believe now that some of mine may have been an unleashing of angers sublimated by years of smoking. Feel angry? Smoke a cigarette. Kids on your nerves? Smoke a cigarette. Feeling put-upon? Smoke a cigarette. At one point I even started smoking after six years of being clean simply because Bruce made the mistake of "forbidding me" ever to smoke again. As soon as I was re-hooked, I realized my retaliation had hurt no one but myself.

I learned some time later, from a Sunday sermon, that most anger and frustration stems from the common human frailty of wanting everyone to think, feel and act just as we do. Knowing that has helped me. I keep trying to remind myself it's our differences that make us interesting, and that this world would be a total mess if everyone felt and acted like Annie Estlund! I also learned that it is easier and less painful for the widow to feel anger toward her husband than it is to feel love. We sometimes postpone the pain of loss by staying angry and concentrating on those less admirable qualities in our deceased husbands.

I expanded the discussion about my intense anger to show how each of us experiences different levels of the various stages, depending on our personalities and on any number of personal circumstances. Most widows I talked to told of going through periods of anger, but a few said they felt none. I suspect some have forgotten that aspect of their grief. Others say they fought anger, believing it an unhealthy emotion. However, most experts say anger is an expected emotion and that we must learn to express it. One counselor suggests we scream into a pillow, pound our fists on a mattress, write (but don't send) a venomous letter, and then pursue a very strenuous exercise, such as running or swimming to the point of exhaustion. I remember wishing I could haul a rug outside and beat on it with an old-fashioned rug beater. I'm sure many an angry widow did just that before we went modern and tacked our carpets down. Vacuuming just doesn't cut it.

Maggie, young and recently widowed, said, "Anger is a very visceral emotion. It helps if I can verbalize that I am angry, even when I can't carry a discussion any further right then. Sometimes it's a struggle to figure out what's causing the anger. I may be feeling hurt or threatened. Sometimes, just figuring that out is enough." When her late husband had lapsed into a semi-comatose state he would occasionally open his eyes in response to his brothers, but he didn't respond to her or to their kids at all. "I felt hurt and abandoned," she said. "I remember crying to my mother, 'I think he's mad at me. He won't talk to me. Well, I'm mad at him, too!'" Who among us wouldn't feel hurt and abandoned in such a case?

Whether you become angry with your husband for causing you pain or for leaving you with insufficient funds or for character flaws while he was alive, or just for dying, it is entirely natural. We are expected to feel anger and, according to most experts, we will get over it best by venting it occasionally rather than letting it stew inside until it erupts in some unhealthy, unforeseen way. Be advised that your grief will find a way to make itself known to you, and some ways can be a lot worse than screaming or crying. As Woody Allen said in one of his outrageous movies, "I'm sorry. I can't express anger. I grow a tumor instead." It would be a far funnier line if it didn't often prove to be true.

—GUILT—

Were you one who felt an incredible sense of relief when your husband died? I don't mean, in this case, the kind of relief one might feel for someone who has suffered a long illness and found peace in death. I mean the kind of relief one feels when a source of major stress is removed. Many women experience this sensation, although most hesitate to admit it. Some wives suffered so in their marriages, for one reason or another, that their first response to his death is profound relief. They are free at last, be it from physical or verbal abuse, from life with an addict, or from the stress of a relationship on the rocks. Although perfectly natural, feelings of relief often trigger overwhelming guilt feelings. "What kind of insensitive beast am I," a friend asked, "to feel relief at his death?" Without expression, that guilt can then grow and become deeply imbedded in her psyche. It may help to learn more about guilt as a natural stage of the grieving process and some ideas for minimizing it.

Nearly every widow feels some guilt. It may be as simple as wishing you had kissed your husband good-bye before he left you for the last time. It may be considerably more serious, like knowing you could have prevented the accident that killed him by glancing in your rear view mirror before passing that semi. Whatever the cause it is best to do some digging to be sure you are not assigning guilt to yourself when it is totally unwarranted. Even if it is warranted, it should be dealt with to prevent ongoing emotional distress.

Sometimes I feel guilt because I didn't respond to clues of my husband's ailment. My only "excuse" is that I was feeling ill myself, and obviously wasn't operating on all cylinders. When I replay those first traumatic minutes of him dying, I recognize that once I woke up and perceived what was happening, I could not have done more than I did. After the fact, however, I realized he had three symptoms I didn't have. He had an aching shoulder (which he attributed to hauling rocks), he was dizzy (which we both attributed to off-kilter electrolytes from diarrhea) and he also felt very cold to the touch. Now I can see that I should have reacted with alarm when we woke up two hours before he died, or even two nights earlier.

Our doctor offered no explanation for our shared symptoms. At the time I believed our 35 years together had so sensitized me to him that I vicariously shared his symptoms, "sympathy pains," so to speak. I have read since that nine percent of spouses share symptoms with the one who dies. But I couldn't let it go at that. I had to keep searching for clues.

I now agree with a friend, who argued at the time that we both had suffered shock from heat exhaustion and dehydration, from standing for hours in the sun on a 98 degree day. After some research, I think she may be right. I also believe his symptoms may have been worse than mine were because he was on a self-imposed salt-free diet in an attempt to lower his erratic blood pressure. It was only weeks after he died that I learned of the first major study showing that many people have a reverse reaction, that their hypertension responds better to additional sodium rather than to less. I'll never know if that was actually the cause of death, but it helped me to think I finally knew. Until I felt satisfied that I knew exactly what had happened, I was stymied in my recovery. I think we each are driven to know all we can about the cause and circumstances of the death, whether it is by illness, accident or suicide, in an attempt to alleviate our guilt feelings.

I concluded that there was nothing to be gained by beating myself over the head with what I "should have done." As my sister-in-law, Nancy, once said about rearing her seven children, "I did the best I could at that time, under those conditions. That's the best any of us ever can do." I applaud that philosophy, and especially for widows. Many widows recognize too late what they "should have done," so know you aren't alone. However, don't let it drag you down like an anchor. That can't possibly help you, much less your deceased husband.

What should you do if you conclude, after much soul-searching, that it is your fault your husband died? I'm not talking about murder here, but maybe you were driving the car too fast when it rolled over, or you insisted on playing singles tennis when it was too hot, or you convinced him to stop taking his medication because it was too costly. Maybe you just didn't register the seriousness of his symptoms. Whatever it is, my totally non-professional advice is to write him a letter. Admit your guilt, apologize profusely and then try to let it go. To spend years battering yourself about it is a waste of your energy and your precious life. And it won't bring him back! It helped me to consider how Bruce would react if the situation were reversed, if he were alive but knowing he was somewhat responsible for my death. It didn't take much time for me to know. I felt sure he would handle the situation pragmatically. If he could switch places with me, and he had another chance at life, he would make the most of it. So should you. End of lecture.

Having tied that subject up with a pretty ribbon, let me admit two things. First, in spite of my advice, I still badger myself occasionally about how I might have changed the outcome; I guess it takes a long time to forgive yourself. Secondly, I am only talking about very natural, dime-a-dozen guilt feelings. For some of you, this simple exercise will not do the trick. If your guilt runs deep, causing problems in your life, you will need to seek professional counseling. Ongoing depression, nightmares, insomnia, eating disorders, compulsive spending, drug or alcohol abuse all can signify acute guilt. *Remember: There is no shame in seeking professional help, only in not seeking it when it is needed.*

We all flirt with other types of guilt as we move through our tunnel of grief. We may feel embarrassed and guilty for enjoying life, for buying something we want, for forgetting him for a time, for looking at another man, for taking a trip he would have thought too expensive, for going too long without crying, for selling his car and other silly reasons. Try to short-circuit the guilt. You are alive and, once your grief subsides, you deserve to enjoy life to the extent you can.

Some authorities say guilt is a cover-up of anger. Others say we only feel guilty if our husbands made us feel guilty when they were alive. Some widows say it's because we feel he is watching us every minute. If you think that, think about this: if he is watching, he is also capable of feeling regrets of his own. What might he wish he had done differently? Quit smoking? Had a check-up? Exercised more regularly? Driven more defensively? Treated you with more respect?

Whatever the cause, guilt is destructive if not controlled. The good news is that you can control it, either alone or with help.

—DEPRESSION—

It's easy to see now that I was sinking into depression when I wrote the entry that leads off this chapter, but I didn't know it then. Depression was the stage I had planned to skip. However, at 14 months, after "our" September 3 birthday passed for the second time, I realized I had felt depressed ever since the party thrown for me by my friends. Though I loved them for the compassionate thought, I felt like I had at their party for me a year earlier—like a zombie or an alien from another planet. I didn't perk up after the dreaded day passed. In fact, my mood blackened as I packed to leave for my seven months in Florida. I blamed having to leave the security of my friends in Wisconsin, but I see now that was just a superficial problem.

I cried often, usually triggered by nothing at all, and my temper flared unexpectedly with friends and relatives. I often slept ten hours at night with an hour's nap during the afternoon. Then I would suffer extended periods of insomnia. Every muscle in my body ached. For weeks I had a headache that wouldn't quit, no matter what I took for it. I joined in fewer social events and when I did I felt transparent, as if others could see my depression. Life was a chore. I know how it feels when novelists say, "her smile never reached her eyes."

My doctor had given me a prescription months earlier for an anti-depressant, "for when you need it." Even though I knew I probably qualified as needing it at this time, I opted to wait and watch as the depression played itself out. I chose not to add to the necessary medications I was already taking. I recognize that anti-depressants—if prescribed properly and used according to instructions—play a vital role in treatment. Recent studies show they are not as safe as once believed, however. Most are addictive and can cause serious side effects for some people. Depression is dangerous, too, though, so when the black tunnel of depression begins to affect those around you or threatens to take you too close to the edge, you and your physician may decide you need them. One serious thought about suicide, for example, and I swear I would take a capsule with one hand and call my doctor or psychologist with the other. That is no time to try to muscle through on your own.

I casually mentioned my depressed feelings to Cindy on the phone one night, to which she replied, "Darn! You sure are good at hiding these things from us." I hadn't realized that. Her next words helped immeasurably. "It's to be expected, of course. Do you want to talk about it?" I didn't; I just thought she should know. What I hadn't realized was how much it would help me to tell her, and to be reminded that this was a stage I had yet to go through. I had been blue often during the previous year and two months, but I hadn't experienced this deeper and more inclusive mental state. I still felt like a great stone face on a dog-tired body, but her concern and reminder helped start my recovery.

I began to visualize my depression as a physical thing. It seemed to me a very dark, cold, uphill concrete tunnel; I could see it had a beginning, middle and end. I tried to picture myself having plowed my way up through most of it, having only a short distance left to go. This took concentration, but it meshed with my philosophy that I mentioned earlier: YOU HAVE TO GO THROUGH GRIEF TO GET BEYOND IT.

I began to sense light at the end of my tunnel by early November, but slid back several notches as I approached the second set of holidays alone. That setback was intensified by the death of a friend to cancer. She had fought the disease for nearly a year and I wouldn't have wished another day of suffering on her, but her death punctured my fragile web of hope and plunged me back into the pit.

In an effort to perk myself up from that tumble one night, I called a "usually ebullient" college friend. When she answered the phone I thought I had a wrong number. Her voice was weak and dead sounding. Of all things, she was incapacitated by very deep depression. This wasn't the first time for her, but it was the first time in many years. I tried to encourage her, but that's hard to do long distance and even harder when you feel depressed yourself. After several frantic calls, I finally spoke to her husband and urgently pleaded with him to get her in to see a new doctor. A doctor who was new to her case had taken her off a regular program of Lithium, on which she had been thriving for years. Her husband admitted that he was scared and that he appreciated my suggestion. He got her in the next day; she's back on Lithium; she's her old bouncy self again. She is one for whom drug therapy is not only effective and liberating, but essential. It's her life preserver.

I learned an important lesson from that session. It slowly dawned on me that my depression was nearly nothing compared to hers. I could fake normality around most people; she couldn't. Our symptoms were similar; they just differed in intensity. We both experienced constant, heavy sadness; sleep problems; lack of energy and spunk; inability to cry, laugh, scream or feel any emotion very deeply; withdrawal from social contacts. We both suffered more than just "the blues," but my depression remained within manageable bounds. Hers was debilitating, dangerous…"too painful to endure much longer," as she put it. She was absolutely incapable of helping herself. The fact I could summon the energy to alert her husband to the danger shows that I had reserves left. She didn't.

Thoughts of suicide are common among the severely depressed. If you find yourself that depressed, you <u>must</u> prod yourself, or someone who cares about you, to action! Just say "I need help" over and over, to anyone who will listen, and don't stop until they understand and take charge of getting help for you. If you are alone, look up the "Suicide Hotline," or call 9-1-1 and ask them what to do! You must get immediate help! I can't pretend to be able to help you out of that kind of despair with this book, or even with a phone call. All I can do is try to make you see how important it is that you get well-trained help if you ever feel suicidal. While it is true that depression can be disabling, try to remember that it takes a certain amount of effort to proceed with suicide. It takes *much less effort* and makes *much more sense* to make one urgent phone call…to 9-1-1, to a suicide hotline, or to your physi-

cian. Get help, even if you must use what seems like your last ounce of energy to do it!

With the passing of the second set of holidays, my melancholy cloud faded and then disappeared. It had lasted four months. Emerging from it, I felt like a butterfly shedding its cocoon. I knew I had turned a major corner on this grief trip. I felt wiser and I appreciated life more. I became more determined than ever to see this book through to publication, and to take control of my life in myriad other ways.

I learned a lot about the stage called Depression in those months:

- *You cannot fully understand depression until you have experienced it first-hand.* In spite of close experiences with depression, with my husband and several friends, I admit I harbored the suspicion that it was self-induced and could be self-treated. Not true!

- *The clinically depressed are incapable of yanking themselves up by their bootstraps,* BUT that's often what others say they should do.

- *Depression has levels of depth,* like a depression in the earth or in the economy, but it is always more than just "being blue."

- *To cure one's depression often requires time, counseling, therapy and medication.* Programs, self-help books and support groups are more available now than before, but you must respect the need for professional help if you are truly depressed.

- *Common advice for helping yourself out of depression is to eat well, exercise regularly and get adequate sleep.* That sounds good, but if you can make yourself do that your depression is very mild. These habits will, however, help you shake the ordinary blues, which you also will experience as a widow, and they will help speed your recovery as you begin to emerge from depression.

I like what M. Scott Peck states in his classic best-selling book, *The Road Less Traveled,* "…the feeling associated with giving up something loved—or at least something that is a part of ourselves and familiar—is depression. Since mentally healthy human beings must grow, and since giving up or loss of the old self is an integral part of the process of mental and spiritual growth, depression is a normal and basically healthy phenomenon. It becomes abnormal or unhealthy only when something interferes with the giving-up process, with the result that the depression is prolonged and cannot be resolved by completion of the process."

—COCKINESS—

I occasionally felt very cocky during my first year or so. I would begin to think the media had over-hyped grief, that anyone with a whit of intelligence could face widowhood pragmatically. After all, death is certain; only the timing and circumstances remain a mystery. Of course I miss Bruce, I would think, and life is hard without him. I knew I would cry on occasion; I might even prompt tears if they were too slow coming. I knew about grief. I had gone through it with others; I had studied manuals, books and articles on the subject. It's mainly a matter of attitude, I would tell myself. Moping endlessly would not bring him back; it would just make others around me uncomfortable. I just knew I would skim the surface of grief without losing my bearings. (I can hear some of you chuckling. Is that nice?)

Cockiness can be a dangerous stage of mourning. It's not only a sneaky way of avoiding the more traumatic stages, but your less perceptive friends may be lulled into believing you no longer need their tender care. Occasionally it's natural to reject your discomfort and pretend that all is well—that you are a normal human being—even if only for a little while. Grief, especially for one so close as a spouse, hurts like crazy. It affects each of us physically, emotionally and intellectually…no exceptions. It's like a constant, unwelcome guest, one you would like to boot out of the house for a time. I'd like to suggest that may be okay…as long as you understand that, like a sneak thief, it will hide in the bushes and wait to attack when you least expect it. As I have noted several times, avoidance of the stress and pain of grief for any length of time usually proves counter-productive, delaying or extending the healing time instead of easing it.

If you find that you are feeling extremely confident about your progress, and you question the sincerity of obviously grieving widows, take a good hard look at yourself. I know I went through several phases of cockiness; I can even spot it in some chapters of this book; maybe you can, too. During those times I knew all the answers and I thought I didn't need to succumb to what I thought of as the self-pitying phases of grief. I now see the fallacy of that bravado. I also realize cockiness, like self-pity and denial, can be useful in small doses. Each provides brief respites from the constant struggle. It's hard always being courageous. However, for plodding upward through the tunnel of grief, cockiness is little help. Unless you learn to recognize and control it, these pleasant interludes can become habit and dangerously disrupt your mission.

If you catch yourself being too cocky, give yourself a good dose of reality—write an honest, tough letter to your husband, take off your wedding ring, or watch a video of the two of you enjoying life. Suffer a bit now; it will pay in the long run. Or as my favorite guru, M. Scott Peck, reminds us in *The Road Less Traveled:*

"To willingly confront a problem…means to put aside something pleasant or less painful for something more painful. It is choosing to suffer now in the hope of future gratification rather than choosing to continue present gratification in the hope that future suffering will not be necessary. Problems do not go away. They must be worked through or else they remain, forever a barrier to the growth and development of the spirit."

—ANXIETY—

Anxiety plagued me the first months, to the point that I became anxious about my anxiety. I used every trick I knew to handle daily anxiety: massage, meditation, exercise, etc. They all helped some, but I was powerless to prevent several anxiety attacks. Recent studies show that as many as one-third of those who suffer from panic disorders or anxiety attacks, develop agoraphobia, the irrational fear of leaving home. I knew I didn't want that to happen to me. In my typical analytical fashion, I tried to discern the exact cause of my problems. I had eliminated caffeine from my diet some time ago, because it caused me to feel anxious for up to 20 hours after drinking it. I was not drinking alcohol. Beyond that, it was impossible to separate the anxiety I knew because of widowhood from that I suffered from quitting smoking from that caused by reaction to a sinus medication. They probably all intermingled. However, I had one attack I know was triggered primarily by my grief.

One morning, about 4:10 a.m., I woke up with a start, my palms sweating, my heart pounding, my breathing fast and hard. Although that had happened often in the two months since Bruce had died, this time my imagination took the reins and ran. I knew I was feeling all the symptoms he had before he died. I knew I was about to die, too. Actually Bruce hadn't moved a muscle, so he probably felt nothing. I paced; I breathed deeply; I tried to exercise; I tried to read or watch TV, but the anxiety grew. My panic caused more symptoms: chills, lightheadedness, the feeling of losing control. I wasn't sure whether I was about to go crazy, faint or die. I only knew I had to get help. I stumbled toward the phone, not sure whether to dial 9-1-1 or Debby's number. I chose Debby, because she was next door and the paramedics were 15 minutes away. I told her I was afraid I was dying and I needed her to come over as fast as she could.

By the time she arrived I was starting to get myself under control. I felt foolish. However, Debby was wise for her 47 years; she pooh-poohed my shame and stayed until I was feeling stable. Her easy acceptance of my erratic behavior reminded me "good friends don't judge, they just listen." Other widows mentioned similar events. One older widow told me, "Waking up in the early morning was terrible! I had anxiety and diarrhea. My counselor and gastroenterologist have been a big help and [at 3 1/2 years] I'm much better." Luckily, in my second year, I also moved beyond anxiety or learned to control it.

The medical community has made significant strides in dealing with panic attacks in the past few years. Among other things, they have learned that "cognitive behavioral therapy" provides better and longer lasting relief than drugs for most people. It teaches you to keep your imagination in line with reality. They also have learned that popular anti-anxiety drugs, previously thought to be free of addiction and side effects, may not be. There are times to use them, because of their immediate effect. I still keep a few on hand but haven't needed one for years now. For some people, behavioral therapy either isn't available or it fails to solve the problem. If you and your doctor feel drugs are necessary, just be cautious. Follow directions and heed cautions. Don't risk compounding your problems by becoming dependent on a drug, or suffering side effects as bad, or worse, than the anxiety you are treating. Opt for the most conservative treatment that works. Give time and nature a chance. It is also nice having a neighbor who won't be upset if you call her at 4:00 a.m.

—ACCEPTANCE—

We know there's a "carrot" leading us on through this maze of grief. That carrot, that elusive goal, is Acceptance. As we go through various painful stages we learn and grow, and eventually begin to accept the death and our new role as reality. Then, and only then, we can move forward with our lives. There is one problem: I'll be darned if I know how to recognize Acceptance in myself. All the stages tend to zigzag along beside each other for awhile, and then they cross over or intertwine occasionally. Some are clear; some are foolers. I think we probably find acceptance, or learn to accept our lot, a tad at a time. I know we can accept the death intellectually before we accept it emotionally, for example. While we accept completely one week, something may trigger a backslide and find us back in anger or depression the next week. It's not as though we suddenly reach the carrot and gobble it up, sure that the race is over and that we won.

A change of scene often prompts a move toward acceptance. About nine months after I was alone, I took my first trip to Europe. I was in a fog most of the time I was there, but I realize I benefited in subtle ways from that journey. I grew up a little, even though I leaned pretty heavily on Ann A., my traveling partner.

For one thing, I found it was pretty hard to maintain one's self pity while viewing the crumbling vestiges of medieval cultures that no longer exist. And, it was pretty hard to remain egocentric while sitting on the steps of Sacre Coeur and watching tens of thousands of people bustling about the city of Paris sprawled below.

During a late evening auto trip back to Paris, after a country dinner in Chantilly, I remember clearly the passing parade of tiny homes, each with a few dim lights. Thousands of them passed by in a blur; the driver was going 80 to 90 miles per hour. Rather than cringing in fear at the speed, I suddenly had a global glimpse of life. It struck me that each home harbored a French family complete with its joys and sorrows. In some of those houses, and in millions of others in countries all over the world, women had recently lost their husbands and were mourning, I thought. As different as we often seem to be, in dress and customs and language, I suddenly realized that we widows probably feel almost the same emotions upon becoming widowed.

I could see similar scenes in the USA, of course, but the impact is startling and memorable when you first see life in another country and measure your life with theirs. One cannot help but gain a broader perspective on life by travel. I believe that every widow who can afford it would profit from a trip abroad during her first year of two of widowhood. It wouldn't end her pain, but it would give her a glimpse of acceptance.

But, even then, be prepared for setbacks. A good friend, June, told me, "All of a sudden some music or other reminder deals a blow and that awful empty feeling takes over again." That is so true. Another grand lady said, "I don't know when I reached Acceptance, or even if I have. Maybe you can tell me." Is it easier for outsiders to judge our progress?

I can see that our counselor or psychologist might be able to read the signs more accurately than we, but I doubt our friends or relatives would be much help. I know that my public self, that part I displayed to others, recovered much more quickly than my private self. As we become more accustomed to our "condition," we all seem to learn how to act the part we know those around us want to see…that role of "recovered" widow. We pretend to be okay before we are deep inside. I think that's okay, and I suspect that most behavioral psychologists would agree. We can improve our selves and our lives by acting like they already are improved. Eventually that pretending becomes reality.

Perhaps we have finally reached Acceptance when we are so busy with our new lives that we don't have time to think about the stages of grief and where we are in relation to them.

Dear Bruce (at 23 months): Today I unearthed three sheets of yellow legal paper tucked into the last bit of work you did on your prospective novel, "Murder in E Flat." I expected them to be jottings of plot twists or research trivia. But they were blood pressure and pulse readings, taken after dinner on July 5. They give no hint that would be your last meal, but since they were taken on the sly and hidden, I know you were worried. Why didn't you call our doctor? Why didn't you tell ME? I wonder if you would have gone in to see the doctor if I had found the readings earlier? I wonder if an exam would have found a problem? Would treatment have been soon enough? Here I go again, head bashing to no avail. And, I thought I was healed. Damn!

5

Holidays and Anniversaries: Marking Them in New Ways

God gave us memories so that we might have roses in December.

—James M. Barrie

Annie's Journal (11 months, 29 days)
Dear Journal: I thought I would never see the day. Tomorrow it will have been one year. Glad I am in Austin with my two older grandkids to keep me distracted. A year seemed such an incredible span of time to grieve, but I soon will have gone through each special date, holiday and anniversary once alone. I plan to sleep like a rock tonight, knowing that when I wake up the worst will be over.
PS: I just thought how nice it would be if Bruce were here to celebrate with me. What does that mean? A

It's true that time seems to creep at first, but as numbness subsides the clock picks up speed and soon resumes its regular, persistent beat. Just like that precision clock, the calendar keeps flipping its pages, relentlessly moving us forward. It doesn't ask if we're prepared to face our first Christmas, Father's Day or wedding anniversary alone. It just flips another page, day after day, with nagging reminders that "the day" is coming. Then, ready or not, one day it announces, "This is it! The dreaded day is here!"

Then we know: *We can't stop the day from arriving; we only can decide how to get through it.*

—CALENDAR HOLIDAYS—

Which calendar holidays present the worst problems depends for each of us on when our husbands died and which holidays were most special when he was alive.

I'm sure the Fourth of July always will give me pause, because the two of us enjoyed it so soon before Bruce died.

Just over 36 hours before his death we drove the convertible to the northern tip of the Door County peninsula to enjoy "Old Ellison Bay Days." It was officially 98 degrees in the shade, of which there was almost none. But we ducked from tree to shop awning to craft tent, enjoying the crowd and ebullient spirit of one of the county's famous small town festivals. The parade, which took more than two hours, had been touted as the county's longest parade...longest in duration, apparently. We laughed with friends about how it could have been over in 20 minutes if they had kept it moving. But it was Door County at its rural/touristy best, and we loved it.

The highlight of the Fourth that year, though, was a telephone call from our son, Dave, announcing the arrival of Marshall, our second male grandchild but the first to carry Estlund as a surname. Dave reported Marshall was blond and adorable, looking just like his father. That evening we had a lovely dinner and good visit with old and new friends next door, and then gathered on our rocky shore at nightfall to watch fireworks across Whitefish Bay. That was Thursday night. Late Friday night I was calling 9-1-1.

From the time we bought our cottage, leisurely enjoyment of the county's mystique set the pattern for our Independence Day celebrations. So rather than pummel myself with memories the next year by engaging in the same ritual, I welcomed the chance to do something entirely different. Cindy invited me to join her family in Texas, because of the dreaded one-year anniversary. We spent the Fourth at a Tex-Mex barbecue on a small ranch outside of town with their friends from the law school faculty. I knew almost no one and I had never been on a real ranch. We messed up the timing a bit, so we missed seeing Austin's spectacular fireworks on our way back. There was nothing about the day, but the date itself, to remind me of our fun day a year earlier.

On my second Fourth of July without Bruce, Eric came up to the cottage from Madison to spend the weekend with me. We played golf (poorly), which Bruce and I had given up years earlier (for the same reason), and we watched fireworks with friends on our shore. Something different; something similar. It was okay, and soon it, too, was over.

That has always been my ritual for these holidays that could be maudlin. Plan something, preferably something new, and go through it like a robot. After all, it is just another day, I tell myself. It has been my experience that anticipation of the day is far worse than the day itself. For each calendar holiday the first year, I expected to feel devastated. However, my supportive friends and family also worried that I would suffer. So on the day itself I would have more than the usual number of cheery phone calls, and someone usually planned something fun to divert attention from memories.

Psychologically, there seems to be an advantage in expecting the worst. When the day arrives, and it fails to live up to your fears, you feel pleased. "This isn't so bad," you think, and glide through most of the day with relative ease. I can't say I wasn't blue or that I never shed a tear. I was and I did, especially after dark when I found myself alone. Sadness is to be expected, so we must let it happen, knowing the next day will be a new start. I always felt better, though, knowing that I would never have to go through that particular dreaded day again.

It is possible to make yourself feel quite miserable if you dwell on happier memories from previous holidays and imagine that you'll never feel happy again, now that you are alone. It's quite natural to feel sad, and if you feel the need to break down and cry, that's fine. A good, healing cry now and then washes more of the pain away. Norma, a friend from my days as a new bride, had been widowed for 16 years when we talked. She said, "Holidays are still difficult! Gene died around the Easter holiday, so that's a tough one. Christmas is remembering and New Year's Eve has its sting. I guess I really treasure hanging on to all the reminders and memories I can. I really don't want to let go." She hung tightly to her memories, and she admitted to crying easily, but don't assume for a minute that she wasted her life alone. After Gene's death she operated several successful restaurants and nightclubs while rearing two daughters alone.

At four-and-a-half months, I hosted an annual Thanksgiving potluck dinner in my small Florida townhouse. Bruce and I had started the tradition the year before, inviting all of our neighbors who had no other plans. This time, 19 of us combined our food, effort and spirits. I remember that day as my first mostly enjoyable one as a widow. I allowed myself to eat heartily, laugh, tell jokes, play cards and tease others without feeling guilty. Part of my elation stemmed from having quit smoking and drinking. I had been "clean" for about ten days, and it was time to celebrate. It occurred to me later that some might have judged me insensitive, but I didn't dwell on that. What did they know of my many, long and sleepless nights or the stress-induced near-ulcer that was trying to gnaw through the wall of my stomach? I knew I needed that dose of fun and laughter more than any medicine ever invented. We all do, so laugh whenever you can.

Later that year, I worried that I would be tagged "Seagrove Beach's Merry Widow," because circumstances forced me into hosting two more parties. I welcomed 20 or so who had been invited to a friend's house for New Year's Day chili when she had to back out because of surgery. Then in February three of us each welcomed into our homes 20 of the 60 people signed up for our annual Snow-birds' Potluck lunch. That was the day we had to slosh through about eight inches of Florida sunshine.

Pauli's husband died on Thanksgiving Day. She cried on that holiday for many years. She says it still tugs at her, 30 years later. She often tells a story of her first Christmas as a young widow, just four weeks after Will's death.

"Humor often carries us through crises," she says. "The Christmas Eve after Will died, the family was at our house for dinner—my first time to entertain without him. Everyone was very somber and sad, of course, but the children (ages 3, 1-1/2 and 3 months) did help take the edge off our thoughts as we lined up at the buffet to fill our plates. Suddenly…kerplop—bang—crash! A favorite uncle had accidentally upended a large molded gelatin salad onto the floor from the buffet. We all laughed uncontrollably—which was exactly what we needed." She says they still love to tell the story. Comic relief had saved the day.

A Wisconsin neighbor, Irene, told me of one of her first holiday-related memories as a new widow years ago. "Death came in winter. We had spent the end of December and all of January with him in the hospital. In February he died." She had had the leisure of waiting 12 years for his death, and she says she didn't mourn. "I cried only once. That was when I returned home in February, after his death, and found our Christmas tree had died and was completely bare."

Karen, another Wisconsin neighbor, decided not to have a Christmas tree the first year, just four months after her husband's death. "I learned after my son's death that flexibility is the key to getting through the holidays, and it is not necessary to celebrate in the same way or even to celebrate at all if you don't feel like it." That is very good advice from a gal who has learned a heap about surviving, through a series of personal loses in the space of only a few years. Keep that in mind as you plan your holidays. You can't try to keep everything the same that first holiday season alone without noticing a gaping hole in the festivities.

My first Christmas, at 5 1/2 months, was sad but soon over. We gathered at my son Dave's temporary quarters in a lovely, big old coach house in Providence, Rhode Island. The surroundings were totally different from those of Christmases past, but much was familiar, even to the usual cases of "grandchild holiday flu." My kids showered me with gifts, in an attempt to stand in for their Dad who always bought me too much.

Our only snafu was due to lack of communication. David had wanted to make this Christmas Eve poignant, with guitar, singing and talking about his dad. However, he neglected to tell the rest of us. Cindy thought, with her kids sick, the best way to get through this first Christmas without Bruce was to just get through it. Pretend nothing had changed. (She's a lot like me in that way.) I addressed my journal entry to Bruce that evening. Before telling him how much we all had missed him, I said, "If you were watching the dichotomy (do I have the right word, dear?), I am sure you smiled. So, what else is new?" Divergent plans and ideas had often been a part of family gatherings. Maybe yours, too. Holidays often prompt edginess. The next Christmas, in Austin, we managed to get through the period better by being enchanted, entertained and distracted by four healthy little ones.

If you are dreading your family's first Christmas, or other special holiday, without your spouse, think carefully about previous celebrations. Which traditions are important to you, to the rest of the family? Can you start a new one that will acknowledge the family's changing nature? For example, you might suggest the family go caroling on Christmas Eve, being sure to go to homes where others are ill or grieving. It also might lower the stress level, for you and everyone else, if someone talks briefly about your husband, and how much you all miss him. Then proceed, doing your best to enjoy all you have left...life and each other.

If you are about to go through a difficult holiday without family around to help, you may have to be more creative. You can invite others who will be alone to join you. You can offer your services to a shelter or pantry to help those in desperate need. You can offer to relieve someone on the job, so they can be with their family. OR, you can throw yourself on your bed and have a crying, fist-pounding and foot-kicking temper tantrum. Whatever your choice, you'll feel better. Or at least it will be over.

When faced with a holiday that had special meaning for the two of you, or one that always prompted a loving gift from your spouse, you can choose how to handle it. You can sulk, which is tempting but not helpful, or you can deny your concern and just keep yourself real busy, which at least postpones the misery. But it might be better to face your emptiness. There are various ways to do that, some selfish and some unselfish. Selfishness isn't always bad; it can serve to help glide you over otherwise rough waters.

Be selfish. For this brief time, think primarily of your self and your own needs. Do whatever YOU want to do for the day. Some ideas:

- *Pamper yourself with a visit to the beauty salon or massage therapist.*

- *Loll around all day in your lace nightie, or read a trashy novel while soaking in a bubble bath.*

- *Doll up and do the town with a friend, eating in your favorite restaurant and shopping in your favorite store.*

- *If a gift was always part of the day, buy yourself a special item you might have gotten from him…even if you wince a little at the price. If it makes you feel less put upon, it may be worth the price. (Warning: Don't go bananas and spend yourself into debt. Just be nice to yourself.)*

Be unselfish. Look outward instead of inward, and try to make the holiday special for someone else. If you have healed enough to be able to consider the needs of others, this often provides good therapy.

- *Help a granddaughter bake a three-layer heart cake for her parents on Valentine's Day.*

- *Make dozens of Easter corsages and boutonnieres for residents of your local nursing home.*

- *Baby-sit for a single mother, so she can go Christmas shopping, or prepare Thanksgiving dinner.*

- *Invite your single women friends over to make holiday cookies, and exchange some with each other.*

- *Take an elderly widow to see the festive holiday decorations and stop someplace special for lunch or a cup of steaming cider.*

- *Offer to provide transportation to a church, mosque or synagogue for special services.*

If a holiday arrives while you are in depression, all the advice in the world isn't going to keep you from feeling sad. I know. My second birthday, Thanksgiving and Christmas were celebrated under the black cloud. I got through them by practicing denial, refusing to think about memories that made me sad. But my temper was short and I withdrew from activities that normally were fun. Participation might have helped, but I suspect it would more likely have ruined everyone else's fun.

Psychologists recognize that, regardless of one's religious leanings or lack of them, the much-hyped holiday season triggers depression for a great number of people. Widows are particularly susceptible. I can only suggest you pay attention to articles and TV shows dedicated to relief of holiday depression, and re-read Chapter Four's treatise on the subject. Always be on the lookout for signs of depression, realize it is to be expected. Just try to make sure you don't become frozen in the stage, unable to grieve and grow.

—PERSONALLY MEANINGFUL DATES—

Birthdays are always tough; especially yours and his. I suspect September 3 was a little tougher for me because it had been both of our birthdays. We never could decide whether we shared "our birthday" or "our birthdays." It's not that they had always been such fun. Bruce dreaded each marker of his increasing age, and his attitude helped deflate my own tendency toward cheeriness. I was five years younger than he was, so I got no sympathy if I worried about my age. The day I fussed about turning 40, he was turning 45, etc. It occurs to me, after the fact, that my complaints about getting old could do nothing but exacerbate his age worries. In a way, I think we both felt a little cheated, like those whose birthdays fall on Christmas. We each wanted the other to bake us a cake and fuss over us, so neither of us did much.

Probably every new widow's biggest challenge is getting through the first celebration of her wedding anniversary alone. The closer that is to his death, the harder it may be. It probably was, after all, a private celebration of the happiest day of your life together. Unless you mention it to others, most won't even know of the date's significance for you. You celebrated it as a twosome. No one else needed to know. We had always told our children to remember our birthday(s), since we'd been thoughtful enough to provide just one for the two of us, and Mother's Day and Father's Day would be nice. Our anniversary was optional for them. That was "our day." But what is it now, when we are alone?

As new widows we face that anniversary date and realize there is nothing to celebrate, and no one with whom to celebrate. So what can we do besides mope? Not much the first year, I suspect. At least I couldn't. I tried to run from my sadness the first time April 14 rolled around, at ten months. But finally I faced up to my need to grieve alone that evening. I closed myself inside and spent time remembering Bruce, our wedding day, early years and memorable anniversaries throughout our marriage. I didn't have my old photo albums with me in Florida, but I did have pictures of Bruce taken during his last year, a tape of him singing five years earlier and 36 years of memories. They helped me recreate those joyous days of youth and passion.

I even found and reviewed our wedding vows. I remember I had always thought the phrase "from this day forward...until death us do part" simply meant *forever*, as in infinity. Maybe we all thought that. Is "forever" only until death, ours or our mates? That night I had to face the fact that whatever "forever" meant in most cases, it didn't imply infinity to a marriage with only one spouse left. Not only was Bruce gone, our marriage was over. I remember developing a very tight lump in my throat, finally eased by the release of a few tears. I knew in my head the marriage was over, but it would take a long time to feel unhooked. That night I felt particularly close to him, as though he was with me in spirit. On my second wedding anniversary alone, at 22 months, I was contemplative and blue, but I managed to make it a fairly normal day.

Advice for surviving your first wedding anniversary alone? Do whatever makes you feel comfortable:

- Talk to others about it.

- Cloister yourself and sentimentalize about your young love and happy memories.

- Plan a totally involving activity, such as rafting down the Colorado River, and get through the day without getting maudlin.

- Go out to dinner and a movie with another widow or two. They will understand if you blubber through a comedy.

As with other crises, just get through it! The second one probably will be easier.

In addition to calendar dates, each of us marks off the days, then the weeks, and then the months since he died. One time I had gotten so involved with holiday preparations and traveling, I said to my son, "How old is Marshall now? Five months?" Dave was dumbfounded. So was I. Marshall was born less than two days before Bruce died. I had, temporarily, lost track of the months. It was six months, not five. I saw that as a good sign, that I wasn't preoccupied with the date, but that probably was the last time for almost a year that I couldn't automatically recite, to the day, exactly how long it had been.

I remember calling my sister on the first anniversary of her husband's death. She said, "Oh, thanks for calling, but I'm fine now. It was yesterday, and especially last night, that I suffered." Now I know what she meant, and I feel the same way. Although the date stated on Bruce's death certificate is July 6, the terror for me is the night of July 5. Unconsciously, I believe we begin each day when we normally wake up, not at one second after midnight. July 6, from daylight on, is always anticlimactic for me. The yearly mark is over, and I sigh with relief. So, now I try to remember to call a widow on the day before the dreaded date, especially if it was an early morning death.

—END OF THE FIRST YEAR—

Those of us who have put our hopes in the "one-year to grieve" promise are nearly always disappointed. Several widows said, "The second year is the hardest." When Thelma first suggested this as a possibility I knew she must be an exception to the rule. I was in my first year at the time. But then I found that most widows agreed with her. I'm afraid I must also, but I think that requires some explanation so those of you in the early stages of grief don't become despondent about the length of the road stretched ahead of you.

During the first year, going through shock and numbness and confusion and denial and anxiety and guilt and anger, I knew things could never be worse. And, in some ways, I was right. The intensity of grief is much worse during the earlier months. What is worse the second year is the sadness. There are reasons for this:

- *We feel let down that it isn't over after one year as expected.* I suspect the one-year myth stems from Victorian Days when mourning was ritualized. The widow wore black, "widow's weeds," and took part in no social functions for one year. Mourning during that year was probably more deliberate than it is now.

- *Our support system of friends and relatives backs off after the first year.* By now most either are sick of hearing us moan about our grief or they are satisfied that we no longer need them. We are on our own before we are ready to be, like unfeathered birds kicked from their nests.

- *Our first year is relieved by "highs" from successes, but the second isn't.* At first we continually surprise ourselves with our resilience, our stamina, our talents and abilities. Left alone to deal with all kinds of foreign problems, we are forced to dig deep into our resources and, *voila*, we find we have a good deal more of them than we knew. Our pride in our survival carries us over the incredible, rocky journey of that first year. But by year two we are expected to do it all—and all alone. The second year is quite a comeuppance.

- *We are (I was) very "I/me/my oriented" that first year.* "Can I do it? Yes, I can!" Every day was a new challenge for ME, a new way to test MY mettle. People hovered over ME. I worried about ME. I barely had time to miss poor Bruce; I was too busy, preoccupied with surviving. With the arrival of the second year we are no longer brave pioneers, proving our worth. We tire of struggle; we each long for our helpmate, our ever-present friend, our protector, our lover.

- *I couldn't envision a healthy Bruce the first year.* That seems to be fairly common among widows who witnessed the death. My image was always of him dying beside me. Then, for awhile, I could hardly conjure up an image at all. It took me until well into the second year to recall the Bruce I had married and to miss all our wonderful times together. It was when I could do that that sadness draped over me like a heavy, damp blanket and depression set in.

We may still continue to prove ourselves after that first twelve months, but some of the lift is gone. We expect to be able to do things; others expect us to, too. Having lost both the self-satisfaction of newly discovered abilities and the support system circling to prop us up when we falter, it's no wonder we feel blue that second year. Many of us move into the stage of depression shortly after the one-year mark, probably for those reasons.

In the second year, when we don't need to funnel all our energies into the grieving process and surviving, we suddenly look around and notice couples our age laughing together, kissing, and playfully teasing each other. Then we begin to realize how lucky they are to be taking cruises together, helping each other in the kitchen, working in the garden, playing tennis together, playing with grandchildren, making love to each other. And we feel melancholy. Just writing about it makes me feel sad.

"Some little thing would set me off," Dale told me, "such as seeing a couple holding hands or just enjoying each other's company." Many others, such as Karen and June, reported similar feelings each time they watched amusing grandchildren who were born after their husband's death. Thelma says, "The grief, of course, has a different quality now. It is more of an ache, an intense longing to be with that person who was so much a part of you."

The first year might be compared to a deep, ulcerated gash in the mid-section; the second year, for me at least, was more like an agonizing backache. Both are very painful, but in different ways. The grief that carries on into later years may be more like a dull headache with occasional acute flare-ups. This later pain didn't prevent me from getting on with my life, but it took some of the fun out of it.

When does it get easier? No one can say, except that it gets easier gradually, and that it can sometimes be interrupted by very difficult setbacks. Progress is neither continuous nor predictable. Some women enter new relationships or exciting careers, helping end the worst of it. Some make a determined effort to "get on with their lives," by volunteerism, travel or a consuming avocation. Dale, for example, says she became so busy and involved with her photography that, looking back, she isn't sure she even gave herself enough chance to grieve.

If your intense grief seems to be stuck to you like crazy glue, for more than a few years, it might be worth prodding a bit. Make an appointment with a professional counselor and ask for help cutting you loose. If you are more the "I'll do it myself type," go to the self-help aisle of the library or the bookstore and plot yourself a course in how to force yourself back into this living world. Diane says she found it helped her to issue a few casual invitations, asking one or two women for lunch or inviting two couples in for a simple supper. "I even shared with one woman ahead of time that it would be difficult for me, but that I needed to learn how to be sociable again." Continuing to grieve inconsolably after several years does nothing to honor your husband or your former life together. It only makes your precious life miserable and it worries those around you.

If what my widowed friends say is correct, our pain should gradually recede until it is no longer the focus of our lives. But we will continue to miss our husbands forever.

6

Saying Good-bye: Not to Forget, but to Move Forward

Life can only be understood backwards,
but it must be lived forwards.

—Soren Kierkegaard

Annie's Journal (9 1/2 months)
Dear Bruce: Writing this letter has been good for me. I realized I'm writing as if you still have feelings, as if you're alive. Guess I am in denial. My counselor says I need to say good-bye to you; that will help me accept your death. I can tell I don't want to. Every time I think about it I cry. Though I have done well, outwardly, since you died, it seems I have not let you go. I am clinging to you in death almost more than I did in life. Where is my strength when I need it?

Mike, my counselor, suggested among other things to deal with my denial, that I write Bruce a long letter. I was to tell him everything I loved and admired about him, and what I missed most. That would be easy. I was looking forward to it. "Then," Mike said, "I want you to tell Bruce everything that made you angry about him and your life together, and about any ways that your life is better without him." He must be kidding, I thought! After only nine months, I not only thought the assignment cruel and unusual punishment, but that I wouldn't be able to come up with anything negative to say.

I have not reprinted that entire letter, although I refer to it occasionally throughout the book. It was too long, and some was too personal and revealing to share with anyone. Did it dispel my penchant for denial completely? No. But it certainly helped. I learned, for one thing, that my subconscious still thought of Bruce as alive, or at least totally present in spirit. In six single-spaced pages of feelings that poured out through my computer, I never considered it necessary to tell him how I was doing or what had happened to me or our family since his death. It was as though I assumed he already knew that, like he had been watching over my shoulder ever since he died, which is exactly where I had been picturing him.

In some ways I know I still denied his death at 22 months. I made note of the fact that I would forget and use the plural "we" and "us." I would still dream of him, although his significance in the dreams had begun eroding, just as I had read it would. Occasionally I would catch myself in the men's department looking for a nice new shirt for him. I addressed some journal entries to Bruce. I still felt disoriented, as though I wasn't quite sure whether I was part of a pair or single.

But now hear this! I suspected then, and firmly believe now, that at some time each of us must consciously unhook from the moorings of our past, bid *bon voyage* to our late spouses and mean it! Only then can we take the helm and bravely set a new course for our lives. The *when* is a problem. Knowing it and doing it are two different things, too. I thought I had done that when we dispersed Bruce's ashes. I said good-bye; I felt it was final. I thought I had wrapped it up for sure when I gave away the last of his possessions. And when I changed our bedroom; and when I sold his little car; and when I endured "our anniversary" and "the one-year anniversary," and...

But my mind clung tenaciously to the idea of his death being temporary. I dreamed several times the first year that he came back to life and to me. I was thrilled, and not terribly surprised in the dreams. My biggest concern was how I could explain this to neighbors, the kids and all those who had mourned his death. How would they accept this phenomenon? The consummate worrier; I even worry in my dreams.

While my conscious mind kept objecting, knowing full well he couldn't come back, my subconscious mind compromised. It let me think he was just one step removed from this life, not quite alive but not quite dead, watching and listening to all I did. I didn't talk aloud with him regularly, as did many of the widows with whom I spoke. But I often carried on a one-sided mental conversation with him and I continually wondered what he was thinking. There were many times I imagined (almost heard) him roaring with laughter, or shaking his head when I lost my glasses or my keys, saying "Annie, Annie, Annie. What AM I going to do with you?" It was (almost) like having him there.

For the record, notes I made after the second year marker indicated a feeling that I was finally letting him go. "Either that," I said, "...or he is finally turning me loose to sink or swim!" I think that was a turning point for me; not the end of my grief, but rather a major step toward the end. Your own "turning point" may be subtle or dramatic, and it may take you more or less time than it took me.

Don't try to compare your progress with others. Just continue to try new ways of helping yourself accept reality so you can move toward a new life alone.

—PARANORMAL HAPPENINGS—

The San Diego Widowhood Project estimates that one third of all widows hear, see or feel their dead partners' presence. From my interviews with nearly 60 widows, I might have guessed that number to be higher. Many of them reported they had felt such things; some after many years. A good number told me about what must be considered paranormal phenomena. They reported hearing their husband's familiar footsteps, or his voice calling them, or doors opening and closing as they always had when he came home at night.

Many women told of feeling solid taps on their shoulders, as though their spouses were trying to get their attention. I have felt that distinct "tap" several times myself, and there is never any way to explain it away. It isn't exactly frightening, but it surely gets my attention. Sometimes I rethink a situation to be sure I'm not making a big mistake.

One woman reported seeing an owl perch outside her bedroom window shortly after her husband died. It seemed to stare at her, watching every move. She felt certain it was her husband. The owl continued to appear every day, until she reached a point where she felt capable of handling her new life. Then "he" flew away and, she believes, left her on her own.

Another widow reported to me, that at about two weeks, when she felt particularly sorry for herself, one of two nearby hanging beds had begun to swing wildly back and forth on its chains. There was no "earthly" explanation for the movement, so she interpreted it as a reassuring sign from her husband. She said to me, "If I ever deny this happened later, don't believe me. It really did happen." But two months later she said she was sure it had been a figment of her overwrought imagination; she had needed the reassurance, so her mind had provided it.

I would like to feel smug and pooh-pooh all such reports (that cockiness, again) or to refer to them as hallucinations spun off an irrational mind, as most psychologists do. It would make life more logical, more in keeping with scientific theory, easier for my mind to accept. But I've had too many unexplainable things happen in my own life, and I've read and heard impressive evidence of forces we can't explain with the scientific method of proof. Whether we attribute these forces to God, angels, an advanced mental state, ESP or a universal spirituality, these "events" seem to be more than pure coincidence or imagination.

Making such an "irrational" statement may put me in bad stead with scientists and secular humanists, but I can only tell you what I believe. After a great deal of soul-searching, I decided to go one step further down the road of possible incredibility, and share with you two experiences I had as a relatively new widow that I have previously only shared with one or two close friends.

When I was trying to revive Bruce I had the distinct and overwhelming impression that he was hovering above me. I even looked up at the ceiling, expecting to see him. I didn't see him, but I "knew" he was there. I had heard of people coming back from near-death experiences, so I yelled up at "him," angrily, "Oh, no you don't!" and returned to my task with renewed determination…to bring him back down to earth. I can still feel the certainty I felt at the time, and I knew it was not just hallucination.

Much later, after almost two years, I saw an incredibly convincing display of "unnatural light" shining on Bruce's little woodland pool, which he had designed and babied into existence. The sun itself was behind the pool and behind miles of thick woodland. It was not reflecting off of anything and no electric lights were on outside at the time. There was NO explainable source of light. I could not create a shadow anywhere by holding my hand near the pool. In addition, it seemed to have a supernatural quality, as if it was more than just light. It was spooky. Not knowing what else to do, I went inside and ignored it. Although this weird episode lasted for at least two hours, it seemed too weird for me to share with anyone. So I tucked it safely into the back of my mind, and got back to a writing assignment with a looming deadline.

Many months later, I heard a very competent woman friend tell how she and three sisters had seen a very strange light glowing in the corner of their bedroom the night after attending their other sister's funeral. They were certain it was their sister, perhaps coming to say good-bye. Years earlier I might have dismissed this story much as I had my own experience and let it go at that. This time, however, it shocked me with the full impact of what my own light might have meant. Was it Bruce? I guess that little pool would have been the place of choice, had he wanted to contact me.

I wrote down my experience in great detail and shared it with two trusted friends, who happen to be Zen Buddhists. They accepted it at face value and assured me I didn't have to figure it out. I should just accept what I saw. That sufficed until I got back to Wisconsin, where I had seen the glow nearly a year earlier. I decided then, looking at that garden pool in the deep shade, that I had to have been hallucinating. I could not have seen what I thought I saw. My logical brain simply couldn't deal with anything so transcendental. At least for the moment I felt more at ease, once I decided it had not really happened.

My experience helped me to better understand those with similar stories to tell; those who had told of mysterious happenings that they felt sure had really happened but later recanted. Many of us are too uncomfortable with the unknown and super-natural to accept such happenings as reality. And yet…

Several women mentioned inexplicable phone calls they felt were messages or signs from their deceased husbands. In some cases no one spoke but they felt a warmth come through the phone, like a big hug. I know of a few cases where a friend or close relative of the widow claims to have spoken by phone with the deceased. One such terrified woman says the deceased man was desperately looking for his wife, and he wanted her to tell him where she was. She did. She claims he even called later with a message to be relayed to his wife. These people were, at the time, 100 percent sure they had spoken with the deceased man, or listened to him, and they were visibly shaken by the experience.

"It didn't just sound like Bruce," my brother-in-law told me, desperately. "I know Bruce's voice better than my own. It was him!" In that case Tom was referring to an operator's message he heard after he misdialed a phone call in Arizona. He thought Bruce might have recorded a message years earlier, having worked for the Bell System. I checked with Bruce's department. He had not. Tom is a perfectly rational man, as are the others who reported such inexplicable events. We recent widows might be considered "temporarily unstable," but what about those somewhat removed from the grief? Their stories are quite convincing. So I've decided to consider it all just "beyond our level of understanding." I'm going to keep an open mind.

I am reminded of a TV interview with Joan Borysenko, Ph.D., author of *Minding the Body, Mending the Mind*, and a researcher of alternative medicines at Harvard Medical School. She said, "It's good to keep an open mind, but don't let your brains fall out." Isn't that wonderful? I guess that's what we all should do, keep our minds open while maintaining a hold on our sanity. I don't think my brains are falling out, just because I am willing to concede that there may be more to life, death, and intelligence than we yet know. Stacks of books have been written on paranormal phenomena for those interested in pursuing the subject, some by revered authorities. I am in no position to comment further, except to say that when it happens to you, it is awfully hard NOT to believe it is really happening. And by the same token, as the memory fades, or the conscious mind becomes too uncomfortable with what it can't explain, it's hard not to rebel and deny that it ever really happened.

Perhaps this is one of life's great mysteries, one we will only know the answer to when our days on earth are over.

—DREAMS CAN HELP OR HINDER—

When I began having nightmarish dreams about Bruce dying, I tried some amateur self-hypnosis. I had heard it is possible to remember your dreams by telling yourself before sleep that you want to remember them. I decided the reverse must also be true, and I didn't want to recall these very disturbing dreams. I am sure they were necessary to the deep recesses of my subconscious, working something out for my own good. But, unless they were to be somehow useful to me in adjusting to Bruce's death, I didn't need them upsetting me the next day. So, each night before sleep I told myself, "I only want to remember good dreams and useful dreams." It either worked, or I quit having the nightmares.

I remember one dream, at 16 months, as if it just happened. It was an odd dream, in that I sensed throughout that I was probably dreaming. Within the dream I kept performing little tests to prove I was wide awake. I stared hard at a rock, for example, and because I was able to see every little grain of sand and fissure in the rock, I was convinced I was not dreaming. I think you will see, as I could, the message of the dream.

Another couple and Bruce and I were at LaGuardia Airport, on our way to Athens, Greece. (In real life Bruce and I never traveled abroad.) I left my luggage with the other three and went shopping in the terminal mall. Suddenly, realizing that I was a little late, I rushed back to find that the three had already left on the tram. (LaGuardia doesn't have trams, does it?) I felt furious, especially that they had taken my luggage with them. I wasted time checking incoming luggage carousels, but then ran "miles" for the tram, which had left without me.

I knew the next tram would be too late, so I started out looking for the manager of the airline, who was supposedly at home a mile or so behind the airport. I had to walk over rugged piles of rocks and debris and climb over fences, trying to get to her house. She was apparently going to stop the plane for me? I remember thinking how absurd this was, but that I had better keep going—even if it was only a dream—because I wanted so badly to see Bruce again. I also realized, in the dream, how unfair it was to be angry with him for taking my luggage with him. He had obviously done so hoping I would catch up in time. The dream ended without drama, but symbolically. I was told the plane and Bruce were gone, without me, and I would just have to find my way back home (without my luggage and with very little money) and make the best of things. Perhaps that explains why, subconsciously, I kept expecting Bruce to return any day.

Some women report simple dreams. Betty says, "I just dream that he is there beside me in bed and then the dream is gone." After three years, Dale said, "I don't dream of him as often as I used to. When I do…and then wake up to find it's not true, I am so sad and disappointed. I miss him even more." Others report they see him, but he won't speak to them. Women who nursed husbands through terminal illnesses often are plagued with nightmares of their husbands being ill, calling out for help, and of not being able to help them.

I haven't dreamed of Bruce for quite some time now, but after the dream I described, when he left and flew away without me, my dreams showed Bruce as being less and less important to the dream. He was there, but he didn't contribute and I couldn't visualize him clearly. In one, for example, I was struggling with some difficult decision and Bruce kept disappearing whenever I would turn to him for help. From what I have read, this is expected and shows that I am finally accepting his death, slowly but surely.

—LETTING GO OF HIM—

It is natural to relinquish our loved ones a bit at a time, as we can. It's as if we each have him on a kite string, which we reel out a little bit, tug back, let out a bit more, watch for awhile, give another few feet, etc. But at some point, we must let the spool unwind completely and snip the cord where it's attached. If we are ready, if the time has come for that break, we should feel a wonderful exhilaration as he floats free of us. Because then we are both free. That doesn't mean we will forget our time together with our husbands. It means we can remember it as the past, without letting it control our present or our future. We can fashion a new life that fits our current needs, rather than futilely hang onto the one that fit the life for the two of us.

Let's hope we're not like my darling granddaughter, Jessica, when she was just three. She loved my pretty kite, as long as she could hug it. But, when I tried to show her how to fly it, she cried inconsolably, for fear it would go away and get lost. We finally had to reel my pretty kite in and take it home to the garage, so it would be safe.

If you are reading this just weeks or months into your grief, don't think that you must cut yourself free from grief just because you have reached this chapter. Grief takes time; don't rush it. But read through this chapter so you will understand that you will need to say good-bye to your husband, and your life as his wife, before you can heal completely.

Eventually, we each should give up the role of grieving widow, and move on in life as independent women. No one can say whether that will happen in six months or six years for you. The timing will depend on circumstances of the death, on your life experiences to date and on your personality. If you are aware of the need for this break, you will do it more easily and more quickly when the proper time comes. Why would anyone kick free of a comfortable cocoon if they didn't know they were supposed to? Caterpillars have built-in alarm systems for when they should emerge as butterflies. We don't always. If we get too comfortable with our grief, we find it hard to cut loose from it. We like the cocoon. It is safe.

An excerpt from my journal at 27 months:

Dear Bruce: I was afraid to start grieving. I knew it would hurt. But now I think I am afraid to stop grieving. This rut is familiar. I expect friends to think, "She's still grieving, poor girl." There comes a time—and for me I can see it is soon—when I will have to square my shoulders and say to myself, "Enough! No more excuses. You, Annie, are a big girl who had a bad experience. Almost everyone does sooner or later. Get on with your life!" Funny…why does that stir guilt feelings, like I would be deserting YOU? I always said, and I firmly believe, that you would have re-married within the first year, had I died first. Knowing that should help as, like the phoenix, I struggle to rise rejuvenated from the ashes."

—TEARS THAT WON'T START, STOP—

One reason I call this book *For Widows Only!* is that there are things about being a widow no one else can understand. There are those who assume if we don't cry during the memorial service that we didn't love him. And if we are able to go out with friends and appear normal within the first months, that, too, means we didn't care. On the other hand I have heard people, even other widows, say about women why cry easily and often, "She must feel guilty she wasn't nicer to him when he was alive," or "That's some act she puts one." We hear that tears are therapeutic, but we see friends and relatives express discomfort if we shed them. So many mixed messages. How can we please all these people who think they know what's best for us?

Don't try to please everyone! Don't worry what others think; cry when you feel like it; help yourself cry if you aren't able; seek help if you can't seem to stop. Tears are for your benefit, not theirs.

Near the one-year mark, I realized I either had been gone or had company all but a total of seven days out of the previous six weeks. I intentionally used those seven precious nights to cry. I read a tear-jerker of a novel four nights, listened to Bruce's singing tape on three. Crying was easy; I probably could have done so reading a dictionary. I was ready. I'm sure some people think that to plan time to cry and grieve is somehow artificial, as though we are just pretending we are sad. Not so. Some of us who are seldom alone, whether it's because of children around, too much company or sharing living quarters with someone, must plan times when we feel comfortable letting down our defenses and crying. Storing up unshed tears too long can cause serious health problems. According to research at St. Paul-Ramsey Medical Center, shedding tears actually washes away toxic substances that build up from emotional stress and sadness. Crying helps correct our chemical imbalance and restores health.

Still, although we may know of its value, some of us do not cry easily. Many of the women I interviewed worried that they weren't able to cry enough, or at all. They felt terribly sad, but tears would not come. This phenomenon worried me, too, at first; I thought I was demented that I couldn't cry. My sister reassured me. "Don't worry if the tears don't come at once," she said. "If your friends judge you by that, it's not important. If you prefer to keep it private or if you embarrass them with too many tears, don't punish yourself about that either. It's YOUR loss; you handle it in your own way." Jeanne said she determined to use all her strength to keep grief and tears to herself. "There have been times I have broken down and cried—at home or in my car alone—and I think this is an emotion which must be allowed to happen, and so I do...but only when I am alone."

After a few weeks I felt I needed to find some way to pull the plug on all the tears I had bottled up. I remembered Bruce's singing tape. Five years earlier he had recorded a 90 minute tape of himself, accompanied by our Singing Machine's background music, singing familiar ballads and love songs. My first thought upon hearing it after he died, was "Wow! What a treasure to have a record of his voice. It's so much more personal than a photograph or handwriting." And I was amazed at how meaningful all the old lyrics suddenly were. But then each song dug a little deeper, dredging up unexpressed love, sadness and, finally, tears. I doubt any widow could listen to her husband crooning the words to songs such as "Sentimental Journey," "Stardust," "Tenderly," "Unchained Melody," "The Way We Were" and "I Did it My Way" without crying. I think I had never really listened to the words before. They are remarkably poignant when the singer was your husband, and he has died. Each suddenly felt like a personal message to me from Bruce. Listening to them worked like magic for me whenever I needed to cry during those first two years.

Other widows read a heart-rending love story, watch a teary movie or read sad poetry their husbands loved. Looking at scrapbooks or photo albums helps some widows. Visiting your husband's grave or crypt may help. One middle-aged lady crawled up and sat in the tree house her husband had so lovingly built for their son years earlier. There she could cry. Writing a totally honest letter to him can do it, too. As they say, "whatever works."

Most women said they had problems crying and needed to prompt the tears. But a few, especially the younger ones, cried rivers. Anna, whose husband died in an auto accident more than 30 years before I met her, says the hardest moment was telling her four young daughters that their father was dead. "Seeing their hurt and disbelief is the most heart-wrenching experience of a lifetime," she said. "My crying began at that moment and it was excessive. I cried for a week, in my own world. I felt separate and alone. One week later my mother-in-law woke me up with these words: 'Your children feel like they lost a father and a mother. Perhaps someone could care for them while you recover.' That stopped the crying and brought me to reality. These were our children; they, too, were hurting, bewildered and feeling abandoned. From that day forward the children were my cause, my reason for waking up. They gave me healing and a positive outlook."

Eunie dug back into her memories of 1942, when she was 31 and lost her young husband. She said, "Howie's death was unexpected and a terrible shock.... In retrospect, I did cry excessively. Often I was embarrassed because I would cry for a reason not apparent to those around me."

Pauli says, "I cried unexpectedly and in various places: the grocery store, visiting with friends, driving the car. I always cried in church because his funeral was there. I cried when the choir sang; we both sang in the choir. I cried over nothing, or feeling scared, or feeling sorry for myself because the children had no father, anything. I cried when I looked at baby Erik, and as he grew older and looked so much like his Dad, I cried. I cried on each presidential Election Day, as Will had struggled so to walk to vote just weeks before he died. He was so thin and weak and the weather was so windy and cold. He voted and I cried."

Eventually these women's lives moved on, and the tears subsided. Eventually most do. But sometimes it takes much too long. If your tears don't decrease and become rare within a few months, do something to help yourself. Read self-help books, visit a widow support group, set up counseling sessions with your pastor or a private counselor. Doing so doesn't mean anything is wrong with you, just that you need supportive help at this time. Those who have moved beyond the copious tears will soon come to see that life continues and that it is worthwhile.

—THE WEDDING RING—

I asked widows if, or when, they had removed their wedding bands and why, or why not? The answers ranged widely.

"I haven't," Betty said, after 22 months. "It's been there so long! I tried moving it to the right hand, but it doesn't fit. I'm thinking of having it and my diamond redone into a cocktail ring, but I have procrastinated on that."

"I did, on the first anniversary." (Several said this or something similar.)

"I removed my ring at eight months, after a retreat where others said they had done so. If I had it to do over, I would do the same thing."

"I keep it on for security." (Several gave this reason for making no change.)

Dale said, "It never occurred to me to remove my ring until someone said I would never have a date unless I did so. I'm not looking for dates—and I don't feel like removing my ring."

"I removed my ring after one year," a young widow wrote. "I had a happy marriage, and I would like to remarry someday. I'm available; why pretend I'm not? Maybe I'm just more candid than some."

"I didn't take mine off until seven years after his death," Pauli said. "It was 'safe' not to do so earlier. But finally my children said that if I continued to wear my rings they would never get another dad. So I had the stones reset into a beautiful ring I always wear."

Signaling availability is one reason for removing the ring. And it is a viable one. You may not choose to announce your own availability, but I would hope none of you thinks ill of others who wish to do so. It speaks well for their former marriages. Pauli says, "I once heard that the greatest compliment a widow or widower can pay a dead spouse is to remarry. That's because their marriage had been good and they would want that good life to happen again. I would love to have remarried years ago."

Another good reason for removing the wedding band is to nudge a stubborn mind that refuses to accept the death of a spouse. At about nine months I felt the need, after my counselor suggested I had the need, to break free of the denial stage of grief. I wanted to arrive at acceptance so I could move on. I also felt young enough in my late fifties to do a lot more living, but I didn't have forever, either. I'm not interested now, but if I am ever to find a new love, it can't be after 28 or 29 years, as it was for those who were widowed in their 20s or 30s.

Most counselors advise removing the ring to aid in healing the mind. But if you don't feel you're strong enough yet, and that doing so would upset you too much, that would seem to negate any advantage. My advice: If you want to remove your wedding ring now, do. If you don't want to, leave it on for now. But try to accept, as you can, that with your husband's death your marriage ended. Be sure your reasons for leaving the ring on are valid, and not just a way of clinging to your "late marriage," when you should be building a new life for yourself.

—WAYS TO SAY GOOD-BYE—

Ask yourself once in awhile: Am I grieving too long? Am I taking the easy way, avoiding the hard task of building an independent life? Am I hanging onto the kite string as though my late husband were my only mainstay in life? Am I ready to let go and face life alone? When you are ready, you'll probably know. Although some women never do move beyond the role of widow, afraid to take the risk, others say they slowly eased into their new life and didn't realize they were changing.

Saying good-bye—and meaning it—isn't easy, but it is important. It's probably easier if you've resolved your own concerns about death, or if you believe in a life hereafter. Some say it's easier if your marriage was happy and you feel no regrets. Others say that's hogwash; they believe those recalling disastrous marriages break away more easily, because they don't feel as much loneliness as those who lost their soul mates.

Your age may make a difference. Younger women are generally more adaptable, on the one hand, but on the other they may be left with burdens they feel unable to shoulder. They may also feel cheated to have their young love destroyed. Older women might have more financial and emotional resources, but feel ill-equipped to forge a new life alone when all they have known is marriage. The widow who approached her mate's death openly with him and said proper good-byes before he died, may find it easiest to proceed, although she still will grieve.

If you feel it's time to say good-bye, to make a noticeable break, consider these suggestions:

- Write your late husband a letter, poem or song. And end it by saying good-bye.

- Remove your ring. Buy another if you, like I, are bothered with feelings of a "phantom" ring.

- Assemble a scrapbook of your years together, give it a hug and then put it away.

- Put away most photos of him, as well as most of his trophies and personal items.

- Replace "his chair" with one that fits you.

- Give away his gun, stamp, or coin collection and start a different collection of your own.

- Cancel his golf (or tennis) membership and buy a symphony (or fitness) membership for yourself.

If you don't respond to such subtle nudges, try these more dramatic moves:

- Sell "his" car, "his" boat or even "his" house, saying good-bye to him when you do.

- After a year or so, move to a new city or state to start your new life. Unfamiliar surroundings can make it easier.

- Make your availability known; tell your friends you are receptive to meeting a man, if you are.

Saying good-bye is more than just symbolic. It's a way for your emotions to tie a ribbon around one part of your life and set it aside, so you can move on to another part. Virginia said, "You have to say good-bye before you can say hello again." I wasn't sure what she meant, and asked. "You have to get rid of your own pain and anger and grief," she said. "Then you are free to relive the wonderful times you had together as if he were still alive."

My counselor said something along the same line at about nine months. I asked why I continued to feel anger. "Why can't I remember the wonderful warm and loving times we had together instead?" He cocked his head and said, "Don't you suppose remembering the loving times will hurt more? You have to be ready for that. When you're still raw with grief, it's easier to focus on the parts about him you won't miss than those you will."

It's important for you to realize that your own grief's chronology will be different from that of mine, or of this book's. It still may help to read and think about it, while you meander, plow or stumble your way through the everyday problems of adapting to life without your husband.

End of my good-bye letter (nine months)...*After some soul-searching I decided to be dramatic and remove my wedding band tonight. I have not wanted to before; I still worry people will misinterpret it as an announcement of my availability. That's not my intention at all. Taking it off will be emotionally wrenching and, I hope, nudge me closer to reality. You really are gone, aren't you? Forever. This time it was real.* **Later that night:** *The ring is off. It wasn't easy; it had built a 35-year-old niche* *around my finger to call home. But I finally did it. I am no longer married. "…till death us do part." I am just Annie Thompson Estlund, alone but surviving, about to embark on the second half of my life…as soon as I can stop bawling. Good-bye my dear.*

PART II
What Now? Living in the Present

If you will call your 'troubles' 'experiences,'
and remember that every experience develops some latent force within you,
you will grow vigorous and happy,
however adverse your circumstances may seem to be.

—Celestial Seasonings Herbal Tea box

7

Alone but Not Lonely—Trying New Activities

You can't prevent birds of sorrow from flying over your head,
but you can prevent them from building nests in your hair.

—Chinese Proverb

Annie's Journal (11 months)
Dear Journal: I'm alone tonight…and loving it! I need time to think, to cry a little, to read, to write. I love all my friends and relatives. I invite them to visit often and I fully enjoy it when they do. In addition I accept almost all invitations these days, whether for dinner or rafting on the Guadalupe or a trip to Paris. It's just that I tend to become overbooked and I desperately need some private downtime to replenish my sagging resources.

"Lucky her!" I can almost hear the chorus, chirping about how little I know about loneliness. Maybe you'll feel better after reading journal entries for later chapters. But I confess aloneness, especially during the first year, probably was not as bad for me as for some of you because of my living arrangements.

In Wisconsin my neighbors and I walked—and talked—about four miles a day. Included in the usual group were two other widows and a divorcee, as well as two intact couples. That kind of support is worth solid gold when you're a new widow. I was active in several women's organizations, with close friends in each, and I knew a good number of other people in the area. In addition, old friends came to visit when they vacationed in this tourist county. During winters in Florida I lived in a small (72-unit) complex of townhouses. The full and almost full-timers, like myself, had established a book club, an ethnic eating society, a pool fitness group and a birthday club. We often walked the beach together, shopped together and socialized informally. In addition, several of my good Wisconsin friends wintered nearby, and we spent time together regularly. I was never alone for very long. I was lucky, and I knew it.

But sometimes I had an embarrassment of riches. It was easy to become over-booked when you lived in the best of two worlds. Bruce and I had picked those spots because we thought they were among this country's most attractive and popular tourist spots. We had welcomed a steady stream of guests, and I continued to do that for awhile after he died. During the first year, more people than usual initiated visits either to my home or theirs, supporting me and checking to be sure I was okay. I accumulated more than 35,000 frequent flyer miles on four airlines, and put 20,000 miles on my car, mostly visiting grandchildren, relatives and old friends. I probably ate half my lunches and dinners OUT, or IN with friends, during that year. It made the year go by fairly quickly.

Occasionally, I felt swamped with activity, though, and complained about being too busy, usually to those very guests or friends who were keeping me busy for my own good. How dumb can you get? If there's anything worse than being overbooked, it's being dropped by your friends. That's a far more common complaint among widows, and a much harder one to contend with.

The frenetic activity of my year helped, but it didn't dispel my loneliness. I learned the difference between being alone and being lonely. It's perfectly possible, I found, to feel lonely while laughing with a friend or while visiting with a whole crowd of people. You aren't just lonely for people, you're lonely for the other half of you, your mate, your love. Nothing can fix that.

Loneliness was by far the most common problem mentioned by the widows I interviewed. Some underlined it many times or drew multiple circles around it on their questionnaires. Loneliness is a problem we all face, to varying degrees, and it doesn't always go away easily. But after the most intense grieving has ended, you often can help to relieve your emotional loneliness.

Let me add a note about physical longing. As time passes you also may experience physical loneliness, the intense longing to share intimacy and sex with another man. For most of us, this takes some time, so I deal with these feelings and what you can do about them in a later chapter. Just know that if or when you have those feelings, it's because you are a perfectly normal woman who has, at least temporarily, been isolated from perfectly normal behavior. Some women find these feelings quite disturbing when their mates have died, filling them with guilt or shame. What they fail to realize is that their bodies, too, miss their deceased mates. More on this subject later.

—SUNDAYS ARE THE PITS—

I was lonely for Bruce from day one. But the first time I recall feeling *"lonely,"* was on a rainy Sunday during my second month alone. No phone ringing, no doorbell, no commitments on my calendar. By mid-morning I began peering out my window for signs of activity and stewing about why it was so quiet. I knew my closest friends were busy, out of town or entertaining guests. Even my kids were occupied and had no time to dawdle on the phone with their pitiful Mom.

I knew if Bruce were alive we would be busy puttering in the yard or garage, reading quietly and companionably, or working the Sunday crossword puzzle together. Or else we would go out for brunch and shopping. But he wasn't alive. I was alone, and I was lonely, for him but also for attention. When there's no one to respond to you, you begin to wonder if you exist. I felt almost panicky. Until that day, I hadn't realized that on Sundays most people pair off with their mates and enjoy private time together. I felt deflated. I didn't have a mate; I wasn't part of a pair. What was I supposed to do? Sundays happen pretty often. Was this what every Sunday would be like from now one? Had everyone gone back to enjoying their time together and forgotten about me? Had I been crossed off all the social lists where the rest were couples? As new widows, our confidence is easily shaken those first months.

After about an hour of this, I mentally gave myself a swift kick. I reminded myself of those times when the kids were small or when a football game was blaring on TV or when neighbors stopped in for coffee once too often, when I had wished for time alone. "Well, now you have it," I scolded. "And what's more, apparently you will have it almost every Sunday. What are you going to do with it?" I knew I had a jillion choices. All I had to do was pick one at any time.

Odd thoughts came back to haunt me. In my "life before" I had often said, in a know-it-all way, "I can understand almost every human condition but one…boredom. There's so much to do and so little time to do it, how can anyone ever say they're bored?" Unless one is depressed, which is totally different from just lacking for something to do, I found boredom totally unacceptable. "If I were bored for one minute," I would continue to spout, "I would pick up a good book to read and then I wouldn't be. Or, I would clean out a drawer, if that appealed to me, or go for a walk and take a different route, or get out the photo albums and update them, or take a wildflower book into the fields and identify whatever is blooming, or open an encyclopedia and read the first thing I came to, or bake a pie to take to my invalid neighbor, or prune the hedge, or call an old college friend I haven't seen for years, or…. There is no end to the ways I could un-bore myself."

But, I soon realized that loneliness isn't the same as boredom. It's not even the same as solitude or aloneness. Loneliness is a feeling of isolation, of feeling disconnected from the rest of your world. It's how I felt that Sunday. It's like you've been "cut off," as you sometimes are from a phone conversation. It is a very real problem for widows, as it must be for widowers, the divorced and other singles in our society. After eight years alone, Peg told me, "Sundays and holidays are the worst. Loneliness is always there."

I finally developed a two-part Sunday ritual that helped me through the most trying months. First, I took a big step for me; I started going to church regularly. I liked the minister who had conducted Bruce's service, and many of my friends were a part of his congregation. I realized I could profit by gentle reminders about living life well and I needed to feel I was part of a "community" of like-minded people. However, that's a very personal decision; it can seem right for some and wrong for others. Several women told me they returned to their neglected religious practices when they were left alone. Some had felt a gaping hole in their lives for some time, but only recognized what was missing when widowhood fractured their lives and caused them to reassess what was important to them. Many had been influenced by their husbands to use their Sundays in other ways. When those patterns were no longer viable, they found comfort in the routine of religious services. Some rushed back to church in desperation, seeking solace and understanding for their misery. Many said they became more devout, and credited God for helping them through their grief. "I felt lonely," one woman said, "but I knew I was never alone as long as I had my church and my faith in God."

For some widows, though, that faith was severely shaken. "How could God do this to me?" Tears came to the eyes of a young friend when she said, "What kind of God would take a fine, healthy young man, and leave me with children to try to raise alone?" Still others had problems going to church because of the flood of memories that unleashed. Pauli said that sitting in church reminded her of the funeral and the choir reminded her of the years she and Will sang with them. Joan said, "…the one thing I allowed to be a problem as a new widow was not going to church every Sunday as we had done for 35 years. It became a 'thing' that I clearly see now is a terrible waste. Hopefully this note will prompt me to add that back to my life." She added this advice: "Religion is most important for some people—but if that isn't your comfort, don't let guilt nag at you. Get to know yourself and go with your own needs." Church attendance helped me, once I moved out of numbness. But, by Sunday noon I knew I would be back home, facing a long and lonely afternoon and evening unless I made a plan to short-circuit that misery.

In my too-busy past, I had often wished I had time to paint, especially with watercolors. So I tried to turn out an instant Monet. I quickly discovered it takes more than time to paint with watercolors. I shopped, and hinted for Christmas gifts, eventually outfitting my studio (the dining room table) with the proper paints, brushes, paper and all kinds of paraphernalia. My attempts were still dismal at first, doing little to cheer up my Sundays. Finally I took a series of classes and learned the basics of painting "wet on wet, inch by inch." I completed one good size painting and several small ones, which are not great, but are somewhat north of mediocre. But I became frustrated that first year because, due to grief and some potent medication, I couldn't retain the instructions well enough to paint alone at home. So after several months I put away my painting supplies and tried to find a new hobby.

A Florida friend taught me some simple techniques for painting pretty T-shirts, sweatshirts and visors. Suddenly that became a passion, and my Sunday pastime spilled over into weekdays and evenings. I had a lot of fun doing that, and my flagging self-esteem loved the bonus of getting raves about them. I painted a few "masterpieces" on commission, but most (about 70 T-shirts, 30 sweatshirts and 100 visors) went out as gifts to friends and relatives. I was cheered to find that I had some latent talent, which I thought had died 37 years earlier when I began college as a mediocre art major.

I became very protective of my Sunday time for painting. Boredom was gone. I could hardly wait to get home from church and into old clothes. I began to turn down invitations so I could stay home, alone, to finish shirts for Christmas or birthdays. I usually listened to jazz or the classics on public radio and sipped from my jug of tasty iced tea. I could think or not; I could hum along with the music or just listen; I could puddle up if I heard "our song"; or I could swear if the paint decided to blob in the wrong spot. When that happened, I refused to let it ruin my day, though. Sometimes I threw it into a sink full of water, to see if the whole shirt turned an interesting color. Other times I just wadded up the offensive shirt, tossed it in the garbage and moved on to another effort. Luckily it didn't happen very often and the shirts were pretty cheap.

I learned a valuable lesson from my shirt-painting spree: I love keeping company with myself. Many people never reach that stage; some become supremely anxious when required to spend time alone with themselves. But I loved it. It's probably lucky I had a little dog who insisted on being walked with regularity, and that I had friends who insisted I crawl out of my cave and be sociable on a regular basis. Otherwise I might have become a happy hermit.

For some women alone, Sunday has become a day to putter in the garden, dressed in grubbies and crusty old garden gloves. For others it's a day to put their feet up and read novels just for fun. Several mentioned they have become addicted to "How to…" arts and crafts or decorating programs on cable TV. One lady writes letters all afternoon. One goes to lunch alone at a nice restaurant, followed by a good movie. A younger woman, who works full-time, says she spends her Sunday "cooking up a storm," for the enjoyment of it and to provide meals for the week.

Advice time: If your Sundays are lonely, construct a plan customized to meet your own pleasures and needs. What makes you feel good? Working with your hands? Reading? Playing piano? Learning something new? Writing? Painting? Watching old movies? Once you decide which activity to pursue, set the stage. Arrange a comfortable place; assemble what you'll need, choose pleasant sounds for background music. In addition, mark boldly on the next several Sundays on your calendar, "*my day*," or "*paint*," or "*read all day*," so you anticipate the day. If none of these ideas appeals to you, try hooking up with other widows or single ladies, who also find Sundays the pits. Each week one of you can plan the day's activity. One might introduce you to the joys of bird watching; another might give you a lesson in baking key lime pie; another might gather a foursome for duplicate bridge. Gee, that sounds like fun. Maybe I'll try that if I ever tire of entertaining myself.

A friend who had recently lost his wife read an early version of this chapter. He reminded me that it isn't that easy to find something fun or interesting to do when your grief is fresh. As he said, "…it takes a while before any activity is able to submerge feelings of loneliness and loss." Good point. As I have moved further away from D-Day, I have to remind myself of what it was like at first. His comment also reminded me that although I never could imagine amnesia happening to me, it has. So rest assured it also will happen to you.

If you are still pulling yourself together during the first weeks or months, your concentration may be poor, your emotions numb and you may feel that nothing has any meaning. That's hardly fertile ground for your imagination to take root. For now, keep your plan simple. Walk in the woods, put your feet up and read a good novel, or watch something fun on TV. That may help ease your loneliness. As your senses sharpen, you can make more elaborate plans.

—LOSS OF IDENTITY—

When we lose our husbands, we not only lose our roles as wives, but perhaps our roles as nurses, caretakers, girl Fridays, partners in sports, friends, comrades, lovers, etc. Although I hate to admit it, being a women's rights advocate, in addition we often lose "prestige" and "common interests" with a group. Most of us had, in addition to any personal esteem we might have earned, identities related to our husbands' careers. Right or wrong, these prescribed social roles often were seen as more worthy than our own accomplishments. If our social life revolved around his work, or his fellow retirees and spouses, as it so often does when we are married, we suddenly find everything has changed once he dies. "The boss's wife" becomes "the widow of the former boss." No pizzazz. No respect.

Whether you were "the cop's wife," "the artist's wife," "the principal's wife," "the doctor's wife," "the bus driver's wife," "the mill-worker's wife," "the minister's wife," or "the salesman's wife," you find you have been demoted to "the widow of the late..." That title might get you lots of attention for a few weeks, but it doesn't sustain most women very long. Your mate's former colleagues get busy, move on to new concerns, and so do their spouses. You soon may feel like yesterday's leftover mashed potatoes with that group. Add that to feeling like a fifth wheel with your couples' bridge or tennis group, and you are bound to feel a sinking sensation. In the past when you felt left out, you could turn to your husband. He might have put his arm around you and said, "Aww, honey, it's okay. You still have me." Now you turn to a void and feel a blast of aloneness as cutting as an Arctic chill.

Try not to judge your busy friends and neighbors too harshly. If the situation were reversed you might be the one with little time for "the widow of the late...." It happens; it's natural. Your question should be, "How can I rise above this...find ways to feel less lonely?"

Several women said they couldn't stand the "quiet" of being alone, so they filled that void with constant radio or TV playing. "I confess I am afraid of my thoughts," an elderly widow said. "I become terrified and anxious if it is quiet. I'm afraid I'll go crazy if I let myself think, so I keep my mind occupied with TV or radio, anything at all." This particular woman's problems go much deeper than just the loneliness of a long-time widow, but I quote her because she was so honest about her fear of silence, where not everyone is. Many widows dread silence when they are first alone, and it is perfectly acceptable to keep a radio or TV on to ease your anxiety for awhile, but if that continues to be a problem, discuss it with a counselor. We all should feel comfortable with our own thoughts.

Some women rush out and take new jobs or dive into avocations to fill the lonely void. Dale said she worked at night in her photo darkroom until she was so exhausted she collapsed into bed and had no trouble falling asleep.

—RUNNING FROM LONELINESS—

Other women run. Caroline says, "I ran away for the first three years." She helped care for ailing relatives; became president of her busy garden club; took a refresher course in nursing; worked in a nursing home; took a computer science course; studied for and passed her Real Estate Board exam; took and passed an extensive appraisal course, etc. She ran at a dizzying speed until she nearly fell apart.

Joan says, "It took almost three years for me to realize I was running anywhere and everywhere—except home. I finally realized that when I returned 'home,' it took only a day or two before I felt the world caving in on me. You need to know that my husband died in a fire at our home—so the home I returned to was not OUR home, but one that had been beautifully remodeled and replaced for me." Her reason for running was special, making it understandable. Maybe yours is, too.

I admit that I ran at a marathon pace for about a year and a half. It's easy to run away, so easy many of us don't even recognize that we're doing it. We're "keeping busy," we're enjoying our enforced freedom and we're maintaining relationships with friends and family, just as we're told to. But, we also might be avoiding the loneliness, which is much more crushing when we are at home alone. I don't necessarily think "running" should be avoided. Running away serves to put some distance—literally and figuratively—between our lives before and our lives now. Like denial and numbness, it cushions us from too much pain too fast. Problems develop when the running lasts too long, and when we fail to go through the painful growth process of grief because of running.

I pulled the plug on my running after about 18 months. I could see that I had been living in a jet-paced dream world; I wasn't facing up to my grief work awaiting me at home. I had to stifle my natural urge to issue and accept invitations freely. I learned to answer, "No, I'm sorry I won't be able to go," a few times, instead of my eager, "Yes, yes, yes." I reserved blocks of time on my calendar for me to be at home without guests. I kept in touch with friends, but I resisted the urge to participate in every get-together. I made myself absorb my aloneness and face it squarely. It hurt, of course, but it helped anchor me in reality so I could learn to make a new life for myself

—WHEN LONELINESS PERSISTS—

What do you do if you find you are still crushed with loneliness long after you sense you should be surfacing and adjusting to life without your man? Either with help, or by yourself, honestly assess your lonely feelings. What, besides your husband, are you lonely for? What do you miss the most? Intellectual stimulation? Small talk? Busy work? Someone to commiserate with you? Laughter? Feedback? Acceptance? If you can pin down what you are missing, you will have a hint as to which direction you should head in trying to solve your problem.

Keep in mind that you are grieving, unless you're reading this after you have "recovered." You will feel lonely for your husband during this time, sometimes acutely lonely, sometimes passively. The first thing you can do to help yourself is to accept that as perfectly natural. Why wouldn't you feel lonely when your best friend, roommate, lover, confidante, debater, companion, helper, decision-maker, fellow parent, fellow conversationalist, mentor and leaning post is no longer there? You even may miss nagging him or being nagged by him. A big part of your life is gone.

Is it possible you feel particularly lonely because you have withdrawn from regular activities? Joan says, "Getting back into the swing of things—job, church, grocery shopping, community commitments, etc., is HARD! But it gets easier each time you do it. Remember that when you're putting off the first encounter." I agree. I felt completely unstrung the first time I went anywhere we had always gone as a pair, whether it was to a party, a meeting or shopping. My heart would be in my throat and every muscle would knot up. There is no way to avoid that; you can only work through it, knowing it will get easier each time you do it. Just be sure you don't postpone that first time too long; the longer you put it off, the harder it becomes.

If, after many months, you feel powerless to help yourself feel less lonely, your condition may require help from a widow support group, a counselor or a psychologist. But most of you can ease your own loneliness with a little effort. You can begin by reading self-help books such as this one, by facing your concerns squarely, by prodding yourself to make a few phone calls or to write a few letters and, generally, by making the effort to get a ball rolling. Once the ball is in motion, inertia will help keep it moving. Remember, inertia is a force that tends both to keep a still item still and a moving item moving.

As I see it, there are two different ways to approach the problem of aloneness. You can try to be alone less or you can enjoy being alone more. My church-going helped satisfy my need to be alone less; my painting helped me enjoy my alone hours more. When you can, try to look at your aloneness as an opportunity instead of a prison sentence. Think of positive, satisfying ways to spend your time. You probably will need to work on both approaches to alleviate occasional feelings of friendlessness and isolation.

Some widows take in a roommate or move in with their children to fill the void. I know several widows who have done this, to ease their financial situations and to kill the loneliness bug. Several years after being widowed, Sue told me, "My ideal would be a group of people in similar circumstances to live with, to share a house…like a sorority house for widows." I imagine she would have had no trouble filling that house if she had started one. The world is full of lonely widows. But if you are interested, you will have to find someone else to start it. She has since remarried.

Over the long haul you will have to work to establish new friendships and avid new interests. If, for example, you have always enjoyed photography, as Dale had, you can ease your loneliness by diving into that avocation head first. Take an appropriate course; subscribe to a photo magazine to whet your appetite; join a national association; talk to clerks at photo stores; attend workshops; enter contests; visit photographers whose work you've admired; and take pictures by the hundreds. WARNING: Although it is possible to delve into photography, or any other avocation of your choice, without winning the lottery, it's also possible to get carried away and spend more that you can afford. Pick the brains of others in the field, and set your own budget limits before you begin.

—GET INVOLVED IN A CAUSE—

If you have no hobby or avocation you wish to develop, maybe your cup of tea is activism. Pick a cause, issue or problem and see what you can do to "fix" it. This can be a local, national or world problem. Choose something that gets you emotionally involved, very angry or very empathetic. Although everything made me angry for awhile, I had special "triggers" that really lit my fire. My life—and I—changed completely, and my lingering grief subsided, when I decided to get involved in a struggle to help eliminate racism and prejudice in my newly adopted Florida county. Civil rights had always been one of my most passionate issues, but I doubt I would have been able to pursue the cause with such passion had I still been married, nor could I have been as effective had I not first gone through the grief process. It is possible sometimes to make lemonade when you have been handed a lemon.

You have so much to gain and so little to lose if you give yourself totally to a mission…a job that needs to be done. Once again you will feel useful, needed.

The key is to determine your own interest, your own passion and your own resources. What is that passion for you? How can you find it? How can you find your special niche? I can only suggest openness. Know that you are seeking an outlet for your interests. Be open to all suggestions. Don't be afraid to dive in head first and worry later about how you will swim. If you believe passionately in the cause, you will survive the trials and come out a better person for it all. There is no end to the problems facing us, and the only way any of them has a prayer of being solved is if people who care make their concerns known and fight for change. Do you see red when you hear the National Rifle Association defend easy access to Saturday Night Specials? How about industries dumping waste into your river; or old zoning laws that allow haphazard development; or homeless families setting up a cardboard village in the middle of your favorite park; or pornographic magazines being readily available to kids; or zealots threatening—and taking—the lives of doctors in the name of morality? Or, does just the opposite viewpoint on one of these issues spark your interest?

Pick your complaint and get to work. Go to the library or log onto the Internet. Read everything you can on the subject. As you run across names of local people with whom you share concern, make a note and contact them. Ask them how you might help. Try to digest your thoughts into a concise and convincing letter, and send it to your local newspaper's opinion pages as well as to your state and federal representatives in government. Work for and support the ones who want what you want; campaign against the ones who do not. Politics can be a great outlet for your feelings, and at the precinct and county level, it is the essentially American thing to do. You will no longer have as much time to think about being lonely AND along the way you will meet lots of people with whom you share a passionate point of view. Lasting friendships are made that way. Most of my newer friends share my political passions.

If you aren't ready for full-blown activism, begin with a selfless pursuit. Give some of your time, effort and money—if you can—to help less fortunate people in your community. Volunteer to drive for Meals on Wheels. Do it for those who need the service, and know that is what's most important. But watch yourself as you grow from the process. Activism or altruism are "right" of themselves, but it doesn't hurt if these pursuits expand your world and help you recover in the process.

—HELPING INDIVIDUALS—

According to Ralph Waldo Emerson, *"the best cure for loneliness is to make yourself necessary to somebody"*. Bonnie expanded on that premise. "Reaching out to others, making a phone call or a visit, inviting friends, relatives or acquaintances over for cake and coffee or ham and rolls can ease lonely feelings. Don't wait for others to invite you. Surprising someone with home-baked cookies, cake, a pot of chili or chicken soup keeps a widow busy in the kitchen, at the store, and in touch with others. Widowhood should make us each a better person, because it should force us to do things for people whose plight we may never have noticed if we hadn't been forced to seek an outlet for our own loneliness." In addition she recommends taking classes to know about cars, finances, cooking, simple repairs, etc. "This not only alleviates loneliness," she says. "It helps rebuild the widow's injured self-esteem."

Most of these tactics presume you have time as well as interest. Widows with full-time jobs or demanding careers may have all they can do to get through their demanding days. Young mothers face special problems of juggling child-care, career, housework and a tricky social life. For these busy ladies it might mean taking time during lunch to visit with new people at work, spending time painting pictures along with their kids, joining a neighborhood book club that meets at the playground, or learning something new from tapes played while commuting or jogging.

From reading accounts of young widows it's easy to see many of their problems are the same ones I have, but they also feel cheated of all those intact married years we older wives had. They might yearn for some peace and quiet, if they have children always underfoot, but they miss their mates keenly and they feel even less prepared than we older gals to live without them. They may never be alone, but they are lonely in a very special way. If you can find the time, consuming interests and charitable projects (and the people you meet while pursuing them) will go a long way toward curing loneliness. They won't make you forget how much you miss your husband, but they might help you spend less time fretting uselessly about it.

—LEARN TO ENJOY SOME ALONENESS—

The other side of the coin is learning to enjoy aloneness. When I am lonely, I try to remember that one or two years from now, I could be desperate for some "alone time." Situations change. I could be remarried, I could be caring for an invalid relative in my home, or financial need might require I take in a roommate. None of us knows what our futures will bring. So, because I relish—actually require—time alone, I tell myself that for the time being I have been granted that time. I shouldn't waste it complaining. I should appreciate it. I can do things now that I couldn't do before, such as activities Bruce didn't enjoy and crazy things I might feel embarrassed to do with someone around.

What might those kinds of things be? For me they have been such things as playing the 1812 Overture at full volume on the stereo instead of watching a TV game show; eating whenever I was hungry and felt like it, instead of when it was expected; sitting on the shore and watching cormorants silently skim the water instead of dusting; painting a glitzy sweatshirt instead of watching a Green Bay Packer game; writing when the mood struck instead of when it was convenient for others; putting on a skimpy leotard and doing my pitiful aerobics with an old folks video instead of joining the fitness club; singing along with the radio instead of humming quietly to myself; reading a salacious novel instead of feigning interest in a pompous bestseller.

Loneliness must be tolerated and understood as a natural reaction to your grief. It takes time to get over the sadness that envelopes you when you want to share a piece of news or a beautiful sunset or a picture of your new grandchild, and he's not there to share with. Your loneliness feels like a gaping hole in your belly, and not much eases it for awhile. Its pain will come and go for several years, but gradually you should learn more tricks to make your life easier. As you try new things, meet new people and begin to worry more about the welfare of others, loneliness will subside...even when you're alone.

8

Taking Charge: Forging Your New Role

An easy task becomes difficult
when you do it with reluctance.

—Terence

Annie's Journal (13 weeks)
Dear Bruce: I need you! The lawn needs you! The house heeds you! I thought the world stopped when you died, that time stood still and all those other clichés. Now I see only "our life" stopped. Life continues. Spiders keep spinning webs; trees keep shedding leaves and needles into the eaves; moss keeps creeping along the shaded roof; shrubs keep spreading, nearly swallowing up the walkway. All that damned outside work to be done and I can hardly keep up with the inside work! What happened to our plan? You know: "your jobs," "my jobs," and "our jobs?"

My sister Joan didn't overload me with advice about learning to live alone when I was widowed, but she did make a few memorable suggestions. For example, she said, "When the car or furnace, or whatever, gives you problems—give it a swift kick! *Nobody* wants all this responsibility, and it *isn't* fair."

I've thought of that a dozen times. Sometimes I stopped just short of kicking the offending machine and smiled, my anger dissipating with the memory of her words. With my luck, if I did kick something, I would realize too late that I had on flimsy sandals and break a toe. More often than kicking though, especially the first year, I got myself into a useless stew about things that quit working and "his work" that kept piling up, railing uselessly at my new uninvited tasks. "This isn't fair," I'd say. "I can't do everything myself! I need my helper," I'd grumble, knowing that in most cases I was "it." Who the heck asked me if I wanted to be "it?"

I have some advice for you. You're probably not surprised at that by now. Next to banging your head against a wall, the stupidest thing you can do is resent your husband for leaving you with his chores. Both are pointless pursuits, and in both cases it feels great when you stop! At some point we each have to try to live with our newly expanded responsibilities. How soon we do depends on whether we have a job outside the home, whether we have a "take charge" or "run away" personality and whether we live alone, with young children or with other adults.

I'm sure I could run away from my new responsibilities longer than Pauli, Eunie, Anna, Norma, Ginny, Agnes or any of the other women who had small children when their spouses died. A young family's needs are immediate; their concerns and crises can't wait for when Mom feels up to it. For most women these days, child rearing had been shared with their husbands. These women have to take charge quickly and try to compensate for the missing parent. That's an awesome task. Some women also are thrust into new jobs to keep their families fed, often ill-equipped and at a low ebb in confidence. A few I met immediately became CEOs of their families' businesses, to keep the income flowing. They may have barged ahead kicking and screaming all the way, but they had no choice but to barge ahead. "I had to take over the wholesale tool business," Diane said, "and I had never even taken care of the family checkbook. But, I had no choice. So I gritted my teeth, took the reins and yelled 'Giddy up.' But I kept hoping that horse knew its own way, because I just looked like I was in charge. I didn't have the foggiest."

I probably took charge sooner than some women my age, just because of my impatience. I needed to move ahead instead of standing still. I also (just barely) had the financial freedom to stay home, giving me time to do some chores, and to hire a bit of help when I needed to. Many of you probably faced greatly diminished incomes when your husbands died, so when things have to be done, you have no choice but to do them yourselves. It is difficult to take charge of any situation when you're in shock, numb, fearful and/or depressed, but if you can see that's your only option, call on all your resources and do it as soon as you possibly can. Otherwise your problems may snowball and become even more difficult to solve.

Some women, who took on brave new ventures to keep the household afloat, changed their lives completely. Toni, for example, moved from her role as full-time wife/mother to a challenging new job in graphic communications when she was widowed in her mid-40s. As the years passed, she accepted more and more responsibility and rose to more and more challenges. "I felt I had to constantly prove I was just as capable as my younger coworkers," she said. "Anything they would do in company training and team-building exercises, I would do. Except for one time," she said. "I refused to bungee-jump when the younger ones did." She succeeded in many ways, soon globe-trotting with the best of the jet-setters, to set up business networking conferences for her worldwide organization. "I had always had an 'I can do it!' attitude," she said. "And I did it. I made a 180 degree turn."

Many women I talked to, who felt forced into jobs, even those who took on major family businesses, eventually grew and gained remarkable confidence in themselves in the process. If you are facing such a challenge, dive in as best you can. You probably will know some tough times, but the payoff is likely to be a spurt of emotional growth you cannot imagine. I doubt you will regret it.

—TAKING CHARGE OF FAMILY CARE—

If you were left with small children to care for, you also may have to "hope the horse knows its own way" part of the time. It isn't fair; that's for sure, but knowing that doesn't make it go away. As I said earlier, I think it is essential for you to seek professional help, in the library or on the Internet if that's all you can afford, to help you understand the trauma your child or children may be going through at this time. Find and read to them age-appropriate books on the subject of loss. Hold them close and reassure them, even when you don't see signs of obvious pain. I was surprised to read recently that children under the age of three need special attention when the father dies, including plenty of reassuring touch, to prevent extreme psychological problems when they are older. One cannot assume that a child is unaffected, just because he or she seems fine at the moment. Hugging your children will also benefit you.

In addition to the reassurance and love your children need at this time, it is important that you appear to be in control of the home situation. I say that, knowing full well that I wasn't always able to appear in control as a young mother, even without the trauma of having lost my husband. Still, that doesn't mean it isn't good advice to keep in mind. It's even more important at this time than when you were an intact family. If you can give your children the impression, as their sole remaining parent, that you are "in charge," and that you won't be leaving them too, they will feel more secure and be more likely to cooperate with you. It's okay for children of any age to see you grieve openly, as long as you explain as best you can. But when you have the strength to act like the family's competent leader, do it in such a way that they notice. Be positive, display a "we can do it" attitude and try to make your home life as routine as possible.

In the movies, and often in real life, it was once popular for the poor widowed mother to say to her oldest son, regardless of his age, "You will have to be the man of the house now." It usually was done to make the child feel important, and it made good melodrama, but we know now that such proclamations caused boys and young men great distress. They knew they could never do all their fathers had done, but many of them tried valiantly, suffering feelings of inadequacy well into adulthood. Psychologists suggest you avoid making that mistake.

On the other hand most children are happier and more confident if they feel needed in the family. From the time they can carry out the simplest tasks, kids benefit from being expected to contribute to the family's well being. Until a few decades ago, the family was an interdependent economic and social unit. Everyone in the family knew he or she was needed to keep the home and farm or business running smoothly. Now, with both parents often employed outside the home, perhaps it is time we revive that pattern. Certainly it is advisable when the father has died, for your benefit as well as for the benefit of your child or children. Just try to keep their chores age-appropriate.

What do you want for your children? When you can think clearly, try to make a list of the attributes you wish your children to have as adults. You might say, "I want my children to become honest, moral, responsible, self-confident, happy and healthy adults." Or, you might say, "I want them to just become self sufficient and happy." Think which attributes are most important to you, and what you think is most necessary for them. Keep these characteristics in mind as you guide them through the daily process of maturing. Expect the best of them when they are young, when you have the most chance to influence them. If you want them to be honest, take them with you when you make a trip back to the store with that $5 too much change the clerk gave you; or make sure they see you leave your phone number when you accidentally scratch a car door in the parking lot. If you want them to be courteous, make a point of showing courtesy to other people. Show your children courtesy, and remind them to say "Please" and "Thank you" to others. Help them see how much better they feel when people are polite to them and how much better they feel when they are polite to others. Kids learn by what they see and experience. Take every opportunity to train them in proper behavior. You will be rewarded a thousand times for your efforts, and so will they.

At a wedding shower a few years ago, I witnessed a casual conversation that kept me awake that night. A young mother, pregnant with her second child, got everyone's attention by saying she intended to instill just one attribute in her children...good manners. "If I do that well," she said, "everything else will follow."

Other young mothers argued, "What about honesty?" "What about self esteem?" "What about cleanliness?" She was adamant that if she taught them manners, which included being courteous to other people in all situations, nothing else would be necessary. I guess we might find a hole in her theory, but think about it for awhile. I have to say that an honest, lifelong habit of courtesy would go a long way toward building happy and successful adults. It might make for a happy and successful world, for that matter. Since that night I have been appalled at the complete lack of manners among so many children and teenagers, and yes, even among adults. Courtesy seems an antiquated trait now. What a shame.

If concentrating on courtesy doesn't seem like the perfect solution to all your child-rearing problems, let me introduce you to *Annie's Helpful Rules for Widows Rearing Young Children.*

Rule #1: From about age two your daughters and sons can, and should be expected to, contribute toward the family's welfare. They can put their toys away. They can throw dirty clothes in the hamper, help put away groceries, put napkins on the table. Gradually their chores can become more sophisticated to match their developing skills. Although it may seem easier to just do it all yourself, you will be doing them a lifelong favor by not doing chores for them, but by letting them know you need their help. Not only will you gradually see your "homework" become more manageable, leaving more fun time with the family, but your children will feel important and begin a lifelong habit of accepting responsibility. For this they should be rewarded with feelings of self-worth and confidence, two things I know I wanted for my own children.

I recall with some fondness my own childhood contributions many decades ago: Saturday morning house cleaning sessions, spring-cleaning frenzies, family wash days, et cetera. We all pitched in, not without the required grumbling of course, but with some pride that we played a valuable role in our family. On Saturday mornings we listened to radio shows while we worked, a big deal in our lives when we didn't have television. Because we lived in a small town near most of my mother's side of the family, I also was able to take part in family "quilting bees," canning sessions, and other "community efforts" among the older generations. This experience gave me a sense of belonging that's hard to match in today's more urban families. Today such strong extended-family ties are usually only found in very small towns and rural America, or in close-knit ethnic enclaves in larger cities. However, even a nuclear family that works together to maintain their home or business certainly will feel closer than one that just resides in the same house.

When the children are young and cooperative, you might let them choose their chores. "Mommy has too much to do alone," you could say. "What do you think you can do to help me?" Job Jars, from which each child selects a new job for the day or for the week, can be successful. Wall charts, showing each child's list of chores, can become a good incentive, especially when gold stars appear as they complete their jobs well. They should be made to understand that they are expected to complete their chores without having to be nagged. Praise them up one side and down the other when they do their job, even if it isn't perfect at first. Children, young and older, love to please their parents and they love getting occasional special privileges "for doing such a great job." *Positive reinforcement works.*

Rule #2: When you say "No," say it like you mean it, and stick to it. Every time you give in to screams and temper tantrums, you encourage more screams and temper tantrums. If young children get what they want that way, why should they quit doing it? It seems simple because it is. *Don't reinforce negative behavior.* On the other hand, don't be afraid to retract a "No" if you and your older child calmly discuss an issue and you can see they have a valid point. Respect their views, but never let them replace you as the one who makes and enforces the rules. Know that they will try, but that this is your job.

Rule #3: Be consistent with discipline and don't let naughty behavior go unnoticed. "Time outs," (removing the child from the scene of his misbehavior) can work well. "Withdrawal of privileges" and "groundings" may be effective for older children. It's hard to be consistent, but the more you are, the sooner the child will cease the misbehavior. If you flip flop back and forth between being firm and giving in, you will still be fighting the same kinds of problems, and bigger ones, years later. Show your love by expecting the best of them. Eventually, perhaps when they have kids of their own, they will appreciate how much you have done for them.

Rule #4: Set firm, but reasonable and age-sensitive, "house rules" that are not negotiable. As a proper grammarian might say: "House rules outlaw behavior up with which I will not put." For young children these may include not hurting other people, not throwing outside toys inside, and respecting "quiet times." For school age kids, they may include homework rules, hours of TV watching, or playing music too loud. For teens and young adults they may include age appropriate rules about curfews, car privileges, and no smoking/drinking/drug use. Make sure you both understand the rules, the reasons for them and resulting discipline, *before* you have to enforce them. And don't change them in the middle of a fight, even if you promise to discuss the fairness of the rule at a later time.

Rule #5: Show and tell your children often how much you love them. This rule should be number one, and underlying all the others, especially when you are both grieving. But, like most really important things, it's not always easy. Let your younger children know how much you love them, by hugging or touching them, especially soon after having to discipline them, for example. Explain to those old enough to understand, that love brings with it responsibility; that because you love them you must maintain certain rules and enforce them. You don't do that for your own enjoyment; sometimes it is very hard work. However, you love them enough to do that hard work so that they will grow into happy and wonderful grown-ups. It might help to tell older children that life comes with rules for everyone, even adults, such as driving according to traffic rules and not spending more money than you have, for example. Learning to live within rules, which often means "delaying gratification," is a large part of what maturity is all about. If you can help them understand that, and that translates into getting more cooperation from them, you won't have to spend all your hours together as enemies.

As children approach puberty, they will try all kinds of anti-social behavior and will need firmer guidance. If, like Ginny, your kids were teens or pre-teens when your husband died, you will have your hands full. She was lucky to have the boys' aunts and uncles willing to step in when things got too tough to handle. Few of us have that kind of panic button available. Tap into any resources you can…extended family, scouts, church, child-rearing self-help books, parent-training sessions. If you tire of battling, and give up on expecting them to behave properly, you are inviting total rebellion and chaos. Then you, and they, may need extensive professional help to get the family unit back in line. If you sense you have reached this desperate level, don't give up. Seek help wherever you can as soon as you can. It can mean all the difference in your future and your kids futures.

Child rearing is a daunting challenge in the best of times. Following the death of one parent, the remaining parent is faced with seemingly insurmountable problems and little of the confidence necessary to deal with them. On top of the usual behavioral problems, you must try to be perceptive about how they are responding to their loss. Your children's grief may play out in much less obvious ways than your own, such as new mischief aimed at attention-seeking, new ways of expressing extreme anger, loss of interest in school, or any number of other ways. As pained as you are, remind yourself often to touch your children lovingly, to show your pride in them and to put on a brave front to reassure them of your steadfastness. They may fear you will go off and leave them, too. Just when you probably feel most like turning your back on your job of parenting so you can recuperate from your own loss, you will have to face that your parenting role has assumed new urgency and gravity. One good plan may be to try family meetings, where you all discuss how you can work together to make your new life work.

By now you may ask "Just who does she think she is, spouting off on how I should rear my children?" Well, I'd like to say I have a secret doctorate in child psychology, or at least that these rules were all tried and proved utterly successful with my own children. I don't; some were; some weren't. However, I'm very analytical, as you know by now, and I have concluded over the years that if I had consistently stuck with these few fundamental guidelines, my children would now be absolutely perfect and perfectly happy. As it is, they all three are "almost perfect" and "almost perfectly happy."

Proper child rearing becomes very clear and simple once your own kids are in their thirties and forties. The trouble is no one seems to care about what you know by then. (I can sense thousands of graying heads nodding in agreement.) Our own children seldom listen to our good advice about raising their children. They insist, just as we did, on making their own mistakes and learning the harder way. Such a waste of the older generation's wisdom. So, I realize you don't want your own mothers and mothers-in-law butting in. But maybe you won't mind these few suggestions from a "fellow widow" who knows you may need a handy, simplified set of rules to cling to in these stressful times. I hope you read my thumbnail sketch on child-rearing as just that...a few hints, in case you might need them, to help you temporarily maintain control of the family or at least to appear in control of it.

If your children are giving you no problems whatsoever, or if you have a favorite child-rearing guru you always follow, I expect you will disregard my suggestions. I offer them as "fast food child psychology" for those who need quick help when their resources are limited by their grief.

Knowing you will have tough times as a young grieving mother, you may want to work out a system of signals with your children. For example: "A closed bedroom door means I need my privacy," "A finger along side my nose means I'm having a bad day and I need you to behave," "One finger in the air means 'Hold that thought. I'm busy right now, but I will listen to you in a minute.'" Don't overuse such signals, but they can help. Kids like to feel they are in on a secret code. Let them make up signals to tell you their needs, too. One for when they feel sad, another for when they want to talk to you privately, for example.

Don't be afraid to ask a friend, your parents, a teacher, or a professional counselor for help when your children's problems swamp you. Seek help. Try to "nip their problems in the bud," to call on an old cliché, and save yourself big-time problems later on. Unless you are very lucky, there probably won't be a mate there to help you then, either. Do whatever you can to build a solid working relationship with your kids now.

—TAKING CHARGE OF HOUSEWORK—

As a new widow I gradually moved from "totally numb," where I didn't even notice whether the house was clean, to "semi-numb," where I noticed cobwebs and dust balls with some interest, to "almost alive," where I noticed and felt awful about encroaching crud, to "fully aware," at which time I decided to do something about it. I scrubbed carpets, I scrubbed furniture, and I made an earnest effort at "spring cleaning" the rest of the house. It was only moderately successful, and not very satisfying. I am not good at this domestic stuff. What few talents I have are limited to the finer arts. Unfortunately, I do operate more smoothly in a somewhat orderly, somewhat clean environment. After a little stewing and snarling and grumping about it, I called in an every-other-week cleaning lady. She's good enough, and worth the money. I knew I was lucky to be able to afford her, at least for the present.

Many of you can't even pretend you can afford that luxury. I understand. When I most needed help, when the kids were very young and incredibly messy, I couldn't either. I had only me, myself and I (and Bruce, but until retirement age he didn't know he could help). If your budget is tight and you live alone, you will have to assign household tasks to you, yourself and you, with some help from the kids. In that case you may learn to live nit-picky clean (so there is less work to be done), become a super-efficient cleaner (so you can do more work in less time) and/or develop a high degree of myopia (so more mess looks like less mess).

If your children are of sufficient skills to help, work out a schedule whereby they materially contribute to the process. Try a few of the suggestions I made about the subject in my child-rearing hints. If you properly present the idea of needing their help, they may accept it with a minimum of grousing. When they do grouse, try saying to them, "Boy, I know just how you feel. I hate this job! I wish I didn't have to do it either. Can you think of a way we can both not do it?" That might work. Then suggest to them that you all stay on the lookout for ways to minimize your own jobs and those of others.

I remember my daughter Cindy telling me in all seriousness, when she was about eight years old, how I could have less housework. One of her suggestions:

"Floors don't have to be shiny; they just have to be clean enough that your feet don't stick to stuff when you walk." She had a point. Sometimes the only answer is to lower standards.

I suppose I had less housework to do, while I lived alone. It stands to reason. However, I was continually amazed at how much damage I could do to a clean house all by myself. Meal preparation is simpler for one than for two, I'm sure, but my stove still got greasy and I still managed to fill a dishwasher in two days. I guess I did pots and pans in the dishwasher, while I (we) used to do most of those by hand. Whatever, I had neither a cleaner house nor as much less work to be done as one might suppose. Apparently the amount of housework Bruce did was mathematically equal to the amount of extra work his presence required.

—CAR CARE—

Many new widows are thrust into the unwelcome roles of family drivers and caretakers of the family car(s). That can be an unsettling prospect. Neither job was completely new to me. Because Bruce's job was 25 miles away, I had done most of the family's local driving for years. Because I held only part-time jobs, I had more time, so I also had been primarily responsible for car care prior to retirement. Bruce and I both had been more comfortable with him driving and me navigating on long trips, though, so I doubted my ability to take over that chore until the situation demanded it.

Some older women have never driven at all. I helped teach my mother, who was then 67 years old, to drive when my Dad died. She had quit driving as a young mother because of a few property damage accidents. I would like to say she took to driving after my lessons like a future Indy driver and put 40,000 miles on her car every year. She didn't. She drove only familiar short hops in town, and then quit driving completely after another very minor accident. It just wasn't her thing. If you don't drive, but driving would make your life easier, don't hesitate to learn. Most people master the skill quickly. Having your own "wheels" can greatly add to your feeling of independence. I highly recommend taking a professional course, though.

Where we often washed and waxed our cars ourselves, I freely used the car wash those first years after Bruce died. If you can't afford that luxury, there are hints that help. Now I sometimes rush out in the rain, or when the car is loaded with dew in the morning, and give it the once-over-lightly with a detergent soaked sponge. For drying a wet car, there is nothing as successful as a natural chamois. Keep it clean and damp, wringing it out when it gets too wet to dry the car.

For car maintenance, I have gotten to know the mechanics at nearby service station/garages. Bruce had established a great rapport with Pete and Jeff in Wisconsin (they even picked up and delivered my car!) and I found two seemingly reliable guys in Florida, although we never got to a first name basis. I bantered with them, asked plenty of dumb questions and then let them know that I trusted them to take care of my cars. If they did, and they didn't take advantage of me, I would become a steady customer. I bought my gas from them when I could, even if I paid several cents more per gallon, and I sent them new business. I don't think they laughed at me behind my back when I described a "lumpity lumpity feeling" to the brakes or "a breathless gasp" when I accelerated. I think they just thought they were better with cars than I was, but I was better with words.

Car maintenance doesn't come naturally to me, however. It took me more than two years to anticipate my need for an oil change and lube job. I never thought to look at the sticker; that was Bruce's realm after retirement. Virginia said this had always been her mate's job, too. His last words to her, though, before leaving to play his fatal game of tennis, were "Don't forget to check your oil." Many years later she still never forgets to check her oil. What saves me is that I often make long trips and I try to have the car in tip-top shape before leaving. When I take it in, I say, "Please do (this and this and this), and check anything else that could cause me trouble on my trip. Don't make any major changes without calling me first." Even knowing I will probably have to okay anything they suggest, I think that lets them know they had better not try taking advantage of me. I've found this entirely successful with local service, where they know I will be a steady customer if they treat me right.

With "on the road" service, I have had a few "misdiagnoses." I doubt I have actually been swindled since I was widowed, although Bruce and I were a few years before he died. At the slightest smell of a rat, I had been told to call my local garage, long distance if necessary, right in front of the mechanic. (That is good advice.) I was told to ask if their diagnosis and estimate sounded right for the car's symptoms. The one time Bruce and I did that—from home after the fact, unfortunately—our mechanic laughed. "I have no idea what that part would cost," he said. "In my 27 years as a mechanic I have never had to replace one of those. You've just been swindled!" Two hundred and fifty dollars of our vacation fund down the drain. So, be careful. There are swindlers out there.

From that experience I suggest you be especially wary of service shops on major highways in busy tourist areas. And, be cautious about advertised specials. If you go in for a free or cheap oil change and they find a part "that could cause a major accident before you get home," do some detective work. Smeared with gunk and black from wear, all parts look like they need replacing. Disreputable repairmen also have been known to switch perfectly good parts with damaged ones they keep on hand, to damage parts intentionally, and even to slash a tire so it goes flat while you are waiting for an oil change. (Come to think of it, I had that happen once, too.) Watch them as best you can, maintain a healthy skepticism and don't be afraid to call a trustworthy friend before accepting a questionable prognosis.

Having to buy a new car can send a new widow into a thumb-sucking fetal position if she isn't prepared for it. I had done that alone several years before Bruce died, so it wasn't much of a problem for me. However, I still asked a good friend to shop with me and to help me establish a fair price. Ask a brother, father, recovered widow or someone else you trust for advice, and do your homework in the library or on the Internet. If you know you are offering to pay the right price, be firm. Don't let them play their game that can cost you hundreds or thousands of extra dollars. Once you settle on an acceptable price, be wary of the final contract. Watch out especially for "automatic add-ons," such as rust-proofing and extended warranties. These are huge profit makers, generally of little real value, and they are sometimes quietly tacked onto the contract. One of the best things a widow can do for herself is to head for the library and a stack of consumer reports magazines. A little homework can save you considerable money.

—MAKING YOUR HOME YOUR OWN—

After a certain grace period, the new widow usually begins to realize that her home is indeed "her" home and that she alone is responsible for making decisions about it. You may recall that I had a mini-version of that realization after only ten days. Some widows hesitate to change a thing for a long time, either because they remain in denial about their husband's death or because they are keeping the house as a shrine to his memory. Either of these is a poor reason to keep from changing something you don't like. No one says you *must* change things; maybe you happen to love everything just as it is. So be it. Just know that you have every right to change things if you choose.

Near the end of the first year, I made several minor improvements to the cottage. The first project was to rebuild our large, raised, double-deck across the back of the house. During the after-funeral gathering the summer before, it had threatened to collapse under the weight of about fifty guests. We had known there was some rot in surface boards, but thought it perfectly sturdy. I remember quite clearly that day some friends and relatives were quite alarmed by it creaking, and they propped it up with two-by-fours just to be sure. I, being numb, said,

"I'm sure it will be okay. Not to worry." As much as I hated parting with several thousand dollars to simply replace an existing deck, rather than to redesign and improve it, I consented in order to eliminate any possible danger to future guests. It actually turned out to be a bit larger, and, because I chose not to stain it dark, it was an improvement over the old one after all.

Next, to ease the frustration I had with our "too small" bedrooms in the cottage, I got rid of the king-sized bed and replaced it with the full-sized one from the guest room, which happened to have a great new mattress set. Then I bought a smaller-than-normal daybed with pop-up second bed for the guest-room. Both bedrooms still had the original, low-quality burnt orange sponge-backed carpet that had haunted me for the seven years we had owned the cottage. So out that went and in came off-white berber carpet to match the rest of the house. I added new inexpensive bedspreads, window treatment and pillows. *Voila!* New bedrooms. For whatever reason, I confess that I sleep better in the new bed.

Bruce and I had planned a kitchen remodeling for that summer, so I took that on next. I replaced the dated orange countertops, added cupboards in wasted space areas, and installed—for the first time—a dishwasher! Hardly a major kitchen renovation, but definitely an improvement. The activity kept me busy, it didn't cost too much, and it gave me a new lease on life. The house was more livable, and sellable. I got a very good price for it a few years later, which I doubt I would have without those improvements. A side benefit of such a project is the confidence you can gain in making good decisions alone. My only regret was not doing it before Bruce died. He would have loved it.

There are other ways to make your home your own. In Florida I turned one end of our guest bedroom into my office. By putting my desk inside the sliding doors of a fairly deep clothes closet, I could close it off when company came or when I wanted the room to look neater. In Wisconsin I consolidated Bruce's workspace in our garage, making space for me to paint there when it was warm enough. His dresser drawers became storage for sewing stuff, correspondence and my off-season clothes. Perhaps I was quicker than some to adapt our homes to my own because of such limited space in both.

Think about your rooms. Could they be put to better use? Could you easily change those masculine touches you'd been so careful to include into something more in keeping with your own taste? Such projects have both practical and psychological benefits. I felt a great lifting of my spirits each summer when I returned to my little cottage and saw how bright and roomy it seemed with my few changes. Sometimes a gallon of paint and/or a roll or two of half-price wallpaper border is all it takes to transform a room from "tedious" into "glorious." It may be very cheap therapy. A side benefit is that each change helps remind us that he isn't coming back; it helps moves us closer to Acceptance.

—OUTDOOR WORK/REPAIRS—

According to Charles Dudley Warner, "What a man needs in gardening is a cast-iron back, with a hinge in it." Make that WO-man, especially WIDOWED WO-man. I wasn't built for heavy work, I admit. We are different, men and women, some of us more than others. Even with a bad back of his own, Bruce could do many times heavier work than I ever could. Partially for this reason I ignored outside chores for the first unreal weeks. I knew I was a poor, weak substitute for the previous gardener/house fixer. When I regained my senses, and noticed the whole place beginning to look seedy, I became frustrated, angry, resentful and depressed about all I now had to do…wallowing in the "poor me" syndrome. Just having to move a big urn of geraniums was enough to send me to the couch to rest and pout.

After I had indulged in self-pity for a week or so, my next-door neighbor spoke up. Divorced and alone for more than ten years, Debby had a much larger and more complicated lawn and garden, which always looked like it was posing for a *Better Homes and Gardens* shoot. That added to my feelings of inadequacy, of course, until she reminded me of her secret.

"You don't have to do it all alone," she said. "Hire help!"

That thought hadn't occurred to me, although I had seen the wisdom of hiring help indoors. However, once she mentioned it, I realized she was not only nine years younger—and a highly talented gardener—she had a young man helping her with heavy work. Luckily her young gardener/handyman had time available, and I engaged him to help me whip the outside into shape. He came every so often from then on to help with those things I was unable or unwilling to do. I tended the annual flowers, most of which were in pots, and I did some artistic pruning, but I "let him" do almost everything else. In addition to routine yard maintenance, he delivered and stacked fireplace wood, cut down small trees, hauled brush away, moved heavy items and fixed almost anything that broke. I considered his reasonable pay to be an investment in my well being, saving both my back and my sense of humor. It allowed me to spend more time writing, and it was an investment in my property, which eventually sold for a handsome price.

Obviously every widow's financial situation is different, as is the cost of help in different areas. I was able to justify these expenses in my own mind, his hourly charges were reasonable, and I had some disposable income.

You may not be able to scrape up the cost of a helper. If circumstances don't allow for this convenient solution, there are a few other ways to alleviate the problem of too much brute work to be done and no brute around to do it. In some areas it is possible to barter your skills. You may, for example, offer to iron and mend for a young college student who can do yard work for you. Or you may baby-sit, cook, write résumés, or whatever you do best, in exchange for work. You may be able to call on your father, brothers or sons for some of your heavier chores or repairs, repaying the favor however you can. Even minor repairs, that wouldn't have bothered us when our husbands were around, can mushroom into gigantic projects that make us feel weak and helpless after being left alone. Caroline said that in her first two years as a widow, everything in her house seemed to need repair. "The doors rattled, faucets leaked, the table tilted. You name it, it needed something done to it." After worrying endlessly about it, her two brothers came for a week and repaired everything in sight. "After that I didn't feel so helpless," she said.

Sometimes, however, moving can be your only answer. If, for example, we had still lived in our bigger house with its extensive, labor-intensive landscaping, I would have had little choice but to move. I couldn't begin to afford as much help as I would have needed to keep that house and yard going. One reason we had moved four years before Bruce died, was that we were unable—and unwilling—to spend the time and money needed to keep it up. I will deal more extensively with the subject of whether or not to move in a later chapter.

—SHOPPING LIST FOR WIDOWS—

Within the first few weeks I began to realize the woman who lives alone needs a few implements she and her husband might not have needed. These are the things I needed to scout up or add to my household to make living alone less daunting:

- Folding two-step, or three-step, stool (smaller ones for bedrooms, etc.)

- Cordless, reversible screwdriver (or, preferably, a cordless drill w/screwdriver bits)

- Smaller hammer, screwdrivers, pliers, monkey wrench and duct tape (in kitchen drawer)

- Assortments of nails, screws, nuts/bolts, washers, hose washers, sandpaper

- Good jar lid opener (the best are old, clamp-types, found at garage sales)

- Easy corkscrew (with arms that extract cork when pulled down)

- Turkey-lifter rack

- Extra sets of keys for house and car (left with nearby friends or carefully hidden)

- Easy wood carrier (if you have a fireplace)

- Fire brick (or other easy-start lighter for fireplace)

- Long-handled squeegee and duster (if you have dirt in high places)

- Light-weight, easily maneuverable wheelbarrow or cart

- Trash cans with wheels

- Assorted fuses, batteries, light bulbs, filters, etc.

- Small metal measuring tape to keep in purse

- Several small, powerful flashlights (for car, purse, bedside, garage, etc.)

Your situation might require any number of other items in addition to these or instead of them. A good friend of mine, who lives in the woods as I do up north, was presented with a pretty little red chainsaw by her husband shortly before he left her for another woman. She probably had some creative ideas for what she would like to do with it, but eventually she sold it at a garage sale to another woman who lived alone. My friend hires a young man for her chainsaw work. Only you can know what items you will need to survive as a widow. Keep a list of those items you need and get them as soon as you can. If you can't afford new, shop rummage sales, auctions or junk shops for some things. Or you might ask for them as gifts. Trying to do without them will only add unnecessarily to your frustrations. Most of us are not as tall, strong or mechanically adept as our husbands were, and some things are just harder for one person than for two. Arm yourself with every labor-saver and back-saver you can afford, rather than spending precious energy struggling with tough jobs.

—BECOMING ASSERTIVE—

Many women become more assertive as widows than they were as wives. They must in order to survive. After months of ineffective dealings with lawyers, bureaucrats, businessmen, bankers and brokers, the new widow often breaks into tears of frustration. "Why doesn't anyone listen to what I am saying?" she cries. Or, "Why doesn't anyone ever return my calls?" or "Why does everyone assume they know better than I what's right for me?" She grits her teeth, rolls up her sleeves and marches into an office demanding attention. It's likely she will over-step the boundaries of etiquette and move directly from "shy kitten" to "angry tiger."

Are you usually wishy-washy, willing to be walked over like a doormat? Or are you self-confident? Or would you say you are demanding? To put those in terms used by assertiveness training manuals, are you non-assertive, assertive or aggressive? Unless you already have taken a course in assertiveness, I suggest that is one of the best things you can do for yourself, your family and your future. Why?

- It will help your self esteem.

- It will help you get, keep and function confidently in a job.

- It will aid tremendously in child rearing.

- It will help you make and reach new goals in your new life.

Thanks to some of the more strident feminists in the 1970s and '80s, assertiveness often has a bad name. People assume it means demanding your rights, even if you must act like a spoiled brat to get them. Most real accomplishments in the women's movement were made by those who knew the better way was by being assertive, rather than aggressive. The relatively recent definition of assertiveness arose out of need. Unfortunately many women, especially my age and older, were reared to be submissive, to keep peace at all costs and never to question authority, especially male authority. Reactionaries say this made for happier marriages, quoting rising divorce statistics to prove that point. But if you think about the marriages you have known, you will undoubtedly see what I have seen in looking, as objectively as possible, at five generations of my own family. Each happy marriage was between two people who openly loved each other *and* genuinely respected each other. In the older generations the husband may have made most major decisions, because it was traditional for him to do so. Within the happier marriages, however, he generally made them with input from his wife and with her and the family's well-being uppermost in his mind. He didn't play lord and master of the house, building a macho image for himself at the expense of his wife's self-esteem.

There are, of course, examples where men ruled with iron fists, and it's true that those unions seldom ended in divorce. Until recent decades, getting a divorce was difficult and considered shameful; it wasn't done without urgent cause. However, from diaries and journals we have learned that many of those long-time wives harbored intense resentment and stayed with their men more out of fear or propriety than out of love. The master/slave routine is usually a recipe for disaster.

Assertiveness, which means behaving with confidence, doesn't always come naturally. It is a trait we have to learn, either by absorbing it through our home, school and work environments, or from study (reading self-help books, taking assertiveness training courses or joining assertiveness support groups). I can't begin to give an entire course on the subject. I am neither qualified to do so, nor is there enough space here to do it justice. I can, however, suggest a few hints that will help you understand assertiveness and how it can help solve some of your problems of being alone.

1) Skip the YOU's; don't accuse. Use the I's and Me's and My's.

The next time someone hurts your feelings, insults you or makes you angry, resist the urge to tell them what you think of them, or how they hurt you. Say, instead, "My feelings are hurt," "I feel I've been put down," or "I feel angry when I hear that." Practice saying things about your own feelings, rather than accusing others of what they have done to you. When you begin to respond that way, one of several things may happen. The person may realize for the first time how their actions are affecting you and apologize. On the other hand, they may become flustered and unsure of how to act when you won't let them bully you. They may become defensive and try even harder to put you down. Don't let yourself get rattled if they do. Look them steadily in the eye and think, "I am a rational, adult human being and I deserve to be treated with respect." I have said that aloud to someone who was being particularly rude, but usually just thinking it gives you the self-assurance you need. It also helps to remember the other person deserves to be treated with respect, but not awe.

2) Just say "No."

We all know kids are to just say "no" to drugs, but take a clue from that motto for yourself. You needn't make excuses for yourself all the time. If a telemarketer calls, or a customer service person gives you a sales pitch, what do you say? I recommend you just say "No." Don't say, "I'd probably better not," or "I'm afraid it is too expensive," or "I would take some, but you see I am a new widow and I don't have a lot of money, and…etc." I remember thinking what a great idea this was, and I primed myself to just say "No" whenever I placed a call and was asked, "Could you please hold?" The first time I tried it, a Sears catalog clerk asked, "Would you mind holding, please?" I squared my shoulders and said, "No! Woops, I mean yes, I would," and hung up. Listen carefully to the question so you can answer correctly.

3) Others can only know what you want if you tell them.

This is an especially apt reminder for the new widow. You will need help; the simplest tasks can defy your determination to be self-sufficient. Just putting in, or taking out, a table leaf alone can be impossible. Rather than struggling and working yourself into a dither about it, call someone nearby and state your need. "I'd like you to stop by for a minute this afternoon and help me put in a table leaf." Stop yourself from saying, "I know you're probably awfully busy, and I hate to ask, but I was just wondering if it would be possible for you to maybe find a few minutes to help me put in a table leaf." State your problem and ask for what you need. You needn't throw manners out the window; you can be courteous without demeaning yourself. "Please" and "thank you" are still viable phrases, but learn to use them as courtesy, not as apology.

4) You will only get respect when you expect respect.

Read and pay attention to the affirmations repeated by recovering alcoholics, abusers, etc. They make a lot of sense for all of us. For example, tell yourself over and over, until you firmly believe it, "I am a worthwhile, capable person, and I deserve respect from others." Another good one, which I think comes from the AA manual, "Every day, in every way, I am getting better and better." Repeated often enough, these affirmations help boost sagging self-images. Listen in on conversations of successful men or women, especially when they are doing business. You can learn a lot about how those who expect respect get respect.

Believe in yourself, be direct, be polite, and be honest about your wants and needs. Say what you mean. You will be surprised at how much respect you'll begin to get. Add to that some study of assertiveness. You won't be sorry. If you study and learn to deal assertively with people, you will greatly ease the taking charge phase of your transition from "dependent wife," if that's what you were, to "independent woman." Best of all you will feel good about your new self.

9

Protecting Yourself: Don't Be Scared, Be Prepared

To conquer fear is the beginning of wisdom.

—Bertrand Russell

Annie's Journal (10 months)
I can't believe it. After 56 years of being the world's biggest scaredy cat, I went white-water rafting with Cindy and Sam and some friends. And I enjoyed it! The infamous Guadalupe River north of San Antonio wasn't all fierce water, but there were plenty of thrills to go around. It's the kind of "danger" that is fun, enlightening, awakening of the spirit. I wish Bruce and I had done such things years ago. It hurts me to think of all the exciting things we didn't do because we were afraid. Afraid of what? Dying? That happens whether we fear it or not. What a shame.

I was feeling euphoric the day I wrote my journal entry about white-water rafting. I felt immortal, indestructible. In fact, even when I wrote the first draft of this chapter, months later, it began, "Nothing scares me anymore." After several months I realized that wasn't quite true, so I went back and changed it. The possibility of a Wall Street crash wiping out my income scared me, when I thought about it. Helplessly watching the increasing power of fanatical terrorists scared me, when I thought about it. The remote possibility of being in the path of a Class 4 or 5 hurricane scared me, when I really thought about it. And, when I first wrote those words, I realized it hadn't been too many months since my imagination had swamped my reason and left me with a good-sized anxiety attack. So, it wasn't true that nothing scared me at all. I guess that would have been too much to expect.

One thing definitely had changed, however. I no longer limited my life to a safe little box because of irrational fears. In addition to the rafting trip I men-

137

tioned in my journal, since Bruce died I also have gone downhill skiing in the mountains of Colorado, Keystone to be exact. I didn't venture onto the black expert runs, but I did ski down "Schoolmarm" once, a run more than a mile and a half long. It was a piece of cake for my young grandchildren, but it was slightly terrifying for an acrophobic older lady with weak knees, who probably skied 20 miles back and forth on the steeper parts and snowplowed the rest of the way down. I also have ridden on all the thrilling rides at Disney World, except for one, which I was cautioned against. I, known by some as "white knuckle Annie," have flown all over this country, to France twice and England once. In addition, although I had never been comfortable on the seas, I sailed from Ft. Myers to the Keys and to the Bahamas and back in a 45-foot sailboat. I think I would like to go more exotic places and do more exotic things, and it's nice to know that now I'm more limited by real factors, such as the cost. It's not that any of these things I mention is innately dangerous, but that I had always projected them to be so. Now I know that, with proper precautions, they can be exciting without being life threatening.

I still become terrified sometimes, but it usually doesn't keep me from trying new experiences.

I continue to be reasonably cautious: no bungee-jumping into mountain gorges or climbing the face of the Grand Canyon. But I usually am not paralyzed with fear when facing modest adventures. In addition, I seldom get tied in knots by "things that go bump in the night." I no longer break into a cold sweat facing a two-day auto trip alone. I no longer stay up late glued to radio or TV weather reports, because we are under a "severe thunderstorm watch." It seems I lost my irrational fears of life by having survived the cold, hard reality of widowhood. I have almost, it seems, "conquered fear…[and found] the beginning of wisdom." I suppose my life is better now…in that one way.

Looking back on our 35 years of marriage, my primary regret is that Bruce and I missed out on having a lot of fun together because of our imagined fears. We seldom traveled, unless forced to by his job. And when we did travel, we were both uptight for most of the trip. If only we had known then what I know now. "If only…." Another thing I have learned, is that the "if onlys" are a sad waste of time.

I suspect some of you will have trouble identifying with this former "scaredy cat." That's fine. Maybe the real question is: *Are you either much more fearful or much less fearful than before your husband died?*

Apparently, unexpected bravado and a numb sense of indestructibility are common reactions for new widows. I initially worried about my new sense of indestructibility. I wondered if I just didn't care that much about my life anymore. I wondered if I was unknowingly a bit suicidal. Was I being reckless, trying all these new activities, and secretly hoping I would die, too? This is not an unusual concern. And it is true that some widows test that new fearlessness, doing really dangerous things. I have not, and probably won't. I have simply learned to be realistically cautious instead of irrationally fearful. Although I am sure I have a lot of company among you, other widows go completely the other way, from "formerly fearless" to "suddenly spooked" by anything and everything. Several widows I interviewed talked of being extremely fearful and anxious for their own lives, in the months following their husband's death..

—BEWARE OF EXCESSIVE FEAR—

Many women said they felt shaken to their very foundations by widowhood. They had felt secure, cared for and protected from harm by their husbands. Without that protection, life suddenly seemed overwhelming, frightening. They said they began to dwell on their own vulnerability and to worry excessively about all the real and imagined threats to their safety.

"I bought a gun and keep it by my bed," Caroline said. She took a gun handling course, where she learned she couldn't just shoot up at the ceiling. The instructor told her, "Anyone who breaks into your home means business. Shoot to kill; a dead witness is the best." He also told her if she didn't mean business, an intruder might take her gun away and kill her with it. "I also keep an outside light on in the front and back of the house all the time, and I play a radio or TV 24 hours a day," she said.

Ginny became super cautious about locking her house, and kept all her curtains closed at night. "I also worried about the kids a lot," she said. "I had to know where they were every minute." The first thing Dale did after her husband died was to install a home security system. "I have a one-story house and my bedroom and bathroom windows are very close to the ground," she said. "So I felt uneasy," She turned the system on at night and whenever she was away from home, easing her anxieties. Karen, whose sleep habits suffered from her fears, said, "I'd be awake every night from three to five and then fall into a light sleep until seven. I felt so incredibly alone! Then I had a security system installed, which gave me the feeling of safety during that time." She is quite independent now, fearing little, even though she lives alone (except for her cats) in a remote and very wooded area.

Thanks to instant media coverage here and around the world, we now can watch horrendous acts of violence committed against innocent people every day.

We can see live-action police chases. We can watch innocents die in the jungles of South America. We can go into battle with front-line generals, from our comfortable seats on the sofa. The whole world's worst atrocities can be going on in our living rooms. There are "crazies" in this world, threatening our otherwise beautiful lives, and we know it. Since September 11, 2001, we have had to face that we aren't exempt from the kind of senseless terrorism we'd only heard about before. There are many real concerns, but studies show that life still isn't nearly as dangerous—for most of us—as we think it is. That is true even in areas where terrorism is a daily occurrence. Until modern electronics made this worldwide coverage possible, most people only knew what happened in their own parishes, families, neighborhoods or small towns. It's easy to get spooked if you watch TV news before heading to bed at night. It is probably wiser not to watch any more television than necessary while you are trying to regain your senses. It's important to think about this problem when you are thinking clearly, in broad daylight. It's hard to keep your imagination in check at night. We widows have to guard against letting our new fears dominate our lives and imprison us in our homes. You probably remember secluded widows from your childhood, as I do. We always thought these old ladies were a little crazy. Well, maybe they were, because of letting their unrealistic fears imprison them in their own homes.

I realize that is much easier to say if you live, as I do, in a comfortable suburban area, than if you live inside a crowded tenement building or only half a block from where drug addicts gather. For those of you who live in truly dangerous places, do whatever you can to make your home as safe as possible. If the situation is intolerable, and you can, move to a safer apartment or home, a safer neighborhood, or a safer community. No place can be absolutely guaranteed safe; bad things can happen anywhere. But having it happen all around you as part of the daily routine, can destroy your efforts to take control and fashion a new life for yourself.

I felt very lucky as a new widow to know several incredibly self-sufficient, active and hardy widows who were 82 years old, or older. Ah, the stories they could tell about their long years, if you could get them to sit still long enough to reminisce. They all lived in rural or small-town areas that are, undeniably, safer than most metropolitan areas. It seems to me each of these ladies faced about the same potential danger on a daily basis, except that one of the five did not drive a car.

It would seem this woman would feel less threat and fear for her life than those who drove. Wrong. The other four kept busy with interesting lives, using their cars to see and do more interesting things than they would know at home alone. But the non-driver lived in a hell of her own making by torturing herself with constant, irrational fears. She listened to news all day and all night, and as is so often the case with those who do, she projected each incident into a larger threat to her world than it really was. If she heard of a break-in in her town or a town nearby, she stayed awake nights listening for the sound of footsteps outside her window. If she heard of a car-jacking in a state two thousand miles away, she called her children, and sometimes grandchildren, and told them to be sure they locked their cars wherever they went. She was suspicious of everyone, whether it was someone seen in a crime report, her neighbor down the street or someone close to her. She feared they all were plotting to take advantage of her in some way. Except for this failing, she was an incredible woman. She taught herself in her fifties how to upholster furniture. There was no piece so intricate she wouldn't try, and stick with, until she succeeded in making it look like new. At about 90 she began to slow down, and had to refuse work on large davenports. She had amazing strength even then, often doing push-ups and backward somersaults for incredulous visitors.

Fear and suspicion are common failings among the elderly. Unfortunately, widows of all ages are especially susceptible to vicious neuroses and psychoses, such as paranoia. Reasonable concern turns to worry, which escalates to irrational, immobilizing fear. I mentioned this woman's fears to a widowed friend, who said, "Oh, my heart aches for anyone who lives with fear." Mine, too.

Luckily the other four women I mentioned remained relatively happy, productive and awe-inspiring to me. One, who was 88 at the time, mentioned that she had recently driven by herself, at night, fifty miles round-trip, just to hear a symphony. "I couldn't miss hearing that Rachmaninoff piece," she told me. "I hadn't heard it for years." She also carried a bucket, shovel and waders in the trunk of her car at all times, just in case she should need to rescue some marsh marigolds or Jacks-in-the-Pulpit from the path of a construction crew.

A widow from the other end of our far flung neighborhood could often be seen biking the seven miles—each way—between her home and another property she owns. In her mid-80s, she sat tall in her seat and wore a helmet, ever cautious but never fear-ridden. When she arrived at her lot, she "rested" by cutting down trees and splitting the logs for firewood.

In spite of trying threats to her health, one of my favorite octogenarian friends travels abroad occasionally, entertains often, participates actively in the community and manages to be one of the most generous, gracious and loving women I have ever known. Her secret: she worries more about the well-being of others than herself.

Another friend, who was still slender and shapely at 82, lost her 86-year-old husband soon after Bruce died. Until her husband's death the couple still enjoyed downhill skiing, and she swam almost every day—when it wasn't frozen—in the frigid waters of Green Bay. Just a few years before, the couple had been skiing in the mountains of New Zealand, had stopped in Hawaii for a few rounds of golf (having taken their own equipment for both activities) and then had flown into the Green Bay airport. Instead of groping for the nearest bed so they could collapse and recover, they were upset because a delayed flight had caused them to miss the first quarter of the Green Bay Packer game they went to. I love it!

I think I unconsciously decided which kind of widow I wanted to be, from studying the lives of these five women. Amazing, inspiring women, all of them. I wish they had known my great aunt Ida, whom I hope to emulate in my advancing years. At 95 she climbed into a huge gnarled old apple tree to cut down a limb for a younger neighbor man, because, she said, "I do have the sharpest saw in town!" That saw was her pride and joy, and I'll bet she decided she would rather climb the tree than let him borrow it. She homesteaded in the Dakotas as a young woman, was soon widowed, and moved back to a farm near her family in southern Wisconsin. She soon became known around the area for keeping the rattlesnake population under control with her trusty Winchester.

The difference between these women and the first one isn't in the dangers around them, but in their mental attitudes and their perspectives of life, especially their perceptions of the dangers they face. One built molehills into unscalable mountains; the others put on their boots and tromped over the molehills on their way to see, ski or hike the mountains. Mark my word, if I am lucky enough to be strong and healthy at age 82, I am going to ask my kids for new hiking boots for my birthday!

I don't recommend carelessness. I hope you will protect and prepare yourself, so you won't need to be fearful and you can enjoy your life. Louis R. Mizell, Jr., says in his book *Street Sense for Women,* "Awareness is the key to saving lives, property and money." His book counsels women on how to avoid becoming victims. Still, even he hypes alarming statistics and headline-making crimes, causing more fear than is useful. But hype sells! Keep that in mind as you read newspapers and blockbuster books, or listen to daily news and docu-dramas. Crime and violence often are played up far beyond their significance to the world as a whole. One crazy gunman who kills one innocent bystander often gets as much or more coverage than the fanatic regime of a foreign country that slaughters a whole generation of innocents. Even the terrorism we're experiencing for the first time in America is (so far) not as life-threatening to the majority of us as it might seem.

Imagine how safe our lives must seem to people in war-weary countries in the Middle East, or drug-war torn Columbia, or eternally fighting Northern Ireland. And, of course, most of us still live well and comfortably compared to millions who know the daily terror of starvation and homelessness. Our lives, even if we are legally poverty stricken, are safer and more comfortable than the great majority of people on this planet. Try to remember that.

—MAKING YOUR HOME SAFER—

I have always lived in fairly safe areas. But, as the professionals remind us, most people think they do until something happens to upset their safe little world. Realizing that, I had to learn to be more careful after I was alone. In my Florida townhouse I (usually) locked my doors when I was inside when it was dark outside, and when I went outside beyond the parking lot where I walked my dog. Usually I also locked up when I would be upstairs writing for long periods. Although a security expert might shiver at this casual attitude about locks, I suspect I was relatively safe because neighbors and friends lived close by and they watched over me like mother hens. In rural Wisconsin I knew I was more vulnerable, and so I was usually more careful about locking doors.

The first evening I was alone in my townhouse (at three months), my good friends George and Joanne came to my door. I swung the door open wide and then turned around to flick on the porch light. I thought George would have a heart event! It was pretty stupid; I hadn't learned to be cautious yet. The next morning he arrived and installed a "fish eye" peek hole in my solid door, and warned me to turn on the light and look to be sure I knew who was there before opening my door. I also had a chain lock, so I could have opened the door a bit and looked before opening it wide. Live and learn. Thank heavens I didn't have to learn the hard way.

I also had a dog. Manda was a 13-pound Shih-Tzu, but she tried very hard to sound like a vicious 98 pound killer pit bull if anyone surprised her by coming to my door unannounced. When I wasn't home, I suspect she protected herself by hiding quietly under the bed; when I was home, she protected me ferociously. As much trouble as she was to me once I began to travel and enjoyed keeping odd hours, she was an invaluable asset. Intruders would rather not tangle with any dog, given a choice; they will usually go to a neighbor's house rather than to one with evidence of a dog.

I lived in the woods in Wisconsin, and my neighbors lived much farther away than those in Florida. At the time we added our garage, we installed a heat-sensitive security light. I didn't know how it worked, but it did. It came on if anything larger than a squirrel ventured into the front yard/driveway area. It was reassuring, especially when I had to walk Manda at night. It came on several times when I was locked inside, but usually only to startle a family of deer who had come for a little juniper and hasta leaf salad from my garden.

It also was comforting when I came home alone at night. We had no street lights and it was blacker than black when there was no moon. The security light would come on as I entered the drive, and then I opened the garage door electronically. At night I usually drove in and lowered the door before getting out of my locked car. I think we all are a bit more cautious in the dark. I had a second light installed at the back of my home soon after I was alone, knowing that is where most intruders attempt illegal entry. I have heard criminals don't like lights, so I find them very comforting.

If I lived in a large city, I might have triple locks and a security system. But I hate them and doubt they are as useful as they are annoying when you live in small town suburban America. If you, on the other hand, feel they would comfort you, go for it. Don't let me talk you into being too casual. If you get locks and window grates though, be sure they allow any people inside to easily get out, in case of fire, which is more likely in many areas than burglary, assault or rape. One frustration I have with electronic alarm systems is that the brain-rattling alarms go off so often, triggered by something harmless, that they fail at their mission. I asked my daughter what to do if theirs were to go off while I was caring for the grandkids. She said, "Go downstairs and punch in the code to stop it." That, of course, would be the wrong thing to do if someone had just broken in. Their house was very secure, sometimes TOO secure.

Several years ago their then two-year-old son, Luke, went inside from the back yard and locked the patio door behind him. Luckily for the parents, Luke became frightened and crawled behind the playroom couch, so although they were locked out they could see that he was safe. After trying every possible way to get inside, they had to go to the neighbors and call 9-1-1. The fire department arrived and removed a second story skylight in order to enter the house. After parents and son were reunited and calmed, and the fire department had left, Cindy decided to hide a key outside in case such a thing ever happened again. Armed with hammer, nail and key, she scrutinized the area and finally picked the perfect spot to hide it, where no one else would ever think to look. She raised the hammer and was about to hit the nail, when she felt something there. It was a nail…holding a house key. Sure enough, the previous owners had picked precisely the same spot as "the least likely place someone would look."

Aside from the comic relief provided by this story, it also serves to remind us that burglars are clever. They try to think like we do, so many of our efforts to foil them are ineffective. If two women picked the same spot to hide a key, it would probably be the first place a burglar would look. Keep that in mind as you hide a key or choose a lock combination.

Since living alone, I have not had much experience with suspicious strangers arriving at my door. One time, though, I glanced out the window and realized I had no idea who the man was at my door. As I opened the front door I turned around and hollered (to my empty house), "In a minute! There's someone at the door right now." It turned out to be an annoying but harmless salesman, so I took advantage of my ruse, and told him I had to rush and help my husband. I had, as always, picked up Manda and taken her to the door with me. It not only stopped her from barking, but her obvious nervousness also might have made someone scouting the neighborhood for places to rob think twice about considering my house.

It is often tricky trying to conceal from phone callers that you live alone when you are a widow. Some are persistent, asking to speak to the man of the house. I insisted that I ran the household and I had full authority to make decisions in its regard. If they continued to insist, I just hung up.

In summary, how do professionals suggest you protect your self and your property? Here is a compilation of suggestions gathered from numerous sources.

- *Lock house, garage doors and windows day and night, when you are there and when you are not.* If your locks are of questionable reliability, replace them. Add good dead bolts to outside doors and rigid bars to brace sliding patio doors.

- *"Extra-lock" double hung wood windows.* With windows closed, drill, at a slight downward angle, a hole through the first and into the second window's center frame. Insert a strong nail. You can easily remove this from inside for opening the window, but it makes illegal entry much more difficult.

- *Install and use outdoor lights, preferably security lights, which come on when they detect a visitor.* Or consider leaving floodlights on all night, in front and back of the house.

- *Hide a key outside or program a combination lock, trying to outwit a wily criminal.* Avoid the obvious.

- *Install large, readable street numbers on your home or near your drive, to help emergency vehicles locate you easily.*

- *Install smoke alarms on each level of your home and near each bedroom.* If you have electronic smoke alarms, install a couple of battery operated ones in prime areas, so they will work even if the house power is off. Maintain batteries, replacing them every year on your birthday.

- *Keep fire extinguishers handy—and in working condition—in your kitchen, basement and garage.*

- *Post signs warning of a burglar alarm system, vicious attack dog and "automatic police alarm if phone lines are cut."* Your best bet is to make intruders stop and think. They may suspect the signs are fakes, but they probably will not be sure enough to risk it.

- *Conceal valuable computers or stereos from windows.*

- *Get a dog (which increases your odds against having an intruder by seven times) OR leave a large water dish and bone near exterior doors.*

- *Cover or "frost" garage windows so no one can see if a car is there.*

- *Leave your home looking lived in, with automatic light timers, radio or TV on, lawn mowed or drive plowed in winter, mail and papers rerouted or stopped if you will be gone a few days.*

- *Install a phone by your bed, with a lighted dial, so you can summon help if you need it.*

- *Rehearse an "alarm code message" with a neighbor.* If I were ever to call my next door neighbor and say, "I forgot to call when I got home. I have your coffee. (Pause) Sure, come on over," she would know to come over as fast as humanly possible. It was our code, saying we had someone in the house we didn't trust, be it a suspicious salesman or an "old buddy" of our husband's.

If you live in a large city, where you feel more susceptible to crime, you also may need to do the following:

- *Install a home alarm system.* Professionals recommend choosing a reputable company. Check out consumer testing lists or contact your local law enforcement agency for recommendations.

- *Install keyless window gates inside vulnerable windows.* They discourage burglary but make exit easy in a fire.

- *Install solid, preferably metal, entry doors AND door frames.* For wood doors, get what are known as police locks.

- *Arm yourself with knowledge and/or implements of self-defense.* If your location and situation are extremely treacherous, it may be necessary to buy and learn to use a gun; keep canisters of mace or tear gas (if legal in your area) in strategic places; learn self-defense strategies.

Then, relax. I don't mean to be facetious. I truly believe we must prepare for the worst so we can enjoy the best. But, remember: *Fear is no deterrent to crime, only caution is.* Fear simply eats at you, caution prompts you to take necessary steps to protect yourself. Most of these suggestions are not specifically for widows. I offer them here, because some of us feel more vulnerable now that we are alone, and ideas we formerly scoffed at may make sense to us now. The point is to protect yourself enough that you can relax and enjoy your life.

—SAFETY FOR YOU AND YOUR CAR—

Additional perils exist away from home, but a few simple precautions and a little knowledge also can help you function more confidently in your larger world. As a woman alone, you need to give yourself some advantages to compensate for your (probably) smaller size and lower level of strength than a man's.

I won't bother including a long list of all the ways you can try to prevent your car from being stolen, because that problem is much the same for men, couples and women alone. There are lots of little tricks and hundreds of gadgets available that tilt the odds in your favor. If you fear for your car's safety, ask around, read up on the subject or visit an auto parts store and get advice from a knowledgeable clerk. Never risk personal injury or death trying to prevent someone from stealing your car, however. Let them have it.

Here are a few simple reminders that might save you the hassle and annoyance of losing your car to a thief. When leaving your car:

- *Close car windows.*

- *Lock car doors.*

- *Take your keys.*

- *Park in well-lighted, preferably attended, lots.*

- *Be sure valuables aren't visible.*

Far less likely, but more frightening than car theft, is the newer problem of "car-jacking." Armed thieves attack while the driver is in or near the car, demanding keys, purses and wallets, and then driving away with the car. It's good to learn more about how to avert this type of crime, because it often involves you and your passengers' personal safety as well as the car itself.

- *Avoid areas you know are susceptible to carjacking whenever possible.*

- *Keep car doors locked whether you are in the car or out.* This simple precaution would prevent most carjackings, according to police.

- *Never, ever, leave a car with the engine running, especially with children in it, even to run into the house for a second or to an ATM machine.* (If you don't appreciate this reminder, let me tell you about the day my 3 1/2-year-old grandson decided to drive the family's van, with his two sisters aboard. Little harm done, thanks to a handy fence and neutral gear, but it scared the daylights out of all of us watching.)

- *Talk, or pretend to talk, on a cell phone when you are in a suspicious area or when you feel somehow threatened by nearby strangers.*

- *Let them have your car, if you believe that will prevent anyone from being injured.*

I would like to suggest that all widows arm themselves with cell phones, so they'd never have to worry about being on the road alone. But that's not always as simple or as effective as it sounds. Several single friends and I took the precaution of getting cellular car phones in the early nineties, before they were so common. Some auto dealers offered "free" bag phones with the purchase of a new car. They turned out to be anything but free, by the time they were installed and activated with a two-year contract. Not only were those old bag phones semi-effective and very expensive, they probably made us inattentive drivers and more vulnerable to accidents because they were so complicated to use.

Even now, cell phones are less than ideal "lifesavers." They are simple enough to use locally, but they still can present quite a challenge outside your local area. Different areas have different rules, etc. Add to all that a scarcity of towers outside urban areas and spotty transmission in hilly areas, which adds up to your cell phone being a "possible help" in an emergency, certainly not a sure thing. It's probably still worth having one, for when it does work, but don't mislead yourself about its value for security on the road. If you intend to buy one, I can recommend the following from my experience:

- *Be sure your phone has a one-button 9-1-1 emergency calling service available even when it is locked.*

- *Insist that you get good, easy-to-understand instructions before taking possession of the phone.* Take notes on and practice the most common actions: dialing local/long distance calls; retrieving messages; answering incoming calls and completing calls; entering and using speed-dialing, etc. If you can't use it easily, without looking up the directions, it will be virtually useless as an emergency tool.

- *Select the service most likely to save you money and serve your needs.* Ignore "1,000 free minutes" plans, unless they are usable when and where you will most likely make calls. Be sure you know whether it is just "free air time," or includes "free long-distance charges" and/or "free roaming." As smart as I think I am, I got an unexpected bill for almost $300 worth of roaming charges for calls I made in Texas to mostly nearby numbers. And I recently got one for $600 because of a misunderstanding of

- *Keep the phone in your purse or pocket so it is handy if you need it, and to prevent theft.*

CAUTION: While a cell phone can be a great comfort when you're driving alone, be rigid about talking and driving. That combination is almost as deadly as drinking and driving. Pull over to a safe spot before placing a call. If you can easily answer an incoming call without losing your concentration, do so but tell them you will call back when you reach a safe destination. If the phone is not easily accessible, let it ring. When you reach a safe place, the number will probably be displayed on your screen so you can easily dial it. A hands-free device may leave you free to watch the road, but conversation still distracts from the business of driving.

—BE A GOOD GIRL SCOUT—

I was a Girl Scout in my youth, a Brownie and Intermediate Scout leader in three cities as a young woman, and briefly served as a volunteer staff member as an adult. Perhaps that explains why I learned so well their motto "Be Prepared." It means, of course, to be prepared so that you can handle emergencies that may occur. I, however, have always taken the warning one step further. I prepare so emergencies won't happen. I believe the adage put forth by Benjamin Disraeli and others: "What we anticipate seldom occurs; what we least expect generally happens." For many years I tried to expect disasters all the time, and prepare for them, so they wouldn't happen. Except for Bruce's death, I was quite successful.

For 19 years we lived in a great contemporary hillside home. The four-level structure and sloping, wooded grounds were not ostentatious, impressively large or terribly expensive, but they were "artistic," pleasing to the eye. The home was, however, a few miles from town and we lost electric service several times a year during wind, snow, rain, sleet or ice storms. It was a pain in the neck, especially because we had our own well: No electricity equals no water. Getting along without water is…icky. No dishwashing, no cleaning up, no bathing, no flushing. For about ten years we put up with periods—from a few hours to several days—without lights, heat and water. Then I discovered the answer, which I share with you in some embarrassment.

A message taped to my refrigerator door for twenty years, said, "There are two kinds of things you never need worry about. Those you can't do anything about and those you can." Author unknown. So, instead of worrying, I called on my Girl Scout training. I prepared. I bought a ten-gallon storage jug for water, a battery radio, extra batteries, flashlights and an emergency heater. In the next nine years we never needed them. Not one storm interrupted our electric service for more than an hour. Unbelievable. My preparedness apparently had changed southern Wisconsin's entire climate. Then I discovered that lighting a candle as a storm approached kept the lights from going out at all. We laughed about that for years. It was spooky to contemplate my powers over Mother Nature.

We also learned the hard way that when you live on the top of a hill out in the country in Wisconsin, it's very easy to get snowed in for extended periods. Years ago it happened at least once or twice each winter. We were only three miles from a store, but downhill all the way (uphill all the way back) and often a treacherous drive in heavy snows. So I packed what I dubbed our "blizzard box" for such emergencies. (Can you tell I'm a Virgo?) This box contained what I considered at that time to be the barest essentials of life after the more elementary emergency box with batteries and water, etc. These were things you just had to have if the power was out for days. It included additional batteries, a can opener, toilet paper, candles, matches, vodka and cigarettes. I laugh now that I ever thought those last two essential. It's been years since I've had any wish for either. Perhaps a few cans of beans might have been more appropriate, and they will take their place in a hurricane box if I ever get alarmed enough to pack one. Unfortunately, the supplies came in handy whenever I ran out of something. So the one time we were snowed in by a two-day blizzard, I had borrowed almost everything from the box. After that I tried to keep it full. Just having the box fully packed was apparently adequate to prevent future snow-ins.

I haven't needed jumper cables for a dead battery since I bought one for each car; or a shovel to get a car out of a snow bank since I bought one to keep in the trunk; or….you get the picture. Of course, eventually I settled on the ultimate solution to most of those winter problems. I moved to Florida's southwest coast. (I'm working on how to prevent hurricanes from hitting this area, and so far I've met with success.)

Even so, I am usually prepared for most eventualities. For years my regular purse had a kit with a Swiss Army knife, bandages, superglue, a mini-sewing kit, floss, first-aid medications and safety pins. I over-pack for emergencies and odd contingencies when I travel, too, saying, "If I have it I won't need it; if I don't, I will." I have, honestly, only needed a fever thermometer when away from home the two times (in 25 years) that I forgot to pack it. It goes without saying I also take along plenty of cash, plus travelers' checks, plus checkbook, plus credit cards, plus ATM cards. I don't keep everything in one purse, in case it might be stolen. So, of course, it never has been.

I tell you all this silly stuff about myself so you will know how much stock to put in my advice here. My "Be Prepared" background is so ingrained I usually perform like a robot when any kind of threat looms. I'm sure it doesn't really forestall disaster, but it does keep me occupied so I don't worry myself to death. So, whenever you are considering how best to protect yourself, your home and belongings, remember these tips and…*don't be scared; be prepared!*

10

Dealing with Finances: Money and Money Problems

O money, money, money,
I'm not necessarily one
Of those who think thee holy,
But I often stop to wonder
how thou canst go out so fast
when thou comest in so slowly.

—Ogden Nash

Annie's Journal (9 months)
Whew! I just had to write checks for income taxes, my quarterly estimate and to my accountant for preparing them. I had hoped my budget could have a month to recover from delayed Christmas expenses. And yesterday I got the estimate for rebuilding our deck! I'll never make it without selling the lake house…or getting a job…or cutting back to the bare bones, that's for sure. I don't care what "they" say.

They say, "No one's so poor as a widow in her first year." That implies that none of us is as poor as we first think we are. Maybe that's true for some; our fears make us feel more poor than we really are. But in money, as in most factors, we each are different. Everyone's balance sheet will be unique. Some widows have dependable employment, with steady paychecks and all the perks. Others have found that they are in possession of more assets than they ever dreamed; money is not their worry.

However, most widows are presented with a less rosy realization: that we are now dependent on finite resources and/or fixed incomes. My income was "fixed" at considerably less than I had expected it might be, due to slumping interest rates on our bonds. If you became a widow during an economic slump, you probably had a similar jolt. Our financial plans for this rainy day had assumed steady or rising rates, as had been the case for years. Instead, I faced my first year with one third less income than projected. I remember getting angry whenever a politician reiterated the favorite brag line of that period, "The economy is in great shape, interest rates are way down." At one point I screamed at the TV, "Oh yeah? What about those of us whose primary income is from interest? What are we, leftover mashed potatoes?" That is one of the advantages of living alone. Until I told you this, no one ever knew of my outburst.

As is so often the case, my decreasing income was met with increasing expenses. I hadn't foreseen the need to rebuild the deck on my Wisconsin cottage, much less that it would be done the day following a rise of 10 percent on all lumber prices. Nor had I expected rising maintenance costs, such as having our holding tank pumped or having the plumber close and open the cottage. Each increase hit me like a brick in the belly! As soon as I recovered from one blow and began to spot light at the end of the tunnel, something broke...or got struck by lightning. Within the first several months I had to pay for a new water heater, major repairs to the Florida air conditioner, a new TV and a new VCR.

On top of these assaults, I got another shocker. I had always thought one could live on about half as much as two! *Not!* I kept asking myself, "Where is the money we used to spend on Bruce and he spent on himself?" When my anger subsided, I had to admit I knew the answer to that dilemma, but I didn't like facing it. I now needed to hire help for repairs and heavy work that Bruce used to do, and because my fibromyalgia became acute during early grief, I needed regular full-body massages to ease the pain. I confess that I also spent more money on clothes and shoes, partly because of its temporary therapeutic value, and partly because I liked not having to justify the expense to anyone. I also traveled more, but I doubt I spent more on travel than the two of us had before.

My first outward sign of anger, actually my first sign of being *alive*, occurred about ten days after Bruce died, when my husband and wife investment counselors drove from Milwaukee to Door County to discuss my accounts and projected income. At first I cocked my head occasionally, frowned or nodded, so they would think I comprehended what sounded like so much gobbledygook. Meanwhile, I remember my thoughts swimming around and around, and up and over and inside out. I noticed, more than anything, how the two of them reacted to each other as spouses. I thought how much nicer they would have treated each other if they had known what I knew about losing a spouse. I also chided myself for not paying more attention to Economics 101 decades earlier. I whiled away some time wondering if Bruce was watching; he knew I was bored by investment talk, even when I could think straight.

Unaware of my distractions, the two talked on. I didn't give a hoot that day about "calls," "loads," "yields," "coupons" and "limited partnerships." I had no interest in the process; I only wanted assurance that they could manage my money so I would have enough to live on.

My first clear thought took shape while I was listening to the husband's "little lecture to the little widow," which he apparently recited at each such meeting. He concluded his simplistic short course on economics by wagging his finger at me, and saying, "You must *never, ever* spend a penny of the principal." My confusion cleared like fog in a dry wind. I bit my tongue and waited until he finished. Then I gave him my "little lecture."

"I am more than four years from getting social security benefits," I recited in measured tones. "And these four years promise to be the hardest, most miserable years of my life in every way. If you think I am going to make them worse by worrying and pinching pennies and going without, just so I don't disturb the damned principal, you're wrong! I will be careful, no yachts or minks or mansions. But I intend to use what I need during these four years, when I most need it. And if that means I have to dip into the principal a little bit, so be it!"

They chose to leave soon after that. I think they liked me better when I was in the fog. I still consider his lecture and warning a belittling insult. I was a new widow and I was in shock, but I was not a moron! I, and I'm sure all of you, know better than to spend much of the principal that earns our income. To do so would be to eat the goose that lays our golden eggs. I hope because of my outburst that couple learned to be more respectful when dealing with new widows. They were more respectful to me after that, but I soon switched to a much more respectful financial counselor.

During her first three months as a widow, Karen says much of her time was taken with estate issues and financial planning. "Gene was an accountant and had taken care of investments, etc.; he had left everything in good order. My problem was my inability to concentrate long enough to get a grasp on what I was studying."

Mine, too! Nearly all widows say the same thing, but especially those who had little experience guiding the family "fortunes." Presented with the challenge at any "normal" time in our lives, we might learn quickly, but to be thrust into this new responsibility at a time when our minds are shattered and not tracking, overwhelms us. Most of us feel inadequate, terrified, stupid, dependent, ashamed and depressed. Not good feelings.

—BRINGING HOME THE BACON AS WELL AS COOKING IT—

Many new widows not only have to struggle with how to manage their finances, they have to go out and earn the money to manage. Their "financial straits" are more than just natural widows' worries. Their very survival depends on working to keep food on the table. For many that situation is complicated by their years working full-time in homemaking and child-rearing. Both are worthy endeavors, but they aren't the best preparation for finding a good job. One good friend was widowed in her 50s. For years she had helped operate a nursery school, earning a pittance but enjoying the work. It became obvious very quickly that she had to retrain herself for a better position. She was lucky that she could take a Spanish immersion class in Mexico to revive her skills as a Spanish teacher. If you don't have such a skill you can easily brush up, you may be what is referred to as a "displaced homemaker." Because there are so many of us, help is available through county extension offices, women's studies departments in local colleges, and other sources. Ask everyone you know, until you find someone to help you become employable. The help is there; it just takes legwork, the Internet or phone calls to find it.

Decades ago Eunie (with children seven and three years of age), Agnes (with boys four and eight) and Anna (with four girls, ages four through eight) were among those who found it imperative that they work full-time to support their families. At that time it was not common for young mothers to work; there were no nursery schools or day care programs to make it easier. But they were not afforded the luxury of choice. They needed to work, and work they did. It's apparent in talking with them that each had a real struggle in those first years, but they now can see the benefits that working provided them. Finding themselves capable of being self-sufficient breadwinners helped them develop into self-actualized women who weren't easily thrown by life's difficulties after that.

Anna says, "I must say I never had any illnesses after Glenn's death, which I attribute to the busy schedule I inherited. Work is the best therapy." Other widows said they credited their need to work with keeping them sane, moving them beyond grief and forcing them to mature and face reality.

Ginny had always worked as a nurse or as a teaching nurse, because she had always been able to juggle her hours to mesh with her husband's teaching schedule. One or the other of them was always able to care for their two boys. When Don died, she found herself in charge of the physical, psychological, and financial well being of her family at age 39. Her husband had taken advantage of a school offer to give up social security contributions, thinking he would outlive her because of her diabetes. He planned to resume deductions as he got nearer to retirement. "It was a gamble we all lost," she said. As a widow who had been a working partner, she wasn't eligible for any of his benefits, and her children's benefits were paid on minimal contributions he had made early in his career. A lot of widows, including this author, learned the hard way about shortsighted financial decisions.

Pauli, widowed at age 29, was able to stay at home with her three small children for six years. But doing so meant living on a very stringent budget. "Our only income for the first six years," she says, "was our Social Security and a small insurance payout. But our house was paid for, which helped." After that she worked, and thrived, in such diverse jobs as bridal consultant for a swanky department store, selling petroleum by the tanker truckload, sales consultant for a funeral home, and working with dysfunctional families.

These younger widows suffered double whammies. They were left with the unavoidable expenses of rearing young families, but they and their spouses hadn't had time to build income-producing estates, nor had they opted to buy sizable insurance policies to protect against such unlikely eventualities. I shudder when I think of how that could have happened to me. We, too, thought we would both live long enough to worry about such cares later. I was lucky; we did. Knowing how dislocated I felt most of my first year as a new widow, without serious financial problems or small children dependent on my strength, I marvel at these young women. I can't imagine having been faced with these kinds of pressures, when breathing, eating, sleeping and grieving were pressures enough. They say they benefited in the long run, that their struggles boosted their self-images, and that they had less time to feel sorry for themselves. Necessity demanded that they not waste time wallowing in their sadness.

I cannot imagine having been able to do that as a young mother, but I probably could have and would have. I doubt they could imagine being able to do it either. If we share nothing else, we widows all learn one lesson from this unfair toss of the dice: *we all can do more than we thought we could.*

—ESTATE/INHERITANCE/INCOME TAXES—

You probably have muddled through your earliest financial duties by now. I mentioned quite a few in chapters two and three. As you recover your senses you will need to get more serious about handling your finances.

Although Bruce's estate was settled without probate, thanks to his foresightedness, it wasn't settled without a lot of busy work. Even with almost everything in both our names, I probably made 200 phone calls and used a roll of stamps getting everything signed, sealed and delivered. I could have used a live-in Notary Public for awhile. For some of you it will be even more complicated.

You probably have been in contact with a lawyer for filing the will or assuming your role as sole owner of property. If she or he hasn't talked with you about filing estate tax forms, ask them (or an accountant) whether it will be necessary for you to do so. That depends on the provisions of your husband's will, if he had one, and the size of the estate he left. I hesitate to get into numbers, because laws change and I can't tell you exactly how to tally your proceeds from your husband's estate. When I was widowed, if his estate included net assets of more than $600,000, none of which was "protected" in a trust, the estate's PR (Personal Representative) probably needed to file and pay federal estate taxes. I suggest you don't try to do this alone, unless you have been trained. If the estate is substantial enough to warrant filing, hire an accountant or lawyer to do it. At the time I was widowed, a widow had nine months from the date of death to file and pay federal estate tax

In general, any estate that pays federal tax also must pay state estate tax. Also check to see if your state requires you to file and pay state inheritance taxes. (ESTATE TAX is levied on the net assets left by your husband; INHERITANCE TAX is levied on the amount you inherit.) Some states levy no tax on money passed between spouses; others levy one percent or more. Contact your state's department of taxation for guidance.

Federal and state income taxes owed by the deceased are due on the normal filing date of the next year, unless for some reason you request an extension. You may file jointly for the year he died; after that you file as a single taxpayer. If you have dependent children, you may file jointly for two additional years. Send for an IRS publication called *Information for Survivors, Executors and Administrators* to answer further questions. The Internet and public libraries have many helpful resources to make your job easier. Don't be afraid to ask for help. *People who know what they are doing usually love to help those who don't.* My son suggests that you double-check that help. "I got a wrong answer from [a firm] that almost cost me $500," he said. Good point.

—DETERMINE FINANCIAL NEEDS—

As soon as possible you need to know what assets you have, what you will have coming in on a regular basis, and what your expenses will be. Only then can you know whether your money worries are realistic. If your records are in order, and your holdings relatively straight-forward, this should not be an onerous task. It's the basic foundation from which all other financial decisions will be made.

- *Have your properties appraised.* Soon after your husband's death, get an appraisal of real estate and other property that has increased in value since its purchase. If or when you sell it, you may use this "stepped up value," the value at the time of his death, as your new "cost," presumably lowering your profit, hence your tax. My lawyer suggested I hire an appraiser to estimate market value of my cottage, because there was no recent, comparable home sale with which to compare. The fair value of the town house and cars were estimated informally by knowledgeable realtors and salespersons.

- *Determine your net worth.* This is fairly simple for most of us, once the above is done. If your situation is complicated by ownership of a business, several holdings of real estate other than your own home(s), unusual investments or legalities, you may need an accountant or lawyer's help.

  List Assets: This includes cash on hand (your wallet and his, etc.); balance of savings and checking accounts; estimated current value of stocks, bonds and Certificates of Deposit (CDs); life insurance proceeds; death benefit and/or savings plan proceeds; market value of real estate and personal property (autos, silver, jewelry, furs, antiques, furniture, clothing, appliances, electronics, etc.)

  List Liabilities: (what YOU owe; debts owed by the deceased may be forgiven or paid by the estate), principal due on mortgage(s), other loan(s) [include those jointly owed or for which you co-signed], consumer debts, credit card balances, etc.

  Subtract Liabilities from Assets: Voila! This is your net worth, the approximate value of all you own at this time, or what YOUR estate would be worth if you died today.

- *Determine your income.* Estimate income you expect from all sources. Unless you earn adequate income to live without a budget, or you know the income from your husband's estate will far exceed your needs, it's important to tally up and project your annual and monthly incomes for the next several years. Include your salary, pensions, Social Security benefits, other benefits, income from investments (rental property, stocks, bonds, CDs, etc.).

- *Establish monthly/annual expenses.* You can determine your monthly expenses in one of two ways.

  Keep track of all your expenses for the first year. Do this in a large 24-column ledger, with headings such as Utilities, Clothing, Groceries, Mortgage, Auto Expense, Home Maintenance, Major Purchases, Vacations, Medical

Expenses, Gifts, Magazines and Newspapers, Business Expense (if you run a business). Your headings will depend on your spending habits.

Determine your expenses during the past year. If you need to know NOW whether you will have money left at the end of each month, or month left at the end of your money, there is a faster way (although it may seem tedious). Go through all your canceled checks and itemized charges for the past year, posting each in a column, such as those named above. Don't cheat; it's tempting to think you will be lucky enough not to have to buy four new tires for your car this year. But, if it isn't tires, it will be something else. Just write it all down, but circle "absolute one timers" (such as funeral expenses or a new kitchen) and expenses that were exclusively your husband's. Then tally up all the columns and add them together. Now you know what the two of you spent last year. By subtracting circled one-timers, you should get a fair "guess-timate" of how much money you will need for the next year, if you make no changes to your habits. However, if you have a known project or expense in the offing, factor that into the equation.

Be realistic. Remember that your husband's expenses may be replaced by expenses you will incur because you're alone. If anything, err on the side of allowing too much for yourself, if that's possible. You will have less stress, and you can always use what's left for an unexpected expense, or return it to a savings fund.

What you do with this information depends on what you discover. My numbers sent me this message: "Just keep on keeping on, but be careful." Yours might shout: "Get a job!" "Marry rich and marry quick!" or, even "Apply for welfare today!" Or it may say, "Relax and enjoy, as best you can. Money isn't your problem." Would that we all could hear that one. As I heard over and over, "having plenty of money eases recovery." But, of course, most of us don't have that advantage.

If your INcome and OUTgo are far apart in the wrong direction, there are two ways of narrowing the gap. You can *increase income*, by getting a job, selling an asset or investing more wisely. OR you can *decrease outgo*. It's staggering how much money we ordinarily let dribble through our fingertips. Plugging the leaks can be a challenge, but as Ginny said, "There is terrific satisfaction in reining in your spending habits." Make it a positive effort, not a prison sentence. We should all heed the words of Samuel Johnson: "Whatever you have, spend less."

—TIPS FOR LOWERING YOUR GROCERY BILLS—

When Bruce and I were young and often cash-poor, I sometimes became anxious or depressed. But most times I rose to the challenge and made a game out of getting "the most bang for the buck." In the grocery store I searched for ways to get the most delicious and nutritious food I could for each dollar I spent. It was good for us as well as our budget. That won't always be possible when you are in the throes of grief, but it's something to keep in mind for when you get more control of your life.

- *Say NO to high cost, low nutrition snack foods and beverages.* Learn to snack on apples, celery or carrot sticks, from-scratch popcorn, iced tea and diluted fruit juices.

- *Cut your meat consumption.* Unless you are on a specific diet for medical reasons, learn to cook with beans, rice, pasta and oodles of fresh fruit and vegetables as often as possible. As any nutritionist can tell you, we usually eat more protein than our bodies need, and especially more red meat than we need. Protein molecules are not as easily digested as other foods. Buy quantities of very fresh fish, fowl and lean meats when they're on sale; wrap carefully in portion or meal-size bags and freeze.

- *Eggs and cheese are good buys.* These can be enjoyed in moderation by all but those who have been advised by their doctors to avoid them.

- *Learn to figure costs "per meal" or "per day," rather than per pound.*

- *Prepare homemade hot cereals.* You will save money and cut down on fats, sugar and salt, often found in large quantities in prepared cereals.

- *Cross most cleaning supplies off your shopping list.* Nearly anything can be cleaned with white vinegar, bleach or ammonia. (Never mix the last two!) I remember reading years ago this tip: If you spot a gooey hand print on the door, don't wait to buy "gooey hand print remover" at the store. Grab a damp cloth and wipe if off. I *try* to remember that. The newer "miracle cloths" make clean-ups very easy.

- *Establish a reasonable budget and stick to it (if you can).* Pay yourself a realistic weekly allowance and put what's left in a cookie jar for something special. This is a good idea, but I've never succeeded in doing it. I have better luck shopping for large quantities of staples and meats at warehouse food stores, and then making regular runs to the farmer's market for fresh produce. I save money, and I eat better.

If you get into the challenge of saving grocery money, you not only will save the money but you will become much more aware of nutritional needs. Try to remember this: If you have limited funds, spend your money on what *you* choose to spend it on, keeping the health and well-being of your family as a top priority. This means steeling yourself against rampant mass advertising that tries to get you to buy what *manufacturers* want you to buy. It's empowering to realize you can be in control of your purchases. An occasional treat for you, or for the kids, will be all the more pleasant.

If you need to pull in the belt even tighter, check the following items to see if any could help you pare your expenses. Use your own judgment about each of these, and how they might be applied by you to your budget.

- *Buy no magazines or books (except THIS one);* use the public library or the Internet.

- *Cut back on going to movies or renting/buying videos.* This can save a lot of money, especially if you have children, but it also can improve a family's enjoyment level. I remember some of the most fun we had with our growing kids, was the whole family playing "hide and seek," off-key sing-alongs while riding in the car, having "scavenger hunts," playing story-telling games, playing cards or board games. Your children need your undivided attention at this time, so give them more of your time instead of more of your money. My son Dave and his wife have successfully withdrawn their kids from most television and videos. They all agree that life is better (and cheaper). It works.

- *Get yourself a good "wash and wear" haircut.* Give up frequent trips to the salon for perms, coloring or styling. Simple is often more attractive, and certainly more affordable.

- *Spend more imagination than money on recreation/vacations.* With the right attitude you can enjoy the benefits of more expensive pursuits with very little outlay of funds. Day trips from home, with a friend or with your children, can include hikes in state parks, bike rides, fishing, picnics, shell/rock collecting, swimming, watching local ball teams, tennis, etc. Try an auto trip on little country roads with your children taking turns deciding which way to turn at each stop sign. Getting lost on a beautiful Sunday afternoon can be fun.

- *Use the Internet to locate money-saving ideas.* Regardless of your age, you can locate advice and great ideas for saving money on the Internet. I just typed "inexpensive vacations" into the search line at Google.com (my favorite search engine) and pulled up many ideas. Try "money-saving ideas" or "cheap fun" or "family fun at home" or something more specific, such as your town's Chamber of Commerce. If you prefer to use "snail mail," send for free or low-cost advice on curbing spending habits from the Consumer Credit Counseling Service at 1-800-388-2227; or from AARP Consumer Affairs Section, 601 E. Street NW; Washington, DC 20049. Or call the extension office of a local college or university. A little effort pays big dividends, not the least of which is a feeling of control over your finances.

After all is said and done, you still may have to take a job or continue to earn what you can in a job. But don't assume your problems are over if you do that. Get control of your expenses as well as your income, or before you know it, no matter how much you earn, it won't be enough!

—GRIEF AND MONEY—

Because she didn't have enough money when she was widowed, a friend told me quite assuredly, "It's much easier to grieve properly with money." Another friend, who had plenty, agreed. She said, "I must say that having the money to do what I want is a big factor in my adjustment. I never have to worry about my future…or my present." Other widows agree; they say those with money have less stress, less anger at their spouses, and they can spend on travel, clothes or entertainment to provide a lift when they are feeling down. I can't disagree with that. It helps, but perhaps not as much as some believe. Those with lots of money still hurt like heck. And, because they may have more TIME to grieve, some may grieve harder and longer than those who have to spend their time on the practical concerns of keeping the family going and the wolf away from the door.

Several of the young widows I mentioned earlier say working forced them to avoid self-pity. They also were helped by the social aspects of working and their intense pride in their accomplishments. On the other hand, Virginia regrets continuing in her job after her husband died. "Looking back, I wish I had spent those precious years with my family," she said. "I could have gotten by without my salary. My job added more stress than satisfaction to my life; it actually slowed my recovery." Obviously, in finances as in all other things, there is no "one size fits all" solution.

There always have been psychological stumbling blocks associated with money that can take the joy out of having enough. That's especially true for women who inherit substantial money through widowhood. Some feel guilty having what they think of as blood money, or they feel it's really not theirs to spend, that their husbands would want as much as possible to pass on to the children. In all likelihood, mature children would rather their mothers spend enough to live comfortably. Other women feel so insecure now that they are alone, they harbor unrealistic fears of running out of money before they die. Some prefer struggling through each month as if they were paupers, as if they don't feel worthy of an easier life. Other women have been entrenched in a savings mode so long they have forgotten how to spend. They just don't see that *this is the rainy day* for which they had been saving.

It's wise to conserve so you don't run out of money, even to build your assets while you are young so you will have adequate income later on. But it's silly to skimp to build savings for savings sake, if you are only responsible for yourself. If you have children, you may have to save whatever you can to help them through college. Higher education is becoming astronomically expensive, so that is increasingly difficult. But don't let that depress you. If you can't possibly save enough, but your children seriously want further education, they probably will qualify for scholarships, jobs, loans or grants. Do what you can to build their desire for knowledge and encourage them to keep up their grades.

If you have inherited a block of money from life insurance proceeds or death benefits, you will probably need to invest it wisely, so it will provide income for you for many years. Stocks, CDs, bonds or mutual funds the two of you owned may need to be redirected into income-producing vehicles to increase your available funds. This is not the time for high-risk ventures, unless you have come into a veritable fortune. *Never invest more in risky investments than you can afford to lose.* I have had to learn and relearn that one, thanks to a volatile stock market. Some authorities suggest the new widow place all but about $10,000 of her new funds into a one-year CD, until she is thinking more clearly about how to invest it, and so she won't be tempted to spend it foolishly. I trusted my financial advisors to invest funds for me, so we got the funds earning immediately. CDs pay very low interest, but they are relatively safe, so consider that option if you are on your own.

A few more cautions regarding early financial decisions:

- *Be sure you are in top mental form when making major investment decisions.* Your livelihood may depend on these investments. Entrust someone you know with the task, or put it into a safe account until you are confident about making a long-term decision.

- *Ask someone you trust to check major decisions before they are final,* until you feel recovered and sure of yourself.

- *Take your time.* A reputable firm won't insist you make an immediate decision. According to AARP warnings, the more someone tries to rush you, the more likely he or she is crooked. Keep that in mind.

- *Do not give or loan sizable amounts of money to your children, relatives or friends.* This includes co-signing notes. While it hurts to deprive the children when you know they need help, you do them no favors by giving away your financial security. Doing so can build tremendous resentments as well as financial hardship for you. If they don't understand your reasons for refusing to "share your wealth," ask your lawyer or financial advisor to explain it to them.

- *Don't invest money with a stranger who contacts you—in person or by phone.* AARP warns that con artists peruse obituaries to identify victims due to inherit large sums of money and prey on their vulnerability. The same caution holds true for buying anything major or contributing funds to a charity because of unsolicited calls. A recent AARP newsletter warned about con artists, saying, "The telephone is the weapon of choice for criminals who talk gullible Americans out of $40 billion each year."

- *Never give your credit card or bank account information to anyone you don't know.* I've heard others say, *"Never give credit card or bank information to anyone who calls YOU."* If you wish to order from a reputable firm by mail, on the Internet or through a catalog of your choice, and you initiate the transaction, it probably will be okay. But, if they contact you, send them on their way.

- *Never pay anything for a "free prize."* AARP warns that if the caller says the charge is for taxes, he has committed a major crime. Hang up!

- *If you have doubts about someone you are dealing with, check them out.* Call the National Fraud Information Center at 1-800-876-7060. Or call your local Better Business Bureau, the state Attorney General's office, the Postal Inspection Service or a local consumer protection agency.

- *Remember that any deal that sounds "too good to be true" probably is.*

Ginny says her situation hit her suddenly. "A neighbor stopped her car, seeing me working in my yard about a month after the funeral and said, 'Are you going to lose your house?' It was a stunning dose of reality," she said. "I realized that I needed to take care of myself and the children, or face the fact that there were more than a few friends who would cheerfully scoop up the bargains at my garage sale and auction, as we slid down the tube to financial ruin." She resolved to get a job that gave her as many hours at home as possible, and to buy nothing she couldn't pay cash for by the time the bill rolled in. After thirteen years she said, "So far it has worked. All I owe is my mortgage!"

—IS HIS DEBT YOUR DEBT?—

Several widows told of being left with debts to pay, because their husbands had little money savvy. "What I'm most proud of," Ginny says, "is that I have come through the test of time without overwhelming debt." She says Don, for all his warm and wonderful qualities, had little money sense and loved credit cards, leaving her with more debts than security. A legitimate question arises. Are you responsible for *his* debts? According to *A Money Management Workbook*, produced by AARP, "In most instances, the ordinary principles of contract law apply. That is, you would not be responsible for debts you did not consent to or derive any benefit from." Their advice to widows: *Do not pay your spouse's debts until you consult a lawyer. You may not be obligated to pay them under the law of your state.* In most cases, you probably are responsible, but it's certainly worth checking. You do owe for all jointly held debts.

—LESSONS WE HAVE LEARNED—

Widowhood is "a learning experience" from day one. Some of what we learn we'll never have a chance to use, unless we remarry and are widowed a second time, heaven forbid! I can think of two things I learned about money that I would do differently if I had another chance. Maybe sharing them will help you better accept dumb things you did and can't change.

- *I would NEVER sign away my survivor's rights to my husband's pension, for slightly higher monthly payments while he was alive.* Never, unless I could see that I would have more than enough money without that dependable monthly income. My reasons for agreeing to sign them away, at the time of his early retirement, were flimsy and typically "non-assertive female." I didn't want him to think that I wanted to be a rich widow if/when he died. Such folly! I should have insisted we discuss the issue with a financial counselor. And I share that wisdom with wives whose husbands are on the verge of retirement.

- *I would not take out a mortgage (or large loan of any kind) without purchasing term life insurance to cover the balance in case my spouse died.* I have heard for years that "credit life insurance is grossly expensive and not cost effective." But advisors almost always continue, "Buying inexpensive term life insurance for the amount of the principal would be much wiser." The trouble is, no one does that. So most of us get caught with our mortgages gobbling a big bite out of our monthly incomes, or out of our investments or savings if we choose to pay them off. Either way, it hurts.

But generally, I have few complaints. I know many other widows whose financial woes put mine to shame.

—BEWARE OF THE "WHAT IFS"—

Caroline made a good point I'd like to share with you. She said, "I worried about where the money would come from if I needed a new roof ($5,000), or a new heat pump ($5,000 to $10,000). I worried about this and I worried about that. They are still okay, and so am I, after six years." In our new sensitive states we sometimes worry excessively about "What ifs." In Caroline's case, she says she kept thinking she should sell her home. It took her five years to decide to keep it, and to know that it wasn't going to fall apart or send her to the poorhouse.

I remember Pauli sobbing over the phone many years ago about how she couldn't possibly put her children through college. Her three children were ages four and under at the time. In spite of her misery, I couldn't help but laugh.

It seems money is very often one of our most trying concerns. We worry that we haven't enough. We worry whether we have the right to spend it if we have it. We worry about living to be 110 years old and running out of funds. We worry about whether to short ourselves and give more to the kids. We even worry about enjoying our money for fear people will talk.

In money worries, as in most widow worries, the best advice is the advice we hear so often that it has become a *cliché*. It is exactly what I said to Pauli on the phone, oh, so long ago: *"Relax, and try to take one day at a time."*

11

Feeling Good and Looking Good: Which Comes First?

When evil times prevail, take care to preserve the serenity of your heart.

—Horace

I'm sorry, I can't express anger. I grow a tumor instead.

—Woody Allen, *Manhattan*

Annie's Journal (7 months)
I had always heard grief described as "work," but I didn't think they meant it so literally. I feel drained by early afternoon, often have to take a nap. In the first weeks there were times it took all my energy to take a deep breath. I suppose this could be because of my erratic appetite and screwy sleep patterns. I don't get much exercise, either. It all takes too much effort. For now I guess I will just keep on feeling sick and tired of feeling sick and tired.

Many of the problems associated with grief are familiar to you by now, probably too familiar. You know about numbness and fear and sadness and loneliness and others you'd just as soon not know so intimately. It's impossible to ignore most of these symptoms; they're recognizable, pervasive and all-encompassing. But did you know…

—GRIEF IS DANGEROUS FOR YOUR HEALTH—

An article I clipped from an old issue of *Friends* magazine, says, "Studies have found grief depletes the immune system, leading some who grieve to illness and sometimes death. About 35,000 deaths are estimated to occur annually in the

167

newly widowed population. And individuals who deny their need to grieve prolong and compound the associated emotions and side effects."

Statistics show that men who lose their wives are three times more likely to die from grief than are women who lose their husbands. This is thought to be because women are more able or willing to grieve, to endure the pain of loss, than men. Men, because of lifelong training and societal expectations, often strive to get beyond their grief without going through the pain. They have been taught to refrain from crying or from showing emotional weakness in any way. They certainly hurt as badly as women do, but many have learned to conceal their pain, to deny it. In addition, because of their stoicism, men usually lack close personal confidants. Few are willing to admit their weaknesses to others, so most lack friends' shoulders to cry on, ears to bend. Many widowers jump quickly into another marriage rather than grieve, but others suffer alone, quietly—internally—and they may not even be aware of it. Their bodies are thus compromised and susceptible to deadly illnesses.

The same can be said for women who don't grieve properly, of course. And all recently widowed people certainly are more susceptible to everything from colds to cancer than are our married or long single sisters. It takes sustained vigilance to head off these demons. Try to devise a comprehensive strategy to preserve your health during this trying period.

- *Allow yourself to grieve.* According to a guide produced by AARP, "Men and women both need to give themselves permission to mourn. Postponing a confrontation with your feelings by filling each day with frantic activity will only delay and compound the process."

- *Strive for mental health as well as physical health.* It's pretty hard to have one without the other. If you feel ill, you usually feel blue; if you feel healthy, you feel happier and more confident. To some extent, the reverse is true, also. Happy feelings can make for good health. So to know optimum physical health, work on your emotional needs as well as physical ones.

- *Switch from "care-giver" to "care-taker."* Although these terms are often considered synonymous, I like to differentiate between them to make a point. You have probably devoted your life to worrying about the well-being of others, giving care, sometimes at the expense of your own health. When life is going along nicely, that seems to work fine for most women. But when faced with the traumatic loss of your spouse, no matter what your age, you move to a higher risk category. You really must take note of that and do everything you can to preserve your health, taking care of yourself. It may be good therapy to help others in small ways while you're healing, but try not to take on their problems until you have worked through your own. Even if you have dependent children at home needing your attention, try to find time for your own needs. With some ingenuity, you might even enlist their help in finding yourself more "Mommy time."

• *Take care of Number One...YOU.* Throughout your life, you probably always have been part of an adult "family." If you became ill, your parents, grandparents, roommate, lover or husband was there to help take care of you. They saw that you got medical attention if it was needed; they carried some of the home load so you could heal. Now, most likely, you are the only grownup in the household. YOU are the only one you can ultimately depend on for your health care. It's true that if you have dependents, they need you more than ever. Try to remember, however, that they need you to be strong and healthy. It's easy to throw yourself into their care, with the best of intentions, and find yourself depleted of energy and wellness. You may have to pretend to be well when you aren't, for brief periods, but you must do whatever you can to forestall the invasion of illness...for the benefit of your family <u>and</u> yourself. Don't let yourself down.

—STRESS AND MUSCLE TENSION—

Stress is the culprit, the thief of grievers' good health. Loss of a spouse ranks number one among life events triggering dangerous levels of stress. It certainly was the most debilitating ailment I have ever known, from the moment Bruce died until many months later. There really is not an ending point, but the stress level, if managed, does decrease with time and intervening experiences. Stress never will go away entirely; modern life pretty well dictates that we live with a certain amount of stress. We each process stress in different ways, though, and differently at different times. Some of us develop obvious physical ailments from it; others develop emotional imbalance, chemical dependency or personality conflicts. Still others of us bury our tension and anxiety so deep that neither we—nor our friends—can see it. That stress, more than any, can make us seriously ill.

Several doctors have assured me that Bruce's death undoubtedly triggered my Graves disease (hyperthyroidism) and it surely intensified my chronic fibromyalgia pain. Since then, I have read several books and Internet articles about stress prevention and relief. I learned to recognize events or feelings that threaten increased stress for me. Then I had to learn how to avoid those situations or deal with them through self-control or exercise. I have gotten a bit better at keeping tension from taking hold and causing problems than I was before I was widowed, but I remain vigilant. My nature is to project problems beyond reason and consider all dire possibilities. A good friend told me, "Women worry about possibilities; men worry only about probabilities." In general that may be true.

I decided early in my mourning process, at about four weeks, to have routine full-body massages to control tension. I cannot say enough for the physical benefits of massage therapy for dealing with stress. But it is costly. I sincerely believe medical insurance carriers should encourage and pay for weekly massages for all widowed persons, to save us from illness and them from the cost of it. Your carrier actually might pay for yours, *if* your physician or counselor prescribes the therapy. It won't hurt to ask. I neglected to do this at first, and I was surprised when I learned that I could get a prescription for a series of massages and have them almost entirely paid for by insurance. If you cannot get them paid for, you should be able to at least take their cost as a medical deduction on your taxes. If you can get coverage or you can afford it on your own, I highly recommend this therapy, especially for the first several months. Some say it is particularly beneficial to widows because we so need the healing touch of another human being. Stress can cause muscle stiffness and pain, actually making injury a concern. More importantly for me, massage keeps my muscles from tightening up painfully and inhibiting routine activity. In addition it slows my metabolism so anxiety doesn't easily take control.

If you decide to try massage, look for a licensed massage therapist, preferably one personally recommended by someone you trust. In an unfamiliar city I usually look for one who works in conjunction with a reputable chiropractor or a sports facility, such as a golf course or fitness center. You are *not* looking for a massage parlor in a disreputable part of town. To date I have gone to six different therapists (five women and one man) in three towns. All conducted themselves professionally and allowed me to maintain a sense of modesty. Be sure to tell them about your needs and your concerns, and ask them ahead of time about their methods and charges. If you don't feel you can afford full-body massage, try foot massage or facial massage. They can be quite rejuvenating. Do-it-yourself alternatives include learning to knead your own tight muscles, learning relaxation techniques from a book or video and/or scrubbing your body with a loofa while bathing; all are helpful but not as physically beneficial as full body massage.

While massage therapy helped me a great deal, it didn't magically erase all the stress manufactured by my grief. At 15 months into my widowhood, I suffered a frightening episode that alerted me to my vulnerability. It was early October, time to pack up in Wisconsin and drive to Florida. It hadn't been such a bad job when there were two of us doing it, and the year before I had been on a "conquer the world" high, so it hadn't bothered me. But, in the hard light of reality I hated packing up alone and all that entailed. I just wanted to stay put in my comfortable little cottage on the lake. But I couldn't. Neither the cottage nor I was physically up to operating through a winter in northeastern Wisconsin. I felt angry, frustrated and resentful. What I failed to see that day, was that I apparently wanted Bruce to come back long enough to help with the myriad details this move entailed.

On the morning I was to leave, I packed up, loaded the car, turned off, unplugged, dumped, notified and protected everything I could think of. As I heaved the final box into the crammed trunk, WHAM! It felt like someone had whacked me across the back with a two by four. I saw stars and crumpled over in pain; I absolutely could not stand up. I also couldn't catch my breath and I broke out in a cold sweat. Had I slipped a disk, I wondered, or worse? It didn't feel like any back problem I'd ever had and I had had plenty; it was too high and the pain was widespread, front and back. I tried to recall descriptions I'd read of sudden heart attacks. Hadn't I heard it described like that? The more I thought about that, the more lightheaded and frantic I became.

I crept into the house, grabbing onto anything I could for support, and headed for the phone to call one of my neighbors. But my phone had already been disconnected for the winter. Then I remembered that every friend I knew for two miles around was at a luncheon meeting in town. I can't describe how terribly alone I felt. I didn't know what to do. I knew I didn't dare take a pain pill; I had a four-hour drive I had to make, to my sister's home in Madison, the first leg of my three-day trip.

After much struggling I was finally able to lock the car trunk, gather my purse and my dog and gingerly climb into the front seat. My rear-view mirror confirmed my pain; I looked pale and pinched. By the time I reached Sturgeon Bay, 15 minutes later, it was pretty clear that I had suffered a dandy back spasm and a mini-anxiety attack, but I decided I had better drive to the emergency room and get checked out for sure. They ran an EKG and concluded it wasn't my heart. It was a back spasm, but of course they weren't comfortable letting me go without further observation. By the time I left, hours later, the pain had subsided and I was embarrassed, angry and late. But, more important, I also had a new respect for the body's response to conflict and an increased awareness of my vulnerability.

I had often heard that most back problems were psychogenic, having their origin in the mind or in mental conflict. When I had severe back problems in my twenties, I was certain whoever had said that had never had back trouble. My pain was real! It was due to two deteriorating disks in the lumbar region. But this "event" made me realize that much of my back pain probably was due to emotional conflict. This episode, especially, seemed directly attributable to my depression and my conflict about leaving for Florida alone. I had been a back spasm waiting to happen, and lifting boxes into the car trunk was a perfect trigger. Keep that in mind and take extra care now, especially when lifting, or you may invite even more injury and pain than you already have.

—ANXIETY AND PANIC ATTACKS—

Stress most often results in anxiety, a state of uneasiness, apprehension, and worry. Most widows mentioned high anxiety levels. Caroline's fear centered on her safety, whether she would have enough money, and whether she could keep up with home repairs. Ginny said she worried excessively about her children when they were out of her sight. Pauli worried about her ability to raise three little children alone and to provide for them as they grew older. Nearly all widows suffer from anxiety, having been thrust into what seems an overwhelming pool of responsibility. If we are young, we worry about caring for ourselves and our dependents; if we're older, we worry about becoming ill or dependent on our children.

Stress-induced anxiety can escalate to the point of panic attacks, as it did for me. It did for Karen, Virginia, and several others as well. These episodes are terrifying, and that fear adds to the anxiety, making it worse. Panic attacks are hard to diagnose, for us and for physicians. The symptoms often resemble those of other illnesses, especially heart attack. The patient doesn't know whether to seek help and, if she does, the doctor doesn't know what to treat. Attacks may last for anywhere from a few minutes to an hour. My few full-blown attacks usually occurred at night, yanking me from sleep with a terrifying jolt and a frighteningly rapid heart rate. They can, however, happen anytime, anywhere. Just knowing your susceptibility to these attacks may help you control your panic.

On the third anniversary of her son's suicide, Karen says she became very angry with her husband (dead for one year) for leaving her the only parent to grieve their son's death, and she began to have panic attacks. "They came at home, in my car, and in stores. Fortunately I recognized them for what they were," she says, "and began therapy immediately." Within several months, the frequency and severity of the attacks decreased. Therapy and treatment are often necessary, and are highly recommended. They can prevent the onset of agoraphobia (the abnormal fear of open spaces, or of leaving your home), a common complication of unchecked panic disorder.

Panic attacks aren't limited to the experience of widowhood, of course. Major incidents of terrorism or natural disasters often prompt an outbreak of anxiety attacks among the general population. It will be a lifelong benefit to your health if you take this opportunity to learn how to stem rampant fears that can lead to uncontrolled panic.

Symptoms of panic attacks can include dizziness, sweaty palms, numbness, tingly feelings, a sense of loss of control, rapid pulse, stomach upset, breathing difficulty and fear that death is imminent. Although doctors still don't understand the problem fully, they know from recent research that panic disorder is biological in origin and it can be treated medically. Attacks often occur in those who have mitral valve prolapse, a common and usually harmless disorder of a heart valve. I happen to have that, as did Bruce and as do several of the widows who reported having had anxiety attacks. Doctors don't yet understand the connection between the two disorders, but they are working on that. The stricken person often calls 9-1-1, races to the emergency room, or contacts a physician or cardiologist. I have considered all these options when in the throes of an attack. With increased interest in this disorder, it's hoped doctors will soon learn to recognize it more easily and find effective ways to prevent it or treat it early.

WARNING: According to doctors, one of the worst things widows can do is to self-medicate for anxiety with alcohol or other psychoactive drugs. Mood altering, psychoactive drugs affect the way a person thinks, feels or acts. As recent widows, we are at our most vulnerable. Our resistance is low in all ways, including resistance to addiction. When we are emotionally upset, anxious or tired, alcohol and other mood altering drugs almost always make matters worse rather than better.

If you have experienced anxiety attacks, ask a doctor or psychologist if you should keep on hand a few fast-acting anti-anxiety pills. If the attacks become severe or frequent, general treatment may be needed. This often includes medication in combination with counseling in behavior modification and relaxation techniques. *The key is learning how not to leap to conclusions that are beyond reality.* After having several panic attacks I began learning methods for short-circuiting those wild thoughts, or shutting them down before they could take a stranglehold on my sense of reason. When that first wild, irrational thought pops into my head, triggering a rapid pulse and sweaty palms, I reject it. I shout at myself (silently if I am not alone), "No! Stop thinking that! That is not rational! Stop that thought right this minute!" If it's convenient, I sometimes do a few quick bending and stretching exercises while breathing deeply and concentrating on winding down the anxiety. That usually works for me.

If you are in a store or in a group meeting, common places for panic disorders to occur, you will have to modify these methods to draw less attention. It is still possible to concentrate on slow, deep breathing and conscious relaxation techniques. It also helped me, when I could, to drink a large glass of water, concentrating on the process of swallowing. I carried a few anxiety relieving pills in my purse, and used one when it seemed absolutely necessary. It really is unwise to let yourself experience this frightening anxiety very often. It can establish an unwelcome pattern that will inhibit your full recovery. As soon as you recognize that you are experiencing panic attacks, seek help from your doctor or counselor. Above all, try to learn how to control your wild and frantic thoughts.

—STRESS AND DEPRESSION—

As discussed in an earlier chapter, deep depression and clinical depression need professional care. You should seek out that care whenever you recognize you have sunk too low to pull yourself up. For "everyday depression" and "the blues," which widows get fairly often, the following home remedies can be successful. If you make them a part of every day, you may prevent many slumps.

- *Get outside as often as possible.* Fresh air and a change of scenery help, as does close contact with nature. If possible, spend time in undeveloped park-like areas. Locked inside our too silent homes, or listening to too many news broadcasts, we can lose our perspective. We forget we are part of an amazing larger world, a wonderful web of ongoing life.

- *Surround yourself with bright light.* When it is dreary outside, or the days are short in winter, use larger light bulbs in your lamps and burn them more often. I also have heard enthusiastic endorsement for "full spectrum" light bulbs for mood elevation. It has been proved that bright light, even when it is artificial, helps prevent depression.

- *Exercise as often and as vigorously as you can without feeling pain (at the time or later).* Physical activity prevents negative effects of stress, which can contribute to depression. It also aids in sleep, so you don't get run down. Try always to maintain good posture and breathe properly, from the diaphragm, when exercising. Proper breathing is always important, but especially when you exercise. This might be a good time to join a fitness club, maybe teaming up with a friend to make it easier.

- *Laugh or smile as much as possible.* Watch funny old movies or silly sitcoms; read comics or books of humor; listen to tapes of comedians or of just irrepressible laughter. For more ideas, read this book's chapter on having fun. Whenever you think of it, put the start of a smile on your face. It will start to grow and help lighten your feelings. If your smile triggers one in someone else, theirs will widen yours. Smiles are quite contagious.

- *Avoid spending time with downbeat and negative people.* Just as smiles are contagious, so are negativity and depression. Spend as little time as possible with downbeat people or situations, and that should include movies, TV and books. Rub up against joy; catch the vibes of happy people, cheerful music, light-hearted activities. Don't be afraid to wallow in your grief occasionally; that can be a healthy release. But, as time goes on try to keep it from becoming a way of life. Seek joy, or encourage it, whenever you can.

Stress doesn't always result in obvious afflictions, such as panic attacks, depression or back spasms, but it remains a major concern of mourning. Stomach pain, loss of appetite, intestinal upset, sleep problems all can be signals. Its work, however, can be more subtle, devious, lurking in the shadows, with no physical manifestations. It can be difficult—or impossible—to repair damages to your body after they occur; it's much simpler to avoid the damages in the first place. Control stress before it controls you.

Start by reviewing good health habits. Most health rules, per se, are not new, although they have been updated to incorporate recent research. What is new is your vulnerability, which makes it necessary for you to review the old rules and give them a new chance. Determine where you need to make changes, and set up a program that will produce the results you seek. I won't attempt to deal with every aspect of women's health, or to provide a lot of detail on the basics. There are hundreds of helpful books, brochures and magazine articles on the subject. Check the Internet, your local library, bookstore or news stand for reliable information. I try here to concentrate on those health concerns especially related to grief, and to remind you of preventive measures that can counteract the effects of grieving.

—EAT REGULAR, WELL-BALANCED MEALS—

Of course, you say. What else is new? I realize the idea of eating regular, well-balanced meals is even older than WE are. However, we must be reminded at times like this to pay added attention to nutrition. Our topsy-turvy emotions can cause offbeat cravings that totally undermine our nutritional foundation. I was lucky in that I often craved pretty harmless foods, such as cream cheese, olive and rye bread sandwiches, nachos, seedless grapes, popcorn, and apples. It is not unusual for widows to crave real junk foods, though, such as potato chips or candy bars. Thelma says she did. "Maybe I substituted food for crying," she said. "Chocolate in particular."

I admit I fight a lingering obsession for some forbidden foods, especially rich, creamy ice cream, my ultimate "comfort food." After I quit smoking several years ago I began to attract fat molecules, seemingly out of thin air. When I began to complain about the results, my dear neighbor (a size 3 or 5, or some such obscene size) said, "Gee, Annie, I hate to be the one to tell you, but ice cream has calories in it." I had been indulging in rich French vanilla ice cream with caramel and chocolate fudge swirls as well as whole buttered pecans, as often as twice a day. I somehow had fooled myself into thinking that was a harmless habit. Once I grudgingly admitted my friend was right, I cut back, allowing myself only one, smaller bowl per day. When that still gathered on my thighs like lumpy barnacles, I switched to soft-serve low-fat frozen yogurt, which I only could get on rare trips to town.

Our appetites are unusually fickle those first months of agonizing grief. During my first days of widowhood I remember that everything I tried to eat tasted like cardboard. I wasn't able to choke down "a real meal" until about the fifth day, and for a long time I had peculiar tastes. I found, for example, that foods Bruce and I normally had cooked together no longer seemed palatable. I developed a gnawing desire for dishes my late mother used to cook regularly. I made batches of meat pie, Spanish rice, Welsh pasties, scalloped potatoes, salmon and cheese loaf and goulash. For more than a year I often ate for breakfast my childhood favorite…graham crackers and milk. I indulged myself, pretending the fiber and extra milk would counteract the effects of the sugar.

At first it's okay to eat almost anything that will go down, but as you become stronger you will want to be more careful about what you put in your stomach. I'm not much of a role model, but I gradually have tried to take control of my diet. I also have tried to blend my emotional needs with my nutritional ones. I do pretty well…most days. Don't be TOO hard on yourself when you're hurting so, but do try to use common sense with your diet.

I try to make easy, good-tasting and healthy lunches for myself by keeping on hand such things as fresh tortillas, cheese and salsa for instant quesadillas; apples, celery and walnuts for Waldorf salad; assorted hearty soup ingredients, such as 15-bean mix or lentils. Explore the packaged soup aisle at your supermarket. Amazing stuff. I also keep handy hard-boiled eggs, lots of fresh fruits and veggies (washed and ready to eat, when I'm on top of things.) For evening meals I try to keep individually wrapped chicken breasts and fish fillets in the freezer for quick-fix meals. I also make or buy large pots of one-dish meals, with leftovers to freeze, such as red beans and rice, three-cheese lasagna, spinach pie and ground-turkey chili.

I seldom snack between meals, but when I do feel a craving, I try to head for the veggies, low-fat popcorn, low-fat pretzels and crunchy apples. Usually, that is. For a time I wondered why I couldn't shed ten extra pounds. I was lucky to find out it was an under-active thyroid left by treatment for an over-active one. Once my doctor and I got my thyroid medication balanced, I found it somewhat easier to maintain my weight. Increasing age, of course, makes it very easy to put on pounds and very hard to take them off. It's hard to believe that I couldn't gain weight for the life of me when I was in my teens, twenties and thirties. It's been a long time, now, since anyone has called me by my teenage nickname, "Bones."

"Cooking for one" is a challenge for the new widow. I haven't ever gotten the knack for it. I had enough trouble cooking for just the two of us. I usually think in terms of whole recipes and leftovers. As a result, I often eat the same dish several days in a row or I entertain those friends who kept me supplied with food and invitations earlier. Sometimes, as I said, I freeze for future meals.

My sister, on the other hand, accepted the challenge of cooking for one. She always has done much better than I in the domestic arts. She sometimes made the cutest little portions of the most complex recipes. It fascinated me. I couldn't believe when she told me she had just made a "one-potato salad." Whenever I made potato salad, I always ended up with enough for eight or ten people and then had to figure out what to do with the extra. She admitted to me years later that she only made the one-potato salad once, as an experiment.

There are more diets around than there are people to follow them, and they vary as widely as people do, so I will resist presenting what I would consider the perfect diet for widows (although it was tempting). We each have different physical needs, different metabolisms and different philosophies of eating. I offer just one main thought. Try to "eat to live, don't live to eat." In addition, here are just a few basic reminders on which almost all nutrition experts agree.

For optimum health, eat...

- *less sugar*

- *less salt*

- *less saturated fat*

- *less red meat*

- *more fish*

- *more fresh fruits*

- *more fresh vegetables*

- *more complex carbohydrates: brown rice, whole grain pasta, breads, and cereals*

The federal government has revised its recommended daily diet, from the age-old pie chart that recommended equal amounts of four basic food groups (meat and fish, dairy, grains and cereals, fruits and vegetables). Nutritionists now recommend a pyramid diagram, *the base of which is made up of large quantities (6-11 "servings" per day!) of complex carbohydrates.* I guess that's best for most people, but I blimp up if I eat that many carbs. *Above that the next larger segments include increased quantities of fresh vegetables (3-5 "servings") and fruits (2-4 "servings" per day).* [I probably eat more fresh produce than carbs.] *Above that are shown even smaller quantities of dairy products (2-3 per day) and also of meats, fish and eggs. The tip of the pyramid recommends sparing use of fats, oils and sweets.* Think about what you have eaten so far today. Could you pass the pyramid test? Or have you adjusted your diet to what better suits you, as I have?

Annie's SPECIAL TIP*: If you have digestive problems, you might try the following: Avoid eating protein and starch at the same meal.* I cured my Barrett's Esophagus (caused by reflux/heartburn) without medication by using this simple rule. A hint borrowed from a classic dietary guide, *Fit for Life.*

Many doctors still tell their patients it is not necessary to take vitamin/mineral supplements, because we can get all we need in a well-balanced diet. I think it's true that many people take way too many supplements, most of which are sloughed off by the body. Some doctors say, "Americans have the most expensive urine in the world." My own doctor admits, however, that we usually don't eat as well as we think we do. Therefore, we SHOULD take at least a multi-vitamin/mineral tablet every day, plus calcium. For what it's worth, a recent survey of doctors shows that, although they are unwilling to recommend supplements for their patients, most of them do take supplements themselves. The majority of them take a multi-vitamin/mineral tablet and extra anti-oxidants: vitamins C, E and beta carotene. Recent research has caused some to cut back to more moderate levels of vitamin C (500 mg/1000 mg per day). Some add soy protein for essential amino acids. They take these because the research they read is extremely compelling that these supplements can help build immunity against cancer and other illnesses, and can improve health in other dramatic ways.

We are all different, however. The primary reason so many think it's necessary to add supplements to our diet now is that even if we eat well, we don't get all we need of some elements. Our foods are raised in more artificial ways than when we were a nation of mostly self-sufficient farmers. Food is often depleted of nutrition by poor soil, early harvesting, over-processing, etc. That might help explain why America ranks 15th in infant mortality, 12th in life expectancy and 1st in money spent on health care among the 22 industrialized nations of the world. Especially now, when your immune system is challenged, taking supplements may make sense. The next time you see your doctor, report what you are taking for your more vulnerable condition, and ask his or her advice. A few supplements have been proved harmful, so consider his warnings, but if you feel strongly about their use, do your own research and present it for consideration.

—DRINK, DRINK, DRINK…WATER—

I remember sitting in class from grades one though eight at least, staring at "healthful living charts." Without fail they pictured full glasses of water, with the advice: "Drink eight (or ten) glasses of water each day." That was to be in addition to all the milk they recommended, as well as coffee, tea or sodas consumed for pleasure. Water was not to be fun; it was a JOB! That seemed like an awful lot then, and it still does. Although our base of knowledge has multiplied many times since, that advice still appears in most health regimens. A great deal depends, however, on how much high water content food we consume each day. For example, I am currently following a regimen of ONLY high water content fruit before noon, so my need for additional "water" consumption may be less than for some.

I agree that water is important. It's important that we wash our insides as well as our outsides…sort of. According to every expert I admire, though, it is NEVER necessary—except for preparation for medical exams—to artificially irrigate or flush the colon, as has been suggested by some nutrition faddists. Drinking plenty of water helps move our food through the digestive and elimination systems keeping us "regular," which aids greatly in weight control as well as good health. It also helps keep our bladders and kidneys functioning properly; it rinses away toxins our bodies manufacture and those we inherit from an imperfect environment; it helps our largest organ, skin, to remain supple and moist; and it keeps our stomachs feeling fuller, less hungry, among other things.

HINT: In recent years more has become known about dehydration. One interesting nugget is that our body often mistakenly sends a "hunger signal," when what it needs is fluids. Next time you think you are hungry between meals, try drinking a big glass of water. If after ten or fifteen minutes you are still hungry, have a bite to eat. I know I feel better when I drink more water, but I'm as lax as most people about doing it regularly. We have simply failed to acknowledge its importance.

Here are some more hints, which I will try harder to heed, and I hope you will, too.

- *Keep an easy-to-use jug of water in the refrigerator, with paper cups nearby.* Refrigeration improves the flavor and quality of water, as chemical tastes dissipate. A filtering water pitcher, widely available today, also can add to your water's appeal.

- *If your water is safe but has an unpleasant taste or odor, float a lemon slice in it.* A slice in glasses at the table encourages most people to drink water with meals, too. Make it optional if you have guests, as some dislike it.

- *Keep a large jug of your favorite iced tea on hand (decaffeinated is best), and keep a glassful handy.*

- *Buy cases of bottled water and keep it accessible.* Soda, diet or regular, should be used sparingly and NOT as part of you daily requirement of water, just like your mommy taught you years ago. There is now evidence that diet sodas actually contribute to obesity, so beware.

- *Contract for delivery of bottled water or install a reverse osmosis drinking water system.* The better your water tastes, the more likely you will drink enough.

- *Make rules about water consumption.* It's helpful to make rules about water consumption, such as the following: Everyone must have consumed three glasses before lunch; a total of six before supper; eight before bedtime.

- *Don't think of water consumption as a painful project.* Make the process pleasant; think about how good and fresh it tastes, how much better it makes you feel. Once you develop the habit, you may feel deprived if you can't have those eight or ten glasses of delicious water each day.

—EXERCISE REGULARLY—

Another cliché! That's what happens when statements are so undeniably true. They get repeated so often they begin to sound trite. Well, trite or not, regular vigorous exercise is great. It helps control weight, improves cardiovascular health, strengthens bones, and provides many other benefits. These are all great reasons to exercise regularly, no matter what's happening in your life. When we are mourning our mates' deaths, however, exercise takes on even more importance. It helps to reduce our stress, prevents or alleviates depression and anxiety; and it releases tension in our muscles, which can prevent injury. Physical fitness contributes to an overall sense of well-being, something we need now more than ever. It requires us to breathe more deeply and more often, filling our lungs with healing oxygen as we inhale, and expelling our bodies' impurities as we exhale. [I do not always practice what I preach here.]

Exercise doesn't have to be torture. If you hate riding a stationary bike, do something else. Pick something you like, or at least something you can easily tolerate. A brisk 20 or 30-minute walk, an hour's bike ride through the park or a routine of water aerobics in the pool can make exercise seem like a treat rather than a treatment. Do something you can enjoy, because the only good exercise is the one you keep doing! At the same time, don't kid yourself into thinking that an occasional nine holes of golf or a rare and energetic doubles tennis game will keep you fit. Rare and extraordinary exercise can kill.

To benefit your body aerobically, psychologically and for relief of stress, you must exercise at least three times per week, involving all muscle groups, working hard enough to raise a sweat, but not hard enough to hurt. If you do exercise every day, cross-train (do different activities every other day) for full benefit. In addition, stretch carefully every morning, and especially when you feel extra stress. Borrow from the professionals: *warm up for 5 minutes, sustain aerobic activity for 20 minutes and cool down for 5 minutes.* Keep that body moving, especially if you are old enough to remember the church bells and cheering of V-E Day! You will suffer less from stress, sleep better, ache less, keep your weight in line, feel more attuned to your surroundings, think more clearly, and recover faster from your loss.

HINT: Experts advise that if you are unable for some reason to do physical conditioning exercises, you will profit by deep breathing. Breathe in and out slowly and deeply for several minutes. The added oxygen helps burn calories, stimulates your muscles and helps keep your brain alert. Deep breathing shouldn't replace regular exercise, of course, but it can have many benefits when you are unable to do more.

—GET ADEQUATE REST/SLEEP—

In addition to exercise, proper nutrition and drinking plenty of water, it's more important than ever that you get plenty of rest. Although we may know that, many of us suffer from insomnia off and on during the mourning period. If that is a problem for you, try to remember what W. C. Fields advised, "A good cure for insomnia is to get plenty of sleep."

If you find that amusing, you probably had a good sleep last night. I did NOT think it was funny when I first read it. I thought it was impudent. I would have bet HE had never laid awake three or four nights in a row. Although, knowing his reputation for drinking, he likely was bothered by waking up after a few hours and not being able to get back to sleep, one of the hazards of drinking as an occupation.

I have never been a good sleeper. I found out a few years ago that this was primarily due to my screwy thyroid and my fibromyalgia. I thought it was just because I suffered from acute hearing. I used to sleep very lightly, listening for any untoward sound. It was always my nature to feel responsible for the whole world, and I took that very seriously at night when everyone else was asleep. In addition, I suffered from burning and itching feet, especially if I hadn't exercised vigorously during the day. I rarely slept through a rumble of thunder or a bug hitting the window screen. I tossed and turned most of the night, even when I seemed to sleep fairly well. It used to bother me that even with all my nightly turmoil, Bruce had no trouble sleeping like a baby next to me. How I used to envy him. I remember on stormy nights, for example, I would bid him goodnight with my rendition of the old motto: "Sleep well, my dear; your National Guard will be awake."

When I added the stress of grief to that mixture, it was not surprising that I often suffered severe sleep deprivation and became short tempered and grouchy because of it. Although I can't claim to be an expert on how to cure insomnia, I do consider myself something of an expert on the affliction itself. For me, the answer lay in medication for my nagging ailments, especially fibromyalgia. Sleeplessness and fibromyalgia syndrome are inseparable. Which is the cause and which is the effect is not clear.

Unless something in particular is bothering me, I now sleep soundly most nights. Ask your doctor if your insomnia is due to any treatable ailment, or medication you're taking, first. If it isn't, you might try one or all of the following. I have tried all of them over the years, with varying degrees of success. Before going to bed at night, try one or more of the following:

- *Munch on an apple or banana.*

- *Soak in a warm bath.*

- *Read a boring book.*

- *Drink a cup of hot decaffeinated or herbal tea.* I had some luck with sleep-inducing teas, but they seemed to contribute to depression when I used them consistently.

- *Write in your journal just before turning off the light.* I did that for years, closing the book when I was done as though I had finished with that day. It helped quite a bit.

- *Meditate.* This works for some, not for me. It unleashes my creativity, so it is great in the daytime, but not at bedtime. It also lowers my already low blood pressure, so my doctor prefers I not meditate.

- *Think of nothing but the color blue.* My counselor suggested this; it often works for me.

- *Take a "power nap" in the afternoon IF that doesn't keep you awake at night.*

I found a 20-minute nap often refreshed me without interfering with sleep at night. Any longer nap did interfere. At first your grieving mind is getting such a workout it may need this breather, regardless of your chronological age. I was fascinated that my brain could work like an alarm clock. I looked at my watch and said to myself: "I just want to sleep for 20 minutes. At (20 minutes later) I will wake up refreshed." I cannot explain it; it just works for me, and for some others I have met.

When nothing else worked, I occasionally resorted to Tylenol PM. One half of one tablet worked better than a whole one for me. I only did this when I needed sleep in preparation for a long drive or a demanding day. Most sleep preparations are habit forming, and could be especially so when you are vulnerable as you are now, so fight the urge to take them regularly.

If you wake up too early and can't get back to sleep, I can suggest a couple of things that worked for me. Waking up at about 3 a.m. became such a habit for me a few years ago that I thought I was doomed to exhaustion for the rest of my life. An article on the subject suggested that for many people this is caused by a full bladder. The solution: Get up immediately and go to the bathroom, BUT do not turn on any bright lights. Our bodies' natural sleep potion, melatonin, will think it is morning and shut down with the introduction of light. Keep a glass of water by your bed so you can have a sip easily if you are thirsty. Do not start thinking about the next day or about your husband or anything else. Think only about how nice and sleepy you feel and how comfortable it will feel to crawl back into bed. If your room isn't dark enough, you may be helped as I was by wearing an eye mask. If noise is distracting you, wear comfortable sponge earplugs. These suggestions solved my 3:00 a.m. wake up calls, as they have for others I know. If you have that problem, try them.

—RELIEVE SEXUAL TENSION—

I often think about the day I visited a Milwaukee area widow support group, and got in on a very wise and frank discussion about the value of masturbation to relieve sexual tension. One wide-eyed widow sat and listened quietly, but finally decided to join in the conversation. "At first it wasn't a problem," she said. "I was numb everywhere. But after several weeks I thought I would lose my mind when I reawakened sexually and had no husband to help me relieve it. I tried running in place, I screamed into my pillow, I did everything...except take care of the problem. Then a widow I met told me it was okay to, you know, do it myself." She blushed, but continued, "It really helps me stay sane and sleep more regularly. But, sometimes I feel really funny about it, like right now, talking about it." Her face couldn't have been redder. The old pros of the group smiled. They had heard it before. Masturbation is not something most women are comfortable talking about, most men either, if truth be known. But the leader said they often see newcomers become visibly relieved when they hear others discuss the issue.

When I discussed this book with Mike, my social worker/psychologist, he immediately asked me, "Are you planning to discuss masturbation? You really must, you know." I assured him I had planned to include the subject. "That's good," he said. "It's important to let women know that masturbation is not only perfectly acceptable and natural, it is healthy behavior." Robert, another psychologist friend, went on to say, "Masturbation is far more acceptable and far safer than choosing to sleep with strangers or letting sexual tension escalate without relief. That," he said, "adds unnecessary stress to the widows' already stressful situation."

Even with their encouragement I felt uncomfortable writing about this issue at first. While I agreed with them both and respected their professional views, I also knew that a majority of more mature readers might feel somewhere between "put off" and "horrified" by reading such a discussion. Most women over 50 or 60 years of age were reared under pretty straight-laced moral dictates. Most are aware of dramatic changes in society's views on sex, and many have come to accept some of these changes. But that doesn't mean all or even most women have incorporated this more lenient sexual attitude into their own lives, especially if they were married to the same man for several decades and/or have deep fundamentalist religious beliefs. For many, a great chasm exists between accepting new ways "for society," and accepting them in their own lives. I have taken this into consideration in espousing advice about masturbation.

Act within your own set of values, or those of your embraced religion. Don't feel you must scrap your entire moral code, just because so much of society has. If you are deeply concerned, it might be helpful to have a heart to heart discussion with your pastor, priest, imam or rabbi. On the other hand, don't feel compelled to stand by rules you learned as a teenager if they no longer seem viable to you. Times and mores have changed, you have changed, and now your life has changed.

Share your concerns with an impartial professional. If you can accept masturbation as a viable option intellectually, but you suffer emotionally because of your prior fears and training, talking with a therapist or counselor can help. In lieu of that, talk with a particularly close widow friend or a support group.

A few women, especially younger widows, are faced with the option of having sex with a new male partner within a relatively short time. This same support group talked about that, generally cautioning about rushing into a sexual relationship. They agreed that the do-it-yourself method was safer.

"I am terrified of having sex with a guy," one member of the group confessed. The others agreed, saying such things as, "Yes, I know. My husband was my only lover and I am 54 years old!" "But, no," the first gal said. "That's not what I mean. I have stored up so much sexual tension I'm afraid I might embarrass myself." Everyone laughed sympathetically, including your author. Since we all are sexual creatures, often continuing to be active into our golden years, we must face that we will have needs when we are alone. Our choices are in how—or whether—we decide to relieve them. As I see it, our choices as widows are limited to the following options:

- *No sexual relief at all,* dealing with the physical manifestations of stress only with increased physical exercise, meditation and deep breathing, for example.

- *Sexual activity with a man you love,* either within or without the confines of marriage.

- *Sexual activity with a man you do not love.* Caution is in order, of course, due to the extraordinary physical threats prevalent in today's world. And, if your upbringing strongly forbade such activity, you also may suffer emotional anguish.

- *Sexual activity with a woman.* This is a perfectly acceptable option for some women, although most of those women would not have been married, hence would not be widows as such. Libraries and bookstores overflow with books on this subject, if you are interested in knowing more.

- *Sexual activity with yourself.* If you are offended by the word "masturbation," think of it as "loving yourself." With or without the aid of a vibrator, pulsating shower nozzle or more adventurous "sex toys," this option is considered the safest, most natural and least complicated of the options.

Your doctor, especially a gynecologist but really any internist or general practitioner, should be helpful to you as you consider your options. You also may require a prescription to relieve vaginal dryness and itching. Consider your doctor your friend. They aren't easily embarrassed, and they are sworn to keep your concerns private, so let them help.

—HAVE REGULAR CHECK-UPS—

Although I have had occasional misgivings about traditional doctoring for years, I lost my cool about it during my early grief process. I targeted the whole profession (not necessarily individuals in it) to lavish with my unresolved anger over Bruce's death. I hear that is common (I am so absurdly normal), especially when the death is sudden and unexpected. Although we might not blame any one doctor for missing symptoms, our frustrating search for answers works on our subconscious, and the profession becomes a ripe target.

I have to caution you; however, this is not the time to give up on doctors completely. At this time you are susceptible to very real ailments, many of which can best be detected by a physician's exam or tests. He or she is, for example, in an ideal position to spot budding depression and to determine when and whether treatment is necessary. Even more urgent, perhaps, is early detection of real, physiological ailments. For example, if you have not had a recent mammogram, Pap smear, EKG or colonoscopy, ask your doctor what tests might be advisable for you at this time.

You know you must take extra care of yourself now, and your doctor can help. This requires regular visits to a doctor you trust, heightened awareness of what is going on in your own body, and a sense of responsibility for your own health. Become alert to the quality of your health care. In today's busy world, you may get precious little of a physician's time and concern unless you demand it. It's essential that every patient be knowledgeable, vigilant, assertive, and uncompromising in their efforts to get proper care. Become attuned to your body and any signals of trouble and then do some research about symptoms or suspected illnesses. Otherwise you may waste your doctor's and your own time. Arrive at your appointment armed with a concise detailed list of questions, and make sure each one gets satisfactorily answered. I have gone armed with a highlighted printout from the Internet, and I usually have found doctors most appreciative. It's important that we do what you can to save doctors time and effort, but still get answers to our concerns.

If you still get the two-minute brush off from your doctor, it might be time to find a physician with more time and/or concern, one who is more than simply a cog in a money machine. Younger doctors sometimes are still a bit idealistic, and oriented to helping their patients. Some people are happier with the care they receive from DOs, Doctors of Osteopathy, or from Doctors of Homeopathy (those who seek to help the body heal itself through holistic practices and minute doses of drugs).

If you sense there is something wrong with you, check it out. Don't play ostrich and poke your head in the sand. You might miss your chance for early treatment or cure. When my aunt was dying of breast cancer she chastised herself, over and over again. "I knew two years ago," she would say. "But I didn't want to know, so I didn't get an exam. Why was I so stupid?" If you check a symptom early, and it turns out to be a problem, early treatment may make quick work of it. And, if nothing is wrong, you can dismiss that as a concern and relax. Once you have been given a clean bill of health, it's important that you try not to dwell on all the things that might go wrong so you don't miss the good parts of your life.

—APPEARANCE MAY BE MORE IMPORTANT THAN IT SEEMS—

I wrote the following in my journal at 4 weeks:

Dear Bruce: I have a new hairdo; a carefree, modified wedge. It's so neat not to have to worry about it or bother with perms anymore. I know you thought I needed lots of "fluff" on top, but I think you would like this. I keep wondering if you are watching me. And if you are, do you like my new look? Whether you do or not, the "new me" still misses the "old you!"

There is great temptation during the early weeks, and whenever we suffer from depression, to "let ourselves go." We feel there is no one left to care anyway, so what does it matter?

It probably matters to you, whether you know it or not. If you slop around the house in a tattered robe, with stringy hair and with dirt under your fingernails, you will soon feel worthless. You will stop treating yourself with love and care. Your self-esteem will sag and depression may become a constant companion. I let down my standards a bit during those first, oppressive days when even brushing my teeth seemed a chore. But I soon saw the error of my ways. The worse I looked, the worse I felt. For as long as I can remember, I have recognized that correlation. When I look dumpy, I act dumpy and feel dumpy. When my mirror reflects back a more attractive image, I get a lift and I feel better. See if that doesn't work for you. Try to keep yourself clean, well groomed, nicely coifed and neatly clothed, even when you don't feel like it. You'll profit from the extra care.

A few suggestions:

- *Work with a hair stylist to find a flattering, easy-care "do" just right for your new lifestyle.* If you can't afford that, keep your hair clean and trimmed and do what you can to make it look attractive.

- *Don't be afraid to try a new hair color, if that might cheer you up.*

- *Take extra care moisturizing your face, neck and hands.*

- *Learn how to apply a little flattering face and eye makeup* for special occasions or whenever you feel down.

- *Determine your most flattering colors and styles.* Wear what makes you feel good about yourself.

- *Check your mirror occasionally, and smile.* A smile is the most attractive thing you can put on your face!

Some of my favorite clothes are wildly colored, with reds, turquoise, lime, orange, and purple, which I purchased in my first year as a new widow. I needed color around to cheer me up, so it showed in my new clothes and in my home. I remember my first major purchase, within six weeks of Bruce's death, was a set of vibrantly colored mix and match separates. A friend suggested I would tire of it, that I should buy something more conservative that would "wear" longer. I stubbornly bought it, and I cheerfully wore it right up until I outgrew it. I always seemed to get an emotional lift from wearing it. It was worth its price and then some.

I worried, briefly, that some people might think I was taking extra care of myself to impress any men I might run into. I decided I really didn't care what they thought. I knew I took the care I did because I was the most important person in my life just then, and I felt better when I looked better. When you think about it, don't you, too?

—SEEK POSITIVES IN THE NEGATIVE—

Off and on again, now and for some time to come, much in your life will seem unfamiliar. Everything seems off-kilter, shaken, hanging in limbo. I think it was for that reason that I decided to begin some self-improvement practices. When you can, think about how you might also turn this otherwise dismal period of your life into an opportunity for positive change. Why not try to turn over a new leaf or two? For most of us there isn't much good about being left alone, but one thing is that you now are in charge of your lifestyle choices.

When feeding two or more people, for example, the cook must try to meet—to the extent possible—everyone's needs and likes. I have heard many wives complain, "I'd prefer to eat just chicken and fish (or vegetarian, or just low fat, etc.), but my husband demands his roast beef, mashed potatoes and gravy every day." This may be your chance to try out some of the new, more healthful meal-planning guides available in books, magazines and newspapers. There are many ways you can plan to emerge from this period a healthier person. I guarantee that if you take a little time and effort you can make your new "good for you meals" as good as or better tasting than your previous menus.

If you sincerely wish to lose weight, for example, look for a sensible guide to help you get started. Forget fads and quick-loss diets; go for a program that teaches you about proper eating and exercise habits, so you will be able to keep off the weight after you've worked so hard to lose it. I, personally, have the best luck by cutting out all processed sugar products and nutrition-deprived starchy products. But I allow myself to indulge occasionally so I don't get into a pity party.

What better time to quit smoking, and/or drinking? Your mind is preoccupied with your grief, the old habits don't seem normal anymore anyway, and your self-esteem could use the lift. I gave up both cigarettes (of which I had smoked a pack and a half for several years) and hard liquor (of which I had consumed two watered-down vodka "martinis" per day) when I was four months into my grief. I suddenly found it easy to quit both, using *How to Quit Smoking*, the bible of the Smokenders group. I have, to date, passed that book on to eight others, all eight of whom also have now quit smoking! The book's message is great, but probably the key to my success was that I knew I wanted to rid myself of smoking forever, and that I would feel better physically and emotionally if I did. Frankly, I quit the vodka to make quitting smoking easier. I knew myself; one vodka before dinner and my no-smoking resolve would dissolve. I would think, "What could one little cigarette hurt?" And that would be the end of quitting. I also got an extra emotional boost by quitting both at the same time. You can't imagine how self-righteous I felt. I am still an obnoxious ex-smoker, but after I knew I was "cured of smoking," I began to enjoy a glass or two of wine with dinner, but still no hard stuff.

If you wish to get control of your high blood pressure or high cholesterol, ask your doctor and read about ways to do that. You can resolve to become physically fit through exercise, or conquer your anxiety, or develop your self-esteem. You will be so proud of yourself. The time will pass more quickly and so will your healing. Most important of all, you will begin to see how much control you have over your own life and health.

If you take special care of your mental and physical health now, when you have healed from the loss of your mate you will be well enough to enjoy the rest of your life. If you don't, well...

12

Learning to Laugh and Have Fun: It's Good for You

You can't do anything about the length of your life,
but you can do something about its width and depth.

—Evan Esar (*Thoughtful Books*)

Life is short; live it up.

—Nikita Khrushchev (*New York Times,* August 3, 1958)

Annie's Journal (8 weeks)
Bruce: I was just sitting here thinking back, reviewing our 35 years together, and I realized my only regret is that we didn't live life as fully as we might have. Why didn't we travel more, participate more, learn more, love more, laugh more, have more fun? What were we waiting for? Whatever it was, it's too late now. I even have to wonder if you might not have lived longer if we had learned how to have more fun. What do you think?

From reading the above sad journal entry and a few of my others, you might believe Bruce and I never had any fun. Not true at all. I just felt really sad when I wrote them. Bruce had one of the sharpest, most finely honed senses of humor I've known, and we always had a large and varied collection of friends. Laughter was a big part of our lives, and over the years we did many fun things together.

However, this experience, my first intimate confrontation with the reality and finality of death, made me more fully appreciate the brevity of life. I realize that we didn't do more, or enjoy more, in part because we naively believed our time together would last forever. Most widows say they felt that way. You probably have your own list of things you wish the two of you had done before he died, unless you are among the lucky few who feels you both made the most of every minute of your time together.

In some ways Bruce and I were worse than most at denying ourselves "fun." Something in our upbringing or the times made us feel that spending time and money on totally frivolous activities was at least shameful, maybe sinful. We often talked about how we both had overly developed needs to be productive with our time and to be practical with our money. We were best at staying home, and saving for a rainy day.

Although I am now sloshing my way through that rainy day, and thankful for what money we saved over the years, I wonder. Shouldn't we have opted for fun more often? We weren't alone in selecting the practical rather than the fanciful. We were "depression babies," reared in the framework of "the work ethic," trained to believe in "waste not, want not" and other trite cautions. I recall a friend writing years back to say they couldn't come visit us in Florida because they had to choose between that trip and buying a new door. I think about how many times Bruce and I had to make a similar choice, and we nearly always chose the door.

It wasn't just our resistance to spending money on fun. We also avoided taking risks. We had been trained to be careful, to worry. Rather than confronting danger or even risking discomfort, we chose to circumscribe our lives, restricting everything we could control to make our lives easier, safer. For all our effort that didn't really work. Our stress levels remained high, often prompted by something so mundane as an hour's wait in a doctor's waiting room, rather than whether we would have the strength to pull our kayak over a turbulent rapids.

Our "life enjoyment quotient" could have been much higher, I suspect. I wish we had been willing to take chances, meet challenges head on and surmount obstacles rather than avoiding them. I wish, for example, we had spent our five years of retirement traveling to every country of the world, maybe on our own without a prearranged itinerary or an expert guide. As our son, Dave, explained after spending three months backpacking through Europe, "Having to solve problems and crises that arise [such as losing his passport and his luggage] is part of what makes travel so beneficial."

Now I understand that, and if I am lucky enough to have time and resources to see more of this great world, even at some risk, I will. How much more fun it would have been doing that together. In addition to the pure joy of seeing new places and new cultures, travel might have provided our lives with more focus. I think we both would have had less time to spend worrying, questioning, self-analyzing, and we probably would have been better off for it.

Don't misunderstand, we had a good life together. I am thankful we got along well and raised a good and happy family. But especially in retirement, after 30 plus years of marriage, we allowed trivial differences to nag at us and cause undue stresses. With my 20/20 hindsight, I think we would have enjoyed life more if we had expanded our horizons and had more urgent problems to consider than whether the TV was too loud or the baked chicken was dry. We should have had more fun, not just so I would have more memories, but because fun and enjoyment promote good mental and physical health.

—HAVE FUN; IT IS HEALTHY—

Ever since Norman Cousins published his famous *Anatomy of an Illness*, fun, laughter and pleasure have gained respect within medical and psychological circles. He tells of beating the odds on a rare threatening illness by watching, and laughing at, hours of old comedies on film. He believed, and proved to my satisfaction, that laughter was indeed the best medicine for him, and is for almost everyone.

"What seems clear," he said, "is that laughter is an antidote to apprehension and panic. As such, its value is not less than that of the fire extinguisher that puts out the flame."

Fun is an essential ingredient in a good life, creating emotional health, which in turn enhances physical health. I sense that's true, but read what Joan Borysenko, Ph.D., author of *Minding Your Body, Mending the Mind*, has to say about how positive emotions affect our bodies positively.

> ...PNI (psychoneuroimmunology) research centers on a group of hormonal messengers called neuropeptides, which are secreted by the brain, by the immune system, and by the nerve cells in various other organs. What scientists have found is that the areas of the brain that control emotion are particularly rich in receptors for these chemicals. At the same time, the brain also has receptor sites for molecules produced by the immune system alone—the lymphokines and interleukins. What we see, then, is a rich and intricate two-way communications system linking the mind, the immune system, and potentially all other systems, a pathway through which our emotions...can affect the body's ability to defend itself.

In a nutshell, she states later that anything that reduces chronic stress in the body helps the flow of chemicals that increase our immunity to infection and disease. That being the case, we shouldn't feel guilty for having fun; we should feel guilty for NOT having fun. If we loosen up and fight stress with fun and enjoyment, we give our body its best chance to keep us healthy. Therefore I prescribe large doses of fun for everyone, and double doses for grieving widows, so that our bodies can fight off the potential ravages of intense chronic stress.

Rx: Laughter: One dose two times per day to start. Increase size and frequency of dosage as it becomes easier to swallow.

If laughter and fun seem impossible to you at this time, try this simple exercise. Look at yourself in the mirror. After studying your serious countenance, force the corners of your mouth to curve up, as though you were smiling. I always think I look like such a fool that I can't keep from laughing, no matter how determined I am not to. Give in to the smile or laugh. You might be able to buy an audio tape of contagious laughter and play it once a day. I have one of radio personalities who got into a laughing jag they couldn't control. It breaks me up every time I hear it. If nothing else, read your favorite cartoon strip, or watch a young baby, new puppy or kitten at play. Whatever it takes, make yourself smile. It will become easier with practice.

Fun and laughter, like other medicines that are good for us, aren't necessarily easy to swallow when we're in the throes of grief. I remember knowing for sure in the first weeks that I would never smile again. Things that used to be fun no longer are, now that you're alone. Those things you know you both would have laughed about are especially hard to endure at first. You may begin to laugh and suddenly think, "I can't wait to tell my husband about this." Suddenly, it isn't funny anymore.

You may honestly believe at this time that you will never laugh or have fun again. But it's important to understand that the time will come when you will be able to smile and laugh again. When that time arrives, be assured that's okay. It's more than okay; it is natural and it is good for you. It doesn't mean you didn't care about your husband or care that he died; it means you are alive and you hope to stay that way. If you want to live long and well, you should take every opportunity to smile, laugh, sing, whistle, hum, giggle, snicker, and snort. Keep those positive juices of joy flowing.

—FIND WHAT IS FUN FOR YOU—

The *American Heritage Dictionary* states that "fun" is a "source of enjoyment or pleasure; amusing diversion...." What's fun for one, of course, may be torture for another. I remember my high school math teacher, telling us his idea of fun. On a snowy Wisconsin day, he said, "Ah, what could be more fun than to settle down in front of the fireplace on a snowy night, with a big bowl of buttery pop-corn and some really tough trigonometry problems?" We thought he was kid-ding; he wasn't.

My younger son, Ric, loves reading, racquetball, golf, cheering for the Green Bay Packers and acting in plays when he isn't working as an editor. But he gets a special buzz out of his private Sunday morning ritual. He turns on public radio's classical music while cooking himself a hearty breakfast. Then he settles down to eat and read the Sunday *New York Times*, winding up by plowing through the Sunday crossword. So far, I think only Smokey and the Bandit, his two cats, can interfere with—or take part in—his "fun."

His older sister, Cindy, enjoys painting T-shirts, softball, playing Jezz-ball and Free Cell on the computer, jogging, traveling and sewing (among other things) when she isn't teaching. But she gets a real high from writing humorous parodies and singing them Patsy Cline style in front of her classes or at faculty gatherings. "I find I have no trouble belting out these songs in front of a sizable crowd," she says, "as long as I know it's a friendly audience, and that they're bound to be impressed with even a modicum of talent from a law professor."

Their brother Dave, who is a philosophy professor, enjoys serious biking, pho-tography, playing classical and jazz guitar, squash, wrestling with his kids and lis-tening to CDs, but he probably most enjoys having a spirited intellectual discussion, especially with another philosopher. Come to think of it, he's a lot like his dad in that way. Arguing—in the sense of debating—about anything with anyone gave Bruce great pleasure. I hated it; he was too good.

I sifted through my reams of interview notes and survey forms, trying to get a feeling for what most of the widows in this book considered to be fun. We didn't deal directly with that question, so I had to extrapolate impressions from their other answers. I would have to say "playing with grandchildren" is a strong first, which comes as no surprise. Kids make us laugh and feel good. Like new puppies, they often give us lots of slobbery kisses and unconditional love, too. We need that more now than ever. If you have no small children or grandchildren nearby, maybe you could offer to baby-sit for brief periods or to volunteer your services as a storyteller at your local nursery school or library. Seek out children who need a surrogate grandmother a few hours each week. They'll have fun and so will you.

After that rather obvious pleasure, I was struck by the wide variety of activities widows undertake in the name of fun after they start healing. I compiled an extensive list of suggestions for fun, which I'll get to a little later, triggered by their comments. It is by no means complete, but I hope it is enough to trigger your own thinking. What's important is that what you pick is fun for YOU.

My good friend Pauli, having been widowed many years before I was, knew the healing power of laughter and enjoyment. After a suitable interval, she began forwarding to me therapy packs of cartoon strips clipped from her *Los Angeles Times*. The "Momma" strip has always been her favorite, and she knew I didn't have access to it in my local newspapers. Pauli's all-time favorite is an old strip showing Momma, a tiny old gray-haired widow, speaking with her dead husband in a dream. "And another thing," she says to him, "you sure did take the easy way out, leaving the child-rearing to me!" As with so many of these strips, Momma echoes the unspoken feelings of widows everywhere. I've saved several showing how Momma deals with her three "grown" children. They were especially apropos of my situation. They make me, the quintessential mother hen, laugh at myself. And I know *that* is one of the healthiest things we can do.

Great cartoonists, like Momma's Mell Lazarus, have razor-sharp wit and see humor where others might not. They condense or magnify an idea, then trim it into a bare bones visual package we can grasp easily. I envy that poetic precision for saying so much with so few well-chosen words and images.

After my first weeks as a new widow, when I finally remembered how to laugh, I became possessed with the need for amusement. I often read the comic section of the morning paper when I didn't have the heart for hard news. I flipped first to the cartoons in magazines; I clicked the TV—when it was on at all—to a well-written situation comedy, stand-up comic, or humorous talk-show host; and I searched out only the funniest books and movies. I needed humor to restore my sense of balance. Those rare moments of "fun," more than anything else, provided glimpses into that other world, the one where grief's dark cloud didn't obstruct every ray of sunlight. They kept me focused on that goal of regaining a more normal life.

Laugher is great! When you can, seek out those activities that make you laugh. Associate with upbeat people, especially those with a slightly irreverent view of life. Encourage joke tellers. They may feel shy or disrespectful about laughing and telling jokes around you at first. Tell them when you are ready for a good laugh. Tell them what Mark Van Doren is reported to have said: "Wit is the only wall between us and the dark." Or quote an anonymous twist on an old adage: "He who laughs—lasts."

Laughter is just one sign of amusement. It is certainly possible to enjoy humor without laughing out loud. I heard Don Ameche tell about his first experience with a Milwaukee theater audience. A new comedy he was appearing in played there, to test it out before heading to New York and Broadway. When no one laughed during the first act, he slipped out to the lobby during intermission to see what they didn't like about it. He understood when he heard a matron say to her friends, "My, that was so funny I could hardly keep from laughing!"

Certainly some amusement conjures up silent smiles. Other amusements cause totally different responses. They cause excitement or even fear. People don't stand in line at Disney World to go through Thunder Mountain, Splash Mountain or Space Mountain for anything other than amusement. But hearing their piercing screams while on the rides, you would swear they were terrified! Who in their right mind would willingly subject themselves to such torture? Millions of people do every year, including yours truly—once. Not long ago, in my Grandma Annie mode, I went with my two older grandkids to Disney World. I have to admit I thoroughly enjoyed the real, temporary fear we experienced on those crazy rides. We watched as hundreds exited from them, laughing and joking about their seeming "near brush with death." Eight-year-old Lucas sniffed as we came out of Splash Mountain, and said, "That wasn't scary at all." A photo, taken as we went over the waterfall, however, shows him grimacing in stark terror.

Think of the millions who flock to see horror movies, knowing they'll be terrified by ghoulish manifestations of some writer's imagination and a special effects crew. Think of those millions who knowingly become engrossed in Steven King's hair-raising tales. Think of those who stand in line in the hot sun to pay big money to go para-sailing or bungee-jumping. The adrenaline pumps, the heart pounds and the skin tingles with fear as suspense builds to a crescendo! Then, poof! It's over, and you laugh, a little hysterically. "Whew! I almost died, but I didn't. Wasn't that fun?"

What is fun about such torment? Why have writers, storytellers, and actors sought to scare the daylights out of audiences since time began? Probably because we all occasionally need to escape from reality, from our own very real and stressful world. For a brief time we become so absorbed in someone else's real or imagined terrors that we can forget our own. We choose to trade our ongoing real worries for a brief risk, one we can be pretty sure will end positively. The experience is akin to banging your head on a wall, because it feels so good when you stop.

How does the body process such intense stress? Dr. Borysenko says, "The acute stresses of life produce temporary physiological responses from which the body recovers. It's the chronic stresses—often caused by conditioned negative attitudes and feelings of helplessness—that are the challenge to healing." So, don't be afraid to be afraid in the name of fun. It can be a big boost, and it can help alleviate other chronic stresses of grief. Not all "fun" causes a response of laughter, screams or even smiles. Many pleasures, or enjoyments, evoke quieter and less obvious feelings of satisfaction. I picture my math teacher sitting before the fire with a contented smile on his face, as he doodles with sines and cosines. But most of life's little enjoyments produce even less visible expressions of appreciation, such as wonder, awe, peacefulness, pride, affection or self-satisfaction. From the following list, I hope each of you will be able to pick one, ten or 25 ideas that appeal to you—if not to pursue immediately, then later on.

—LEARN SOMETHING NEW—

Although you would have a hard time convincing most sixth graders, learning can be fun for almost everyone, when it is voluntary. I learned a valuable lesson, really a "secret," as a young adult that I wish I had known throughout my earlier schooling: "Always try to learn more about a subject than you are required to know." This became especially clear to me when I was asked to present a program to a woman's club on "The Declaration of Independence." I couldn't imagine how to make that interesting, when we had all heard about it so often. Then I started researching the lives of all the signers. I became caught up in the subject, fired by the incredible sacrifices they made for the sake of assuring our precious liberties. Nearly all lost fortunes, family, property, reputation and/or their health. The audience caught my enthusiasm, so the talk proved fun for them and for me.

When I returned to college at the age of 42, I was terrified of the whole process and I was sure that I would flounder because I thought I had forgotten everything I had ever known. The world—especially the world of mathematics—had totally changed since I was a young coed. I was terrified, but armed with my "secret," I studied every subject more than I had to and I'm proud to say I graduated—six part-time semesters later—with a 4.0 GPA. I accomplished my goal, but more than that I really enjoyed the process of learning. I confess that I also thoroughly enjoyed receiving my first kudos in many years. Success is fun, too.

I would like to say my pleasure was silent, to follow through with my above premise. But I admit that this 45-year-old sat in the field house on graduation night with all those 21-year-old kids, ripping up programs so we could throw confetti and holler and scream and laugh and sip champagne after getting our diplomas. I am sure my college-age son and my husband in the balcony hid their faces in embarrassment.

Cindy told us when she was nine years old that she wanted to be a teacher when she grew up. Her selection wasn't unusual for a girl of nine, but I always thought her reason was. She said, "I want to be a teacher so I will never have to stop learning. Learning is more fun than anything." As a professor, teaching—and learning—still seems to be great fun for her.

Learning anything new can be fun. You don't have to graduate from Yale or Harvard, or even take courses for credit to enjoy the process of learning, although doing that might be fun for you. You only need to find out what you would like to know more about, and then seek ways to learn more and more about it. The process can be mentally stimulating and leave in its wake a flood of self-satisfaction, pride and self-confidence.

What might you like to learn about? Maybe you would like to learn how to arrange flowers, grow orchids, upholster furniture, make window treatments, braid rugs, bake sourdough bread, speak Spanish, French or German, trace your family tree, restore an old home, fly a plane, country line-dance, play duplicate bridge, use a computer, sing barbershop, tailor a suit, play the stock market, paint like Monet, identify wildflowers and grasses, discover the history of your town, speed read, play the tuba, write Haiku poetry, propagate geraniums, make homemade beer or wine, take photos worth exhibiting, write a steamy novel, or braid your own hair? Most of these are "pleasures" mentioned by recovering widows I met.

Something in that list might trigger for you an idea that's been nagging in the back of your mind…something you have always wondered about or wished you had time to learn. You may decide to learn how to do a craft you saw on television, without ever leaving home. But your results are bound to be even better if you do leave home. Check books out of the local library, sign up for a course, contact the community extension department of your local college, or make an appointment to meet with a recognized expert in the field of your choice. You'll find that enthusiasm is contagious, and most people love talking about their favorite subjects. Start something today and watch what happens.

After being widowed, Karen learned everything she could about refurbishing old houses. By the six-month anniversary of her husband's death, she and a friend had formed a business partnership. "Within two months we had bought two houses and were rehabbing them," she said. These projects rekindled her interest in antiques, so now she haunts flea markets, garage sales and antique shops on weekends and vacations. She always seeks to learn something new that she can incorporate in her business. But even more important, her learning is why she is having fun in spite of having endured several personal tragedies in recent years.

Gretchen, too, loves antiques. A year or so after the auto accident that killed her husband and teenage son, she joined a suburban Milwaukee group who collected, refinished and sold quality antiques. "I especially liked learning how to do the refinishing, which I can do at home," she said. "But I also like spending time working in the shop."

Dale said the best thing she did for herself after her husband died was to renew her interest in photography. They had shared the hobby—and their home darkroom—until his death. Because she had no money worries, she was able to expand that interest into a new life. Through membership in a group of photography collectors, she met and became friendly with several well-known photographers. "I have learned so much from them. One has become my mentor," she says. "He has been wonderful about guiding me and reviewing my work as I learn. Meeting these men and women has been a stimulating and exciting experience for me." She says she gets additional satisfaction and enjoyment by traveling to interesting photo sites around the world and meeting other travelers along the way.

After Ginny's husband died, she obtained a second masters degree in nursing, which boosted both her self-esteem and her much-needed paycheck. In addition she learned through volunteer activities in her church, her homeowner's group and a nursing organization, that she was a capable person and that she enjoyed feeling in control of her life.

You know from previous chapters that I revived my interest in art, learning how to paint T-shirts, how to draw and a bit about how to paint with watercolors. I have also traveled to France twice, where I just barely recovered my skimpy knowledge of French and learned a lot about a lot of things, most especially myself.

I guess Cindy got some of her love of learning from me. If I had the time, or could capture more of it, I would be delighted to throw myself into learning about almost any of the subjects I presented earlier for your consideration. In going over that list I suddenly realized that I learned that "secret" of always learning more than required from my years as a feature writer for a daily newspaper and as a freelance magazine writer. I still recall wrinkling up my nose when I was given an assignment to interview a local couple who had collected 4,500 specialty pencils from all over the country and abroad. I grimaced again when asked to "do 2,000 words on coin collecting." Both projects, and almost all the others I pursued, turned out to be fascinating. Even the most mundane-sounding subject can become interesting when you delve deeply enough into it. If your life lacks "fun," try to learn as much as you can about something entirely new to you.

—APPRECIATE THE GLORIES AROUND YOU—

It takes a little time and a little knowledge to fully appreciate all the glories around you, but it pays off in increasing the quality of your life. If you are sadly unaware of the flora and fauna around you, sign up at a nearby private, state or county park for a guided nature tour. You will add to your enjoyment by doing some homework ahead of time about what you expect to see. Check your newspaper, call your Chamber of Commerce or tourist bureau for free or inexpensive tours or workshops to increase your knowledge, hence your appreciation. Learn to ask questions of people who know about such things. Take along a sketch pad and keep notes with identifying sketches.

The same process works for learning about any of the many art forms around us. Consider architecture. If you have always admired the architecture of public buildings, read up on the subject. Check out illustrative videos and search the TV listings or the World Wide Web for in-depth reports on the subject. Attend seminars and speeches by local architects. Introduce yourself to the speaker later, ask questions and take notes. The same method works for such subjects as sculpting, interior design, regional history, local geology, etc. Knowing more, and knowing the people who know even more, can fill your life with focus and fun.

Joining with others to enjoy learning about something new can add to the fun. If you are over 60 you might try joining Elderhostel, and spend hours studying their catalogs of exciting learning vacations throughout the U.S. and the world. Some people get so hooked on these unique learning vacations they spend almost the whole year moving from one to another. I doubt there is a subject or an interest they haven't covered. The sessions vary, but typically each domestic vacation lasts about one week, is held on a college campus and mixes intense study with socializing. Some of the more exotic International Elderhostel vacations take place aboard a ship; or take you to intriguing secluded spots with little civilization nearby. Some may involve tiring and strenuous hands-on work, such as a remote archeological dig.

Those of you who are very active women may be interested in something like Rainbow Adventures, which organizes local and worldwide adventure travel for women over 30. They offer a variety of trips, rated easy, moderate or expert, according to the level of physical activity required. Friendship Force is an international organization that works toward bringing the world together through citizen exchanges. Any of these ideas can be explored on the Internet. Just type a few descriptive words into the "search" line of any search engine and press "return."

—JOIN THE WORLD ON THE "WEB" AND THE "NET"—

Which reminds me, you ARE using the Internet and World Wide Web, aren't you? Of all the possibilities I can offer, I don't know of any activity that can be as much fun or as gratifying as "going online." I had used computers for many years in my writing and for laying out newsletters, but I was introduced to the larger world of electronic communications just two months after Bruce died.

My children decided I needed to expand my horizons and have an easy, inexpensive way to stay in touch with them. As a birthday gift, they "gave me" e-mail, assuring me that this would save me lots of time and money. I would be less than honest if I didn't tell you that their gift ended up costing me a small fortune by the time I upgraded my computer, bought a new modem, signed on with a "server" for two years of monthly payments, etc., etc. That having been said, I still believe that no matter what your age or experience, you will get more of a lift out of "going online" than almost anything else you can do.

It is no longer necessary to lay out thousands of dollars for a computer and commit yourself to semesters of study just to use e-mail (electronic mail) and to find information on the Internet or the World Wide Web. Unless you are young, a really quick learner, or you want to also be able to write the great American novel or play the stock market from home or keep books for a business, you probably do not need a desktop computer. No matter how inexpensive they have become, getting one may invite more troubles than it is worth. My son has forced me to put in a plug for Apple. An iMac or an iBook *can* be as simple as an "internet appliance," but you still have the option of exploring or expanding as far as your interest takes you. Plus, you have the confidence of knowing you share a standard for software and hardware with millions of other Mac users.

If you choose to keep your experience limited to e-mail and the Internet, try a dedicated Internet terminal. They are simple to use and inexpensive. That, and a few pointers from a Web-friendly friend or relative, can move you right into the twenty-first century. For even less money (or none at all) you may be able to buy or "inherit" a used appliance. If all you want and need can be satisfied by a simple appliance with limited features, you will enjoy your new toy immediately instead of having to endure a gigantic learning curve. I am still sometimes frustrated by PCs (Personal Computers), after using them for 22 years! If, after using this appliance for awhile, you find you really need a full capacity computer, you will feel much more competent, and ready for it, than if you try to begin that way.

If you think you are too old for this new-fangled nonsense, you will feel reassured by connecting with SeniorNet.com, Seniors Online, etc. Often, local libraries also sponsor Internet or computer training for seniors. Study your local newspaper ads or inquire of your library for more information. There is a veritable mountain of information available for those interested in getting started with computers or the Internet, so I will say no more on the subject.

—USE YOUR TALENTS—

Whatever your talents, you will find that expressing and strengthening them will bring you pleasure and pride. If you think you don't have any talents, you're wrong. You may not have discovered any yet, but I can guarantee that if you pursue something that truly interests you, and you spend time learning about it and practice doing it, you will find you have latent talent. If not in the first thing you try, in the second or third. When you do discover that talent, your life will become fuller than you would have believed.

If you've always wished you could draw, for example, but you have been discouraged at every turn, try what I did. I had had some art training, but I always felt my drawing skill was lacking. I bought what I consider the all-time best drawing instruction book, *Drawing on the Right Side of the Brain* by Betty Edwards. I began going through it chapter by chapter, doing all the exercises along the way. Although I didn't complete the book, I am amazed at how much better I became at drawing from the half I did. The trick is not in learning to *draw*, but in learning to *see* what you want to draw. If you think you would be lousy at it, find the book and look at the "before" drawings of many of the students who have taken the course from the author. Most are pretty child-like; the "after" drawings, done only a few weeks later, are inspiring. Try it. It's fun.

"Talent" doesn't just refer to abilities in writing, art, music, dancing and acting. Talented seamstresses produce works of art all the time, as do quilters, needle-pointers, gardeners, cooks, hair stylists, home decorators, and tennis players. Even mechanics who make an engine purr are using their talent. Just figure out what you love to do and work to develop your talents. They are there, believe me.

—SHARE SOMETHING WITH ANOTHER—

Sharing what you know with others is thrilling and rewarding in many ways. You not only have the fun of learning a lot about the subject yourself, but you double that by passing it on and making someone else's world brighter. If you become something of an expert, you may have an opportunity to teach a class. Or you can share your skill with a friend. Several women I know take turns teaching each other skills. They gather in each other's homes to learn how to make crusty French bread from one woman, arrange flowers from another, can pickles from another, and make Chinese food from another. Someday I plan to invite them over to learn how to make glitzy T-shirts. Then maybe they will invite me to learn something from them. Do you have a craft or skill you could share with your friends?

Make and give gifts to double your fun. One year I made several batches of green pepper jelly to give as gifts. Except for the batch that just wouldn't "set," that was a fun project. I keep thinking someday I'll have time to perfect a flavored mustard or a new homemade flavored vinegar or olive oil to present in attractive containers as hostess gifts and such. I have given away oodles of hand-painted T-shirts and visors over the past few years. Making the gift is fun, and presenting it to someone you like is an added pleasure. If you needlepoint, write poetry, take photos, bake fine desserts, crochet, knit or grow the juiciest tomatoes on the block, try giving them as gifts. Dress them up with a bit of colorful tissue, curly ribbon and a gift card.

Entertain others. Entertaining can be a consuming and amusing venture and some women raise the activity to a fine art. They not only perfect dishes and menus that delight the taste buds and the eye, but they enhance their gastronomical treats with beautifully decorated tables and attractive floral arrangements. Then they learn how to ensure that everyone has a wonderful time. I sometimes try to do all that, but I usually make sure I fix easy, do-ahead dishes so I can join in the festivities. I hate to miss a good party by puttering in the kitchen.

Participate in sports. Sports can be beneficial in many ways—physically, mentally and emotionally. There are all kinds of sports, some competitive, some team-oriented, some risk-taking, some social and some that appeal for the solitude they provide. Some especially appeal to the young at heart, such as skateboarding and in-line skating, and some appeal to the more mature, such as shuffleboard or bocce ball. Some cost a small fortune and some are free. My son tells me he just read a report about how lack of sleep is related to weight gain, and lack of exercise is related to lack of sleep. That's an interesting twist on it.

Ideally, everyone who *can* would participate in at least one sport on a regular basis. Which sport, of course, would depend on your age, level of fitness, interest, climate, pocketbook, availability, social needs and goals. I intended to reprint all the sports and activities listed in the *Random House Word Menu* by Steven Glazier, one of my favorite word books. But there are several pages of such listings, so I selected from the list and then added a few mentioned by widowed friends. There is no shortage of activities for those willing to be active. Which of the following might be YOUR sport or activity?

- **Team Sports:** *Basketball, crew, cricket, curling, doubles tennis, field hockey, handball, ice hockey, softball, soccer, volleyball, water polo, yachting?*

- **Individual Sports :** *Alpine skiing, archery, arm wrestling, baton twirling, bicycling, bowling, canoeing, cross-country skiing, diving, fencing, figure skating, golf, gymnastics, hiking, horseback riding, ice skating, in-line skating, jai alai, kayaking, lawn bowling, lawn tennis, ping-pong, racquetball, roller-blading, running, snow-shoeing, speed skating, surfing, swimming, tennis, walking, water skiing?*

- **Athletic Events and Activities:** *Acrobatics, aerobics, backpacking, ballooning, calisthenics, fishing, gliding, handsprings, hang gliding, hunting, judo, jujitsu, karate, martial arts, mountaineering, rock climbing, sailing, skeet shooting, skin diving, skydiving, snorkeling, tae kwon do, tobogganing, tumbling, trap shooting, whitewater rafting, windsurfing?*

- **Outdoor Games:** *Badminton, bocce, broomball, croquet, Frisbee, horseshoes, paddleball, roller-skating, shuffleboard?*

Develop a hobby or craft: A hobby or craft can be, as it was for me, a way to fill otherwise lonely Sunday hours. Or it can become the entire focus of one's life. I won't list the thousands of different hobbies available, but here is a representative list because sometimes we need a memory jogger to get us started. *Bird-watching, bridge-playing, camping, carpentry, ceramics, collecting, (square, line, ballroom, or modern) dancing, jewelry-making, crocheting, embroidery, knitting, needlepoint, sewing, pottery, quilting, spelunking, weaving.*

Play board/card games: Games help adults as well as children learn the joy of play. I recall times when card games or board games have had me, and everyone else in the room, laughing to the point of tears. There is something about sharing in a game, be it Charades, Pictionary, Tiddlywinks or Trivial Pursuit, that loosens people up and gives them a chance to perform or act silly. Such activities, if they help you relax and enjoy life, are anything but a waste of time. They are valuable tools for your "health chest." I remember as rare high spots during my first few months of widowhood two evenings of gathering around a table and playing a silly card game, called Pass the Ace. For a brief respite, I felt happy and engaged in life,

Join an interest group: An interest group can pick up your social life and provide a sense of accomplishment. Over the years I have belonged to a sewing group (which did little sewing), a marathon bridge group, three book clubs, an ethnic eating group, a birthday lunch group, an open-housing pressure group and several writers' groups. I know friends who belong to an "old movie buffs" group, political discussion groups, bible study groups, garden clubs, women's issues discussion groups and music appreciation groups as well as any number of self-help support groups. In addition, there are unlimited associations, clubs, fraternal organizations, civic betterment groups, etc. Your shared interest provides fertile territory for the growth of friendships and pleasure.

Although I had often thought travel would be fun, it would not have been for Bruce, nor would skiing or scuba diving, etc. Hence they wouldn't have been for me either, had I insisted. His fun, and ours together, was often more homespun. We enjoyed mental challenges, quizzes (he loved trying to guess what odd words in the dictionary meant), crosswords, reading, building wooden furniture, family sing-along sessions, telling jokes, watching a lazy fire in the fireplace, tromping the beach or a snowy woodland path, watching birds and hand-feeding raccoons in the backyard, listening to music, etc.

We did have fun, although we didn't always enjoy the same activities. Bruce loved tennis, especially a good hard singles game with someone who could *almost* beat him. I was never good enough to be a challenge, so I usually played only in doubles games or with women friends. I learned to play golf as a child and grooved a pretty good swing, so for many years I enjoyed playing golf. Bruce, on the other hand, started playing later in life and hated it with such a passion that knocking the game and telling derisive jokes about it became one of his favorite pastimes. He loved telling about the day he quit golf. On his fourth try at getting out of a steep sand trap at the edge of a green, he hit his best drive of the day. It landed not just beyond the green, or on the nearby fairway, but over a fence and on a fairway for the other nine holes! It was fun hearing him tell it, but it wasn't fun being his partner that day. He was wise to quit the game; it provided more stress for him (and those playing with him) than it relieved. Keep that in mind when you choose your fun.

I suspect that even if we had enjoyed the same sports, or if we had done ten times as much to enjoy life, or Bruce had lived 20 years longer, the shock of it being over would probably still cause me to pause and to think of my regrets...my "if onlys." There always would remain "undone things," pleasures not enjoyed, places not seen, music not heard, activities not tried.

Our time with our husbands has ended, for you and for me. So now we must teach ourselves how to have fun in new ways, alone or with friends, so we can make the rest of our lives more worthwhile and healthier.

13

Maintaining Relationships: Friends and Family, Yours and His

…the only way to have a friend is to be one.

—Ralph Waldo Emerson

Annie's Journal (13 months)
Dear Bruce: I miss you more than ever now. I especially miss you tonight. I just found out Paul and Vi are moving to Pensacola! They'll be 60 or 70 miles away instead of minutes. Not only that, but most of our old friends in Door County are either moving away or have become too busy to get here very often. Even my mainstay, Debby, has a new friend and is busy with him a lot. I feel more alone and lonely than I can ever remember. I feel abandoned, like an elderly Eskimo set adrift on an iceberg.

At about nine months, someone asked me what in the world I did all day that I was always so busy. I had been trying to figure that out for some time. I considered asking a friend to watch me, recording absolutely everything I did. I seldom found time to read a book; I watched a minimum of TV; I didn't read a single newspaper the first few months, and then I did so only sporadically. My writing at that point was minimal, and heaven knows my house needed professional help. So where did my time go? To be honest, I finally realized that a lot of my time was vaporizing like a morning mist for lack of focus. Time has a way of doing that if you aren't careful…or if you're in grief. Sometimes I would catch myself reading and rereading the label on a jar of plum preserves or spending two hours on a 15-minute crossword puzzle. I also did a lot of lake-watching without really seeing the lake. Obviously I wasn't as busy as I seemed to be.

I also discovered that I was spending an inordinate amount of time visiting with relatives and friends in person, on the phone, by e-mail, fax or letter. When I first recognized this pattern, my former self recoiled: "time-waster, time-waster, shame, shame." Then I realized how appropriate that was for me at that time of my life. This "occupation" made sense. I had three main jobs in those first months (years) alone: to grieve, to learn to live alone, and to write this book. I had been open with my good friends and most had been open with me, so I think I made a lot of progress on all three fronts. A couple of really good friends endured endless repetitive talk about my loss and the death itself. Sometimes I felt guilty unloading so much on them, but other times I saw them profit from my outpourings…a little more tenderness between spouses, retraction of a cutting remark, a little more appreciation for the beauty of sunsets watched together. Some even profited by reviewing past traumas they had known. If they can love life—and each other—a bit more because of what I put them through, some good will have come of it.

Some friends have made lifestyle changes they attribute to the shock of losing Bruce so young and to hearing my anguished feelings on the subject. The shock reminded them of their own mortality and prompted them to reevaluate their goals. Some chose to more fully enjoy life, and their money, while they could. In general they loosened up, opting for earlier retirement instead of more money, for example, or spending some of their nest egg on travel, a boat, a luxury condo. I see their changes as positive, as determination to live more fully while they—and their spouses—are well enough to enjoy it. As a friend of mine likes to say, "We will never, ever, be any younger and healthier than we are at this moment, so let's not put off the good stuff." Hooray for him! I like that kind of thinking.

Recently I have taken a new tack. When people ask what I do with my time, I say, "I spend a lot of time nurturing my friendships. Friends are my most valuable resource at this time, so it's important that I spend a lot of time with them, letting them know that I appreciate them."

—OLD FRIENDS—

We have always heard "old friends are your best friends." There is some truth in that. Pauli and I have remained steadfast friends for half a century now, despite being as much as 3,000 miles apart (she in Minnesota, then Arizona, then California; I in Wisconsin, then Florida). We might not see each other for years, but the minute we get together, live or by phone, it's as though we have never been apart. There is a thread between us that never breaks. Our occasional 90-minute phone calls may have something to do with that.

After Bruce died, I reconnected with several other old friends from years ago. Some read the obituary, or were told, and called me. In other cases, because my travel plans were more flexible after I was alone, I made an extra effort to visit when I was nearby. Bruce's death was a hard reminder that we won't be around forever, so I felt the need to visit with people when I could. It was great fun getting reacquainted, and although some of us hadn't seen each other for 30 or 40 years, no one had changed (much). None of us looked a bit older, once our eyes adjusted to the years apart. Myopia and cataracts aren't all bad.

On first blush I felt lucky in this friendship game. Most couples and groups of couples we had socialized with were wonderful about welcoming me back into the comfort of their fold when I was alone. I felt perfectly comfortable, once I had moved beyond the sadness of being with them, but without Bruce. I had heard so much about the isolation single women, especially widows, find in this couple-oriented society that I expected it to be worse than it was. June warned me of the possibility, so I knew it wasn't just myth. "Ann," she said, "one of the things that really surprised me was that some of the people I thought would be supportive dropped away. No matter," she continued, "I've made new friends, although that takes effort. And there always are some old steadfast friends standing by."

Her letter prompted me to look a bit more critically at my friends. While it is true that I wasn't really dropped, or entirely excluded, by most friends, I definitely noticed a decrease in attention from those we had known through Bruce's work. That's predictable and understandable, as is the fact that I had been "forgotten" by a few couples who had known Bruce long before they met me. It still hurt. What made it tolerable was that we had a varied and long list of friends. Excluded by some, I just saw more of the others. But, if your social life had always revolved around the same few friends, and they let you down, you may feel as betrayed and abandoned as I did when I wrote my journal entry. You may have to think fast of ways to make new connections and build new friendships.

I feel quite certain most friends who exclude widows don't even realize they do so. They make vague invitations in passing, but no specific ones we can accept or reject. I told most of my friends, "Don't issue any idle invitations, because I plan to accept them all!" Maybe that scared them, or maybe they sometimes just forgot to include me in their activities. I have tried not to feel angry about their neglect because I understand, perhaps too well, how this happens. Bruce and I were at least as negligent as they have been about shunning recently widowed friends. It seemed awkward to us, for example, to have a dinner party for seven people instead of eight. But, it also seemed odd to have five women and three men. I see now how ridiculous that is, but recalling our silly concerns has helped me to understand how innocently it can happen. If you feel left out, think back. Were the two of you always careful to include single and widowed friends socially? If you were, I congratulate you. If you, like we, failed to do so, that doesn't make it right, but it might make it easier to understand.

There is no way to predict how old friends will accept you as a widow. Most will probably be as friendly and close as ever. If you find you are having a major problem, think about it and be certain that you aren't unknowingly causing the problem. Consider the following words of caution:

- *Accept any invitations you can, even when it's painful.*

- *Expect to be included in most of their regular activities.* If you expect them to shun you, it may come across as *you* shunning *them.*

- *Pay most attention to the women.* While you might have enjoyed spirited conversations with husbands before, doing so might trigger jealousy now. Sad but true.

- *Invite old friends for drinks or dinner as soon as you feel up to it.* Talk about how different it will be, but that you hope they will be patient and continue to include you in their activities.

- *Don't panic the first time you feel you have been excluded.* Or, even the second time. The third time may warrant attention. You might call one of the women you know best and ask if anyone in the group feels uncomfortable having you around in your new single status. Take your cue from her answer. If you conclude that there is a problem, try to remain friendly when you see them, but you probably will no longer consider yourself "one of them."

- *Remain calm if there is uneasiness with you in the crowd.* It may seem totally unfair (<u>it is</u>), and it may hurt to the core when your core is already damaged. Keep in mind, however, that millions of widows have survived by finding new friends, sometimes even better friends. You will, too.

—NEW FRIENDS—

Although that last statement may be hard to believe, it's often true for widows that some of our new friends will be our best friends. The friends you make after you are alone have no adjustment to make. If they didn't know your husband, they won't feel that dread of his death looming whenever they see you. They won't be super sensitive to comments you make about him. They will think of you as a single person. Even intact couples you meet now will accept you for yourself. So when new acquaintances appear interested in pursuing friendship, welcome their overtures and invite them to your home when you feel up to it.

You will undoubtedly find yourself drawn to other widows, widowers—and to some extent—those who have suffered the loss of a child or other very intimate trauma. A bond develops quickly between people who have suffered similar tragedies; you understand what makes each other tick, sometimes without speaking about it. In my early months as a widow I was desperate for proof that it was possible to survive this tragedy. I attached myself like a barnacle to anyone who had known stark tragedy and recovered some sanity. Even if I didn't always say it out loud, I was crying out to them, "Tell me I will survive. Tell me this pain and fear and anxiety and torture are natural." Usually, within a few sentences, I knew they understood my need and they let me know that they had, indeed, survived a trauma not unlike mine. From such beginnings many new friendships have sprung.

To a lesser extent, but still viable, is the connection with recently or painfully divorced people. There are differences between the experiences of divorce and widowhood, of course, and there are many different variations of each. However, there are similarities, too. A totally unexpected break in a long marriage can feel much like the unexpected death of a spouse, both providing that wretched feeling of having been ripped apart from one's other half. I suspect there also is a lot of similarity between the conflict divorcees know when broken apart from a long withering marriage and widows who have weathered a long death by cancer, for example. Widows and divorcees often go through very similar stages of recovery, which can provide rapport between them.

Which is worse, divorce or widowhood? I was stunned when early in my grief a divorcee said she thought divorce was worse than widowhood. At that moment I knew nothing could be worse than what I was going through. After a year or so, however, I concluded that sometimes divorce is worse than death of a spouse. It can leave a woman feeling embittered and worthless. In addition, the man can, if he chooses, continue to make his ex-wife's life pure hell. It even can be dangerous, life-threatening. With widowhood at least you start a completely new life the moment he dies, and after the shock subsides, you have some control over it. I remember thinking how much worse I would feel *about myself* if Bruce had suddenly run off with a younger woman and abandoned me. That process not only can do serious damage to the wife's self-esteem, it is likely to leave her with strangled finances and messy division of property issues as well. Multiply the potential for conflict by a hundred if the divorce includes custody issues. With an unfriendly divorce, the conflict can get thrown up in her face for many years, keeping her trapped and unable to recover. With widowhood each day is one step forward in building your new life, although some days that progress is hard to see.

In general, singles attract other singles, just as couples stay glued to other couples, so it is likely that the bulk of your future friends may be single. However, some women carry on with their previous groups of coupled friends, and see little or no change in their social life. This is something over which you have some control, but not a lot, so don't spend time waiting and wondering what will happen to you. Instead, spend your time being a good friend to others. Here is a list of suggestions. Sometimes I am able to heed them. Sometimes I am not.

- *Show others you still care.* Call or send a card if you haven't heard from someone you care about for awhile. E-mails are better than nothing, but less rewarding than snail mail or phone calls.

- *Try not to judge others, and hope they don't judge you falsely.*

- *Learn to appreciate each other's differences.* That's what makes life interesting. What could be more boring than an entire room full of clones of yourself? Make a point to meet different kinds of people.

- *Learn to keep confidences,* just as you expect others to keep yours.

One of the better reasons for joining an organized support group of widows is that you are encouraged to bare your wounds to each other in a protected environment. In addition to being therapeutic, this process can create fertile territory for establishing lifelong ties. I noticed an almost tangible intimacy within the groups I visited, and several interviewees mentioned that intimacy in their written responses to me. Sharing a trauma doesn't guarantee a lasting friendship, though. You may find after a time that you share only your misfortune, which is not a good enough base on which to build a lifelong friendship. The shared wound does present an opportunity to reach intimacy quickly, though, and if other factors are in sync, friendship can grow and bloom.

Because you are alone, you probably will pursue different interests than you did before and you will develop new friends who share them. In all likelihood you will look back in a few years and find that you have more friends, and closer friends, than you had when you were married. That makes sense, of course, because so much of your time before probably was spent nurturing the one relationship around which your world turned.

—YOUR FAMILY—

The shock and aftermath of death can cause families to grow closer than they have ever been. Having shared an intimate crisis, they experience similar reactions. Their shared grief can reestablish the familial bond. To a certain extent, that loss also can remind us of how much we treasure each other, and how important it is to let each other know we care.

On the other hand, crises also can provide the potential for conflict within the family structure. Some relatives try too hard to "help" the new widow, which can cause resentment. I know, for example, of a stepson who apparently thought he could solve all his mother-in-law's financial problems by offering to buy her house. She was insulted, angry and suspicious of his motives. Previously unspoken grievances can become magnified and explode during this unsettled time, when tact may easily give way to the cathartic need for expression. Tempers may be more volatile than usual and feelings can be more easily injured. The biggest danger within families lie folded up in the years of accumulated baggage we each carry around. In this time of edgy nerves, it's quite natural to feel the need to get rid of the load. It is easy to spout off in anger, or to misinterpret others' comments. I know I was unpredictable, swaying between complacency one day and hypersensitivity the next. We often are more sensitive to criticism from family members than we are from others, and we also may feel free to say things in anger to family members that we probably wouldn't say to friends. Hostilities left from childhood can come tumbling out in response to something as innocuous as a discussion about what to do with the leftover ham.

Several widowed friends noted that they finally had to move to a new state to get away from the over-protective, meddling habits of their own parents or in-laws. The older generation, trying to be helpful, may offer "suggestions" that feel like "criticisms," creating a great deal of tension and eventually a chasm in the family. Grown women said they felt they were being treated like little children again, and they were unable to deal with their grief as grown-ups until they struck out on their own. Older siblings may be tempted to "mother" you. My sister admitted that, while she was driving to my home the day Bruce died, she made frantic plans to move me into the apartment above hers in Madison so she could "take care of me." Thankfully, as she pulled into my driveway four hours later she suddenly realized how ridiculous that was. I was 55 years old, the same age she had been when she was widowed. In addition, I had always been stubbornly independent, so the chances were pretty good that I would choose to handle this in my own way. As indeed I have.

Although you may be powerless to prevent all potential family problems, your understanding of these dynamics may help you avoid triggering a fight. Studies show families in crisis often respond poorly to each other, and it seems the deeper the pain the deeper the wounds that can be inflicted. Divorce rates skyrocket, for example, among couples who suffer the death of a child. Unable to deal with anything more than their own loss, each spouse lashes out at the other instead of offering the love and support the other needs. That same dynamic can break apart mothers and children when the husband/father dies. Awareness of the pitfalls may prevent your tumbling into them.

It's ideal, of course, to stem hostile feelings before they erupt into long-lasting problems, but because of our instability during grief, that's not always possible. Once we've moved along, though, and we recall how to express our thoughts more positively, the likelihood of such problems begins to taper off. That's the time to mend fences, if some of yours have taken a beating. Your heartfelt apology can prevent years of discord in the family. Even if you think the other person is to blame, you may derail long term hostility by saying something like, "I'm so sorry about our disagreement. Let's try to be nicer to each other from now on." *It is not necessary to establish blame.*

Much was written a few years back about the superiority of Japan's workforce over ours. It was generally established that their "corporate culture" was responsible for their high productivity. Americans would find some of Japan's methods for increasing productivity quite unacceptable, but I think we all could gain from considering its widely acclaimed "no blame policy." When something goes wrong at a Japanese plant, it seems that not one second of time is spent on establishing blame and assessing punishment. Everyone's effort is poured into solving the problem. Think about that when dealing with family and friends.

Sometimes a widow's children march in and take charge, assuming the parental role for their weakened parent. They make decisions quickly, while she is in deep shock and disabled. They might pack her up and take her home with them, putting the family home on the market, or they may get her enrolled in a retirement home, assuming she will never be able to manage her home alone. Sometimes such decisions are necessary and to the widow's benefit. Other times the widowed mother feels trapped by the rapid changes. Unless you are elderly, penniless, or very frail, you need to be allowed time to regain your senses and make your own decisions. A widow friend in Florida, only in her late sixties, told me of being moved by her son "...lock, stock, and barrel..." into his home up north within weeks of her husband's death. "I hated it," she said. "I missed my lovely house and garden, my bridge group and my church friends. But more than anything, I resented that I wasn't consulted." She had moved back to Florida when I met her, but not without hard feelings on both sides, and not into the house she had so loved.

If we always seemed totally dependent on our husbands—their fathers—it's natural for our children to assume we might not have what it takes to live alone. They may, in their own grief, feel it their duty to step forward and assume the caretaker role. I can't know your situation, but I can urge you to resist making any major changes before you have had time to heal. That includes letting others make a change for you. If your children are pressuring you to make a move you don't want to make, enlist the help of your doctor, minister, lawyer or counselor to convince them you need time alone, maybe a year or more, to recover. Then YOU will decide how and where you wish to spend your future.

Children, even if they are in their 30s, 40s or 50s, don't like their only surviving parent to be anything less than "in control." My own children were immeasurably helpful and insightful, as are most kids, I imagine. But my situation may have been completely different from yours. I was 55 years old at the time, relatively healthy, financially sound—and well known to be stubbornly independent. I'm sure my children had misgivings about my inner strengths those first months, as those were sadly crippled. I was quite obviously thrown by their father's death, but they had the foresight to see that I needed to be allowed time to grieve by myself. They helped me feel I was still competent in many ways, just "temporarily stymied." For the most part we have been able to maintain good, mature relationships. I still forget and treat them like children once in awhile, which ruffles their feathers of course. I just can't stop myself. I have an irresistible urge to share my "wisdom" with them, even knowing they don't want to hear it. But mostly we have been lucky and avoided the parent/child pitfalls so prevalent in early widowhood.

—RELATING TO CHILDREN WHILE YOU BOTH ARE WOUNDED—

If you have young children at home, they may present an incredible challenge to you during these first years alone. Even without the trauma of a parent's death, child rearing is a daunting job. With the added stress of their father's death, the kid's increased psychological needs may threaten to push your own aside. Eunice, a friend whose husband died ten years after their 1932 marriage, said she still remembers the awesome responsibility of being a single parent. "There was no time for self pity. That doesn't mean I was brave; neither was I stoic. I felt terribly sorry for my children. Howie was a wonderful father; he had great plans for the kids. He was a demonstrative dad; he loved them deeply and verbally expressed his love. That they were deprived of that broke my heart."

Agnes related a story about bridging the gap left by her husband's death years ago when her boys were four and eight. About two weeks after the funeral, they were at the kitchen table, with Agnes in her late husband's chair, to help prevent the "vacant chair syndrome." Suddenly the ceiling light bulb burned out. "My boys were rather alarmed," she said. "My four year old asked, 'Do you think Daddy could come back just long enough to fix the light?' From somewhere, my inner being perhaps, came my answer. 'Your daddy can't come back, no matter how much he would like to help. But if you and your brother help, I think the three of us can replace that bulb.'" From that time on she says they handled their problems more or less in the same way. "We did not always succeed, but we tried awfully hard most of the time," she said.

My good friend Pauli offered this advice, tongue-in-cheek I think, to widows with young kids. "Raising my three children alone was an experience I wouldn't wish to do again," she said. "To all new widows with young children, I say 'Remarry immediately!'"

I asked several young mothers what they would say if they could telephone their husbands for five minutes. Pauli answered, "That he sure did take the easy way out by leaving the child-rearing to me!" That was, as you may recall, the tag line on a "Momma" cartoon she still treasures. Several other young women expressed a similar sentiment, although they all did so in good humor.

Children's grief can add incredible stress to the parent-child relationship. How does one determine what behavior is a result of grief and what is a natural part of growing up? Should misbehavior be treated with discipline or cuddles? The topic is far beyond my expertise. I can only suggest you turn to professionals if you are having significant problems. I know that grieving children sometimes become whiny and insufferable, but don't most children at times? Sometimes they become fearful, accident prone, withdrawn and/or uncertain. How can one know the source of the problem? My gut instinct, which is about all I have to go on here, is to reassure, reassure, reassure. To the extent you can muster the where-withal, show them your strength and your constancy. Let them know you won't leave them and, if possible, enlist their help in getting through this period. Helping you deal with your grief may help them express and deal with their own.

One single mother described surviving her children's teen years as very much like surviving a prisoner of war camp. Ginny admitted it wasn't easy for her, either. "All through the teen years I knew Don and I would have dissolved in humor, where, alone I was feeling totally desperate." What helped her get through the "testing of their independence," was a safety net. Both her sisters and their husbands had offered to take the boys (ages 13 and 10) for any period necessary, "if we ever reached an impasse where we could not resolve the clash of my caution and their desire for independence." She only had to take them up on their generous offer once, but knowing it was there gave her great comfort.

Teenagers often become surly and obstinate in the normal course of maturing, and they would not be above taking advantage of a grief-weakened mother. We have always blamed surging hormones, but a recent medical study shows actual differences in teenagers' brains. Whatever the cause, they can become frustrated, confused, anxious and angry, often without apparent cause. The tricky part for the bereft mother is figuring out how much of her teen's behavior is "normal" and how much is ill-expressed grief. Teenagers can appear untouched by the loss of their father. Because their lives revolve around their peers, they may be totally unaware of any real sense of loss. But they almost surely are deeply disturbed by it all and unable to understand why.

You should know that they may need more help than you can provide. You are not at the top of your form, and natural parental struggles can blow out of all proportion with the added stress of mourning. If you can manage it financially, a few sessions of professional counseling for the two of you might do wonders. If your checkbook can't stretch that far, and you aren't eligible for aid, ask a brother, brother-in-law, neighbor or minister or rabbi to help. Most likely your frustrated teenager needs a good, understanding and mature friend they can trust. Even in the best of times a parent isn't always the one who can fulfill that role.

Grandchildren, depending on their ages and closeness to your spouse, suffer in various ways from the loss. Jessica and Lucas, my two older grandchildren, questioned me for several years about their Grandpa Bruce's death. They were three and four when he died, so this was their first experience with death. They asked me the questions I would like to have asked, and to which none of us knew the answers. "Where is Grandpa Bruce now?" "Why did he have to die?" "Can he still see us?" I was frustrated not to have better answers for them, but our struggles to understand brought us closer.

Otherwise, all I can say about grandchildren is that they make the struggle worthwhile. They give us hope; they offer us unquestioning love; they make us laugh and they make us cry. They remind us of our own kids when they were young and that they will someday have children of their own. They remind us that life goes on. It changes constantly, of course, but it does go on. That is an invaluable message for the grieving widow.

My sister Joan wrote, "Little children are God's medicine for a new widow—their freshness and their 'happy to be alive' attitude are more help than anything!" I say, "Amen."

—IN-LAWS CAN PRESENT SPECIAL PROBLEMS—

About half of the widows I asked about their in-laws confessed that they had had problems, ranging from minor misunderstandings to total alienation. Some of the worst rifts occurred between young mothers struggling to rear children alone, and one or both of their husband's parents. "My in-laws seemed to be watching over my shoulder, making sure I did everything just right. Or, rather, just the way they would have done it." Another said, "Even if I thought their way might be right, I needed to know I was in charge. Actually, I needed my kids to know I was in charge." A good friend, who was still estranged from her in-laws many years later, said, "Nothing I did satisfied them. And what made me maddest was that they insisted I should never work or even go on a date. They insisted that I should dedicate the rest of my life solely to my children. Bull!"

The special problems that arise with in-laws are due in part to the fact that his parents are deep in grief themselves. They have lost a child, which has to be wrenching in a way that we who never have, can only imagine. I suspect some cling to their son's offspring in desperation. In addition, they can see your struggles and may feel compelled to "help you" rear the kids during this trying time.

I can't guarantee that I wouldn't present that same problem if, heaven forbid, my son died and left my daughter-in-law in charge of my precious grandchildren. It is an agonizing exercise to even contemplate such an event, but I have done so hoping it might help me to empathize with young mothers. If, in such a case, I interfered with Meg's efforts, it probably would have nothing to do with my intellectual views of her child-rearing skills. I know she is entirely competent—when she isn't grieving. But the temptation might be awfully strong to "be helpful" when she was foundering with grief. It hurts, but I can see that my help probably would not be welcome. I know for sure that I probably would have rejected any meddling by my own in-laws, had I been widowed when the children were young.

When relationship problems occur, especially with in-laws, it is helpful to remember, "They also grieve." Give them space; try not to judge them. When tempers are in complete control, you might try to discuss what you see as meddling, explaining that you don't want there to be any problems later on.

Looking back, I can see that I committed one unforgivable transgression around my in-laws. In the early months I occasionally spoke ill of the deceased, not in anger but just in being too honest about his shortcomings. I know of few widows who haven't done that while in the throes of grief. I believe it is part of the healing process to bare our souls, reminding those around us that this man was not a saint. I referred to my own brief episodes of forthrightness, relatively early in my mourning process, as "Bruce-bashing." I can see now that, although it may have been a necessary part of my mourning process, hearing those negative words about him must have been extremely painful for his mother and siblings. Try to remember that; perhaps you can learn from my errors. Think how you would feel if someone said negative things to you while you were grieving about your deceased partner, or how it would feel if you were the one grieving about your child or one of your siblings.

I didn't realize this at the time, of course. I considered my comments as innocent, irrational bits of mental lint fluttering out of a rattled brain. I had to trust in the expansiveness of their love to rise above it, and they did. If you think you may have hurt your in-laws in this way, ask them. If they agree that you have, perhaps you can explain to them that such actions are part of a healing stage of grief. Or simply apologize and assure them that you loved their son or brother, warts and all (if, indeed, you did).

I also was bothered by role changes, or changing nomenclature, brought about by Bruce's death. "What am I to his family now?" I asked myself. I am not their daughter-in-law or sister-in-law; I'm just the widow of their late son/brother. It actually took a few years for me to feel comfortable in my new role with most of his family. I care about all of them, probably much more than they realize. Life does, however, interfere. I get way too busy and I forget to stay in touch regularly, and so do they. E-mail is alleviating that a bit. We're all human. Unfortunately, we live far apart and seldom get to see each other. All any of us can do is the best we can do. When we are healing from life's greatest hurt, our best sometimes simply isn't quite good enough.

My inter-family struggles pale in comparison to those where divorce was involved. If either you or he was previously married, and especially when any ex-spouses have remarried, what can I say? It is tough. You not only have to consider his parents and his siblings and their spouses, but maybe an ex-wife, her new husband, maybe their family, plus the impact on your children, and maybe their spouses. This presents lots of chances for misunderstanding, lots of opportunity for familial fireworks! There are no blanket palliatives. You will sometimes have to trust others to hang on until you have more energy and clarity of thinking.

—MEN YOU HAVE KNOWN, MARRIED AND SINGLE—

Several widows said they were surprised that some men they had known for years treated them differently after they were alone. A few others felt confused by new romantic feelings they suddenly felt for men they had known for years. Others spoke of fantasies about men they had never known as anything but their friend's husbands. I have to admit, that in my new life as an unattached woman, I found my whole framework of how to act with men went kaplooey for awhile.

I first became aware of the potential for trouble just weeks after Bruce died, when a good widow friend warned me, "Be sure you never look a guy straight in the eye anymore." At the time I honestly thought this woman had lost her marbles, that she was paranoid. None of our friends would see me any differently, I was sure. Besides, I was more than 55 years old! Who would even care that I was single? But I soon realized she was right.

To some long-time male friends it was apparent that I suddenly had become "a woman," rather than just "a friend" or "a friend's wife." Only one of these men was insensitive enough to express this crudely. It was usually noticeable only in subtle ways, in more tender, but searching looks, or the solicitous way in which they tended to my every need. And then I realized that when I looked directly in the eyes of a few male friends, I got back something more than just innocent, honest response. I had to admit it seemed like I was getting silent "invitations," or responses to what they thought were my silent invitations. Please remember, this was only a few of the men I knew, but it was enough that I had to think about it and learn how to deal with it.

A Florida woman said she was suspicious of comments made by husbands of her friends. "It was clear there was more to their offers of help than immediately met the eye. I was irate when I realized these men suddenly saw me as a sexual challenge." She had all the challenges she could handle, she said. In addition to grieving, she had two children to rear and critical financial needs to meet.

Another reacted with disbelief to an offer from her neighbor's husband. "He shows up at my house one night, all slicked up, asking if I would like him to help me out...*in any way at all?*" She said it was the leer on his face and insinuation in his voice that jolted her into action. "He must have thought I was desperate for sex. I knew his wife was out of town, and it made me madder than hell that he thought he could use me for a little interlude!" She maintained her cool, thanked him politely, then closed the door and locked it. "The kicker," she said, "was that he told his wife how rude I had been to him. That jerk!"

There was a brief time when I blew such reports out of proportion and concluded all men were sex maniacs, and no widow was safe from them. I soon realized, however, that this was unfair. Plenty of guys, both married and single, were sincerely concerned about how I would manage life alone, and they were willing to help in many totally innocent ways. In addition, I soon realized that when I was faced with a husband on the prowl, I could easily control the situation. I think it is safe to say that most (middle-age) widows do not want to encourage sexual attraction with married men, especially if those men are married to their unsuspecting friends. We want, as neatly as possible, to restore a simple, legitimate friendship between us. Once I got this straight in my own mind, my eyes steadied and told their eyes to "forget the fantasies and get back to being friends." I often used humor to change the mood; it's a great stress reliever.

If you are a fairly recent widow, it might save you from falling prey to a man on the prowl, to take my friend's advice for the first year or so. Try to avoid meeting a man's eyes directly, unless you know him like a brother or you are prepared to follow through with what he may interpret as a non-verbal invitation. I decided it was far easier for me to avoid an invitation in the first place than to reject it, explain it away or deal with it.

I think we can agree that not all men are perfect. But, for all their idiosyncrasies, they do make up a large chunk of the population and most of us still enjoy having them around. Most of us would just prefer to avoid any messy interludes, and retain the kind of relationship neither of us will regret later. Let's face it, we widows aren't all perfect either. We, especially newer widows, occasionally have our own fantasies. I admit to engaging in some very early fantasizing as a new widow, about old boyfriends, single neighbors, men I met for the first time.

But, until one of my married women friends began treating me like a pariah, making it clear she thought I was a potential threat to her marriage, I had never given one thought to any of our coupled male friends as being "desirable" or "attractive." Once I sensed her concern, I sat back and reviewed each of the men in my various circles of friends. Could I be attracted to any of them? I didn't think so. Perusing the list, I realized that I had great affection for most of them, but not one tingle of desire. Except…what's this? Much to my chagrin, I found that I could imagine becoming attracted to her husband, if he were available. I did not, nor would I ever, encourage such an attraction; but recognizing it served to increase my awareness of the potential hazards accompanying my new role. I go out of my way now to concentrate on her whenever we are together. I need my friends; I don't wish to make either her or him uncomfortable.

Within a short time of being alone, however, I became extremely conscious of being single when I was around single men. I had known a couple of these men comfortably for many years, but I suddenly felt uneasy with them. The last time I had been a single woman alone in the company of a single man, I was 19 years old. In a few cases, both then and now, I froze up and was struck dumb, unable to think of a single word to say. As a 55-year old widow I had reverted to my old, insecure teenage self.

I often think of a good friend from our church's singles group, who invited me up to his apartment to see his new stereo. "Oh, sure!" I thought. Although I had been single for several years by then, I sat primly on a chair, wound up tighter than a snare drum, scared to death. Now I can laugh at myself and see that there was a whole lot more going on in my imagination than in his. He really was just being nice. [I learned something else of value that day; a lot of men are very impressed with things electronic, and they expect women to share that passion.]

One of the pleasures I had found of becoming 50 plus, was the general social acceptance of women hugging old male friends without any stigma attached. Correction! Make that *"...happily married women hugging old happily married male friends."* During the first few weeks after I first became widowed, I hugged everyone in sight, eager for human touch. Then, I was brought up short by a few nervous glances when I did that, so I decided to limit my hugs to men who initiated them, and then only in the company of their wives. Like I say, I can't afford to lose any good friends.

Some men, instead of pursuing widows, become visibly anxious and shy away from them, especially from those who were wives of their close friends or peers. Some men are uncomfortable being reminded of their own mortality. Their statistics are lousy. Every funeral of a male friend is another grim reminder of those numbers, like another nick in their armor. Bruce admitted that being around new widows caused anxiety for him, although he fought it quite successfully. I guess that's why I could spot it in other male friends after he died. It was as though they were afraid I might be a "carrier of death," that they might catch it from me. You've heard of Typhoid Mary? Sometimes I felt like Grim Reaper Annie.

I learned several lessons about friendships during the early years of widowhood. Some of your trusty old friendships will continue without change, some will change to accommodate your new status and some will fade away. If you pursue your own interests, and take care to be a good friend to others, you will maintain some of your old friends and you will make many new friends.

The key to any of these relationships is, at least partially, up to you. If you show that you like and feel comfortable with people, most will probably like and feel comfortable with you. With any luck, most of your relatives and friends will help rather than hinder your recovery.

14

How Are You Doing? Finding Help If You Need It

Give sorrow words;
The grief that does not speak
Whispers the o'er-fraught heart
And bids it break.

—William Shakespeare

Annie's Journal (10 months)
Dear Bruce: You often said you would be unable to survive losing me, but that I
would do fine without you…because I was much stronger. I've thought about that, a
lot. Some days I feel strong, but then life strips away that strength as if it were only a
mask. I have finally concluded that if surviving IS easier for me, it will be for 3 other
reasons. (1) I have friends with whom I can confide my deep feelings; (2) I recognize
my limits and seek outside help when I need it; and (3) our society allows its women to
show weakness. Most men have no confidantes, they shun outside help and they are
expected to hide their weakness. That would be tough!

"How are you doing?" Have you gotten sick of hearing that? During the first
year or so I must have heard the question a thousand times. And it kept coming,
not just once per person, but nearly every time anyone spoke with me. Every
friend, relative and bare acquaintance seemed compelled to ask. I wanted to
shout, "How the hell do you think I'm doing?" But, as the months passed, and I
began meeting even newer widows than myself, I found myself asking them
exactly the same question. The difference was that I really wanted to know!

That was when I realized that some people really DO want to know, in detail,
while others just want to hear that we are doing fine…without their

223

help…whether we really are or not. If you pay attention you will soon learn to recognize the level of their sincerity, by their tone of voice, their eye contact or lack thereof, and by their posture or body language. Are they inviting a meaningful response by stressing their sincerity and opening themselves to your honest answer? Or are their eyes darting around the room, looking for an escape hatch, in case you start telling them more than they care to hear?

I kept some practiced replies ready to use while I sorted out their level of concern. Depending on my mood, I would answer: "So-so," with an uncertain waggle of my hand. Or, "I have good days and bad days, of course." Or, "Except that I often feel like screaming at the top of my lungs, I'm doing quite well, thank you." I tried not to dismiss their inquiries with a meaningless reply, such as, "I'm fine, how are you?" But neither did I want to belabor my grief if they were not really interested. I tried to let them know that I wasn't slipping through this tragedy unscathed, but they (usually) didn't need to worry too much about me. If they wished more information, they asked for it. And, when they did, I gave it willingly.

So, here you are among widowed friends who truly care. And we really want to know….

—HOW *ARE* YOU DOING?—

Think about that. Have you progressed satisfactorily along the dark road of grief, or have you been hiding your pain, even from yourself, hoping it might just disappear?

While you are subconsciously noodling that question, let me share with you a deep, dark secret. This may come as a shock, even to some people who think they know me pretty well, but—I am shy. I have spent most of my life practicing how not to be, or rather, how to appear not to be. I am way, way less shy than I was in high school, but my veneer of self confidence is pretty wimpy and can evaporate at any time. Maybe some of you have discerned as much, throughout these chapters.

Perhaps because of that shyness, or because I am a true-to-type Virgo, I have always been introspective and analytical. Oh yes, *and* self-critical. I continually take my emotional pulse, asking probing questions of myself to see whether I am on the right track and growing emotionally, or quietly slinking back toward the warm and protective womb, as I am so often tempted to do. So, whenever someone asked me how I was doing, I usually knew. I could tell them in minute detail exactly how I thought I was. However, I had to be careful not to give them a complete book-length answer when all they asked for was a one word answer or, at most, a three by five card's worth.

Few people are as introspective as I am, so my question of you should be: "Do you *know* how you are doing?" Do you think about how you are handling this crisis compared to other widows you know? Do you watch yourself with the critical eye of a stranger, measuring your progress? Do you read articles, pamphlets and books about grieving to see how you measure up? Has anyone indicated you might be grieving too long or too hard? If so, have you thought about that, or sought other opinions? Do you keep a journal, and compare your earlier feelings with how you feel now? Are you surprised at your reaction to grief? Take a few minutes and think about how you feel right now, deep inside where others can't see. Try to answer the following short questions:

- Do you cry and feel sorry for yourself all the time? Occasionally? Never?

- Are you usually laughing on the outside, but crying on the inside?

- Do you keep yourself very busy, so you won't have time to think?

- Do you bury your pain, or do you share it with anyone who will listen?

- Do you notice danger signs in recent journal entries?

- Do you tremble with fear at things that go bump in the night?

- Do you feel that because life will never be the same, it will never be worth living?

- Do you often feel hopeless, helpless?

- Do you just feel blue or are you in depression?

- Do you often feel you have no control over the rest of your life?

- Do you feel guilty about your husband's death?

- Are you extremely angry at him for dying?

- Do you think you are doing remarkably well for such a recent widow?

- Do you feel like you are crumbling under the weight of stress?

- Do you worry that recently you have acted totally irrationally?

Your answers will depend, of course, on how recently you lost your husband, whether you are having a good or bad day, your coping skills, and myriad other factors peculiar to your situation and personality. Keep the list around and ask yourself these questions from time to time. If you don't feel capable of recognizing your own weaknesses, try sharing "the quiz" with another widow. Discussing the questions together may help you see your progress better.

Another thing that helped me was to close my eyes and picture, as clearly as I could, exactly how I had felt at an earlier time…at one week, one month, one year after the death. That was often the only way I could determine whether I had moved forward or backward. I remember that I felt very stressed-out at about nine months, so I tried to recapture the feeling of my first weeks. I was surprised to remember the intensity of the stress I had felt earlier. There had been times those first months that I *knew* I couldn't survive another week of that debilitating tension. My muscles were knotted, my heart raced wildly, and I hurt all over, with what seemed like life-threatening pain. Compared with that time, I realized that I had indeed moved forward. The stress was often terrible at nine months, but it was not anywhere nearly as bad as it had been at nine days or nine weeks. Then I knew that I would probably recover, slowly but surely. Knowing that actually helped reduce the current stress level somewhat.

You will have to expect setbacks occasionally, especially during the first year or two, but if you don't see yourself improving little by little over time, you may need to seek help from someone trained to recognize and help emotional problems. This is no small adjustment you are being asked to make. Welcome support from wherever you can find it.

Karen, a trained nurse, began having anxiety attacks a year after her husband died. His death was one in a string of personal tragedies, and in spite of her incredible effort, her coping mechanism finally reached "overload." After a few months of counseling her attacks subsided. Her quick response helped nip the bud of a growing problem.

Dale, too, reported alarming ailments that led her to seek help. "Waking up in the early morning was terrible," she said. "I often had anxiety and an upset stomach. My counselor and my doctor both helped me solve this problem. I am much better."

I felt great comfort after each of my conversations with a psychologist. He helped me recognize which of my thoughts and behaviors were natural and which indicated problems. He suggested specific exercises to help me wade through the mire. A good psychologist can help relieve a lot of your pain and anxiety. Here are a few more questions to help you analyze how you are doing, if you still aren't sure. If you spot a familiar pattern among the following, or one of them jogs loose an entirely different concern, you, too, might find great relief from discussing the issue with an objective, non-judgmental professional.

- Do you tell others how you miss your wonderful husband, while silently swallowing bitterness about his not-so-perfect private life? Was he guilty of infidelity, abusive behavior, obsessive control, drinking episodes or workaholism, for example, which added stress you don't miss?

- Do you act like a tough survivor or a happy-go-lucky super-widow when you are with others, and then cry like an abandoned baby when you crawl into bed at night?

- Do you feel guilty because you feel utterly relieved to no longer have the everyday stress of power struggles and personality clashes you often had with your mate?

- Do you focus on your spouse's negative behavior and the uncomfortable times you shared, and have trouble remembering the many good times you know you had?

These questions are designed to help you recognize your own level of recovery, but some of us have trouble doing that. If you are displaying obvious craziness, which we all do occasionally, those around you might see that you need help working through your grief. Even if you are concealing problems, and fooling yourself and most others, a close friend or relative who has been watching you like a hawk might perceive a problem long before you do. If someone suggests you seek help, thank them for their concern. Don't become rebellious and defensive. Give it credence. They might be right, and seeking help might provide just the key you have been looking for to help you open another door toward recovery.

There are warning signs that should inspire you to seek help quickly. You really MUST seek help if you suffer any of the following for more than a few days.

- Frequent anxiety attacks that leave you faint, heart-pounding and/or breathless;

- Deep depression that causes you to feel alienated from others, or to consider doing harm to yourself;

- Extensive insomnia or excessive sleeping;

- Unreasonable fear or suspicion of others;

- Severe headaches, abdominal pains or loss of appetite without apparent physical cause;

- Increased use of alcohol, nicotine or other drugs to relieve stress.

Such symptoms can indicate severe problems, or conditions that can become more serious if left untreated. Remember that *to seek help is to be strong, not weak.* Try to think of a professional counselor as an objective friend, whose only purpose is to help you ease your pain.

—WHO CAN HELP?—

There are many different places you can turn for help with your emotional struggles. Which of the following you should choose depends on whether you have a serious long-term problem, a new, critical one in need of urgent care, or you just want to see how you are doing. Your choice also may depend on what is available in your area, how deep your pockets are and the type of help to which you best respond.

Among mental health professionals there are several choices. They will vary in their realm of expertise, level of training and fee schedules. They also will vary greatly by talent and personality. It is most important to find someone with whom you feel totally comfortable and with whom you find it easy to share your intimate thoughts.

Psychiatrists and psychoanalysts usually are the most expensive, because their training is most extensive. They are fully trained physicians who have specialized in—and had experience treating—the mentally and emotionally ill. They treat patients individually and/or within groups. They are the only mental health practitioners who can prescribe drug therapy for depression or other disorders. If you are seeking help for a lifelong problem that seriously affects your ability to grieve properly, for example, this might be your best course of action. However, if your concern is grief, and how to do the work of it, going to a psychiatrist or psychoanalyst might involve much more commitment than you require.

Psychologists do not have to complete regular medical school, but their mental health training may be very similar to that of psychiatrists and psychoanalysts. Their approaches to group and individual therapies also may be similar, although most psychologists are geared toward shorter-term problems and treatments. Their fees are generally considerably lower.

Social workers may follow any number of training patterns following basic undergraduate studies. They are certified to treat people with emotional problems, whether or not they have achieved doctoral degrees. Like others listed above, they can treat patients individually or in groups. Their services usually cost less than psychologists, although their fees vary with their background and training.

Psychotherapists may be licensed in any of several categories, but the title itself may be used by anyone with or without education or training. Psychotherapy is not a licensed practice, and as such can be claimed by almost anyone, sometimes giving the title a bad name. That's unfortunate, because the practice of psychotherapy is of great value in the hands of an educated and trained professional. Just check credentials of anyone listed as a psychotherapist. If they have no license at all, you may want to consider someone else.

Certified professional counselors generally hold masters degrees, having specialized in one of several areas of concern, and they are licensed in much the same way as other mental health professionals. Their fees are usually comparable to social workers. Of particular interest may be those who specialize in grief counseling. But family counselors and women's counselors also can help.

Finding that perfect combination in a therapist can be difficult. Rather than closing your eyes and picking a name out of the yellow pages, ask for a referral from your physician, if he knows you well. Ministers and other religious leaders also might know who would best serve your needs. Ask someone who knows you pretty well for suggestions. If the cost of treatment is a big concern, mention that.

If you function well with self-guided education and cannot afford the services of a therapist, many Internet sites provide self-help programs for grief of all kinds. Try "grief stages," "widowhood," "anger grief," etc., in your search engine window. There also are many dedicated sites (for example: www.coping.org; www.grief-recovery.com; www.widownet.com) that may help you understand what to look for and how to find the help you need. As I have said before, I usually go to www.google.com first and use that as my search engine. It is more selective in what it brings up and it seems to more accurately interpret what I am looking for than other Internet search engines I've tried.

You also can consult the community services listings in your phone directory, your county Mental Health Association, social service agencies operated by your state or by religious organizations, your local Women's Crisis Center, your state's department of health, or one of the professional associations listed in the yellow pages. Make several phone calls. Ask for suggestions, and make notes. Remember, the best therapists may not advertise in the yellow pages, while some of the less respectable, less popular ones may run impressive yellow pages ads.

If you are uncertain about whether you can obtain insurance coverage for such treatment, contact your doctor, health insurance agent, or your company's benefits office. If you already have selected a professional, speak with their account manager. They often know how to approach doctors and insurance companies, and they may help you get coverage, as mine did.

However, if you need help right away, *just get it* and work out the financial details later.

—WHAT WILL PEOPLE THINK IF I GO TO A "SHRINK?"—

Several acquaintances—even a few widows—expressed dismay when I mentioned my visits to a social worker/counselor. Most said they were surprised, because they thought I was doing so beautifully on my own. From some I heard an echo of, "Oh dear, I wish I had known she needed someone to talk with," but more often it sounded like, "Wow! Can she really have been THAT bad?" A flurry of thoughts always tumbled around in my mind before I answered their concerns.

"Did I do too well at concealing my pain from friends?" I'd think. Or, "Maybe I shouldn't have gone to a professional after all." But more often I would wonder why, in this enlightened age, there is still such a stigma attached to getting psychological help. I can't answer that, but I can and did answer my own questions. I went to a counselor on the advice of a bright young physician friend who recommends that ALL widows spend at least two one-hour sessions with a mental health counselor. Having followed his advice, I wholeheartedly agree. Could I have made it without help? Undoubtedly, and most widows do. But I think I recovered more fully and easily than if I had tried to muscle through on my own.

Counselors aren't magicians. They can't wave wands to make our pain go away, but they can clear away some fog so we can better see our way, and they can provide us with tools for handling crises on the path. Aside from the overall support I received from my sessions, which reassured me that I would eventually surface from this morass, I believe that my counselor…

- …helped me see that I was working too hard at appearing strong.

- …gave me tools for tearing down the wall of denial, so I could work on the real pain.

• …encouraged me to use my journal and letters to Bruce as aids in recovery.

• …helped me refine my technique of meditation, for relief of ongoing stress.

When I asked him why I still felt so angry after six or eight months, he said, "Perhaps you buried many little angers over the years to keep the waters smooth, as most wives do. Now they have shaken loose and need to be expressed."

When I asked why I couldn't recall the Bruce I had known who was happy, and the wonderful times we had had together, he said, "Don't you think it hurts less to feel anger, guilt and resentment than to face the pain of all the love and happiness you have lost?" When I nodded, he said, "Those happy memories will come when you are strong enough to face them." And they did.

My widowed friend Virginia, also a trained social worker/counselor, told me the same thing, but in poetic language. "You have to say good-bye before you can say hello again," she said. When I looked confused, she explained. "You have to get rid of your own pain and anger and grief. Then you are free to relive the wonderful parts of life you had together as if he were still alive." She said she felt closer to her late husband after 10 years than she ever had since he died.

When I realize how much help I received in my sessions with a counselor, I wonder again why so many people fear seeking help for emotional distress.

—WHY DO WE NEED HELP?—

If you broke your leg, you wouldn't even consider muddling through the pain and recovery without help from a licensed doctor. You would know she could set it, so it would be straight when it healed. She could prescribe a temporary regimen of medication if the pain was bad and she could suggest exercises as therapy designed to strengthen the weakened muscles.

Losing a spouse is something like having your emotional leg amputated. You might think it compares more with losing all your limbs, than with losing a single leg. But for my purposes, the analogy works. We are still able to function, in many respects, without our leg, or without the loss of our love. But we aren't whole; we hurt all over; every activity has suddenly become more difficult; we can hardly remember being whole; and we need to lean on someone or something until we heal. We need help to get us through the trauma itself and to ensure that when we heal, we heal properly.

To carry the analogy one step further, an amputee that has gone through a period of loss and counseling to deal with it, often emerges emotionally stronger than before. With a little help we widows, with our wounded psyches, can do the same.

I believe we all could profit from external help as we progress from wounded widow to self-sufficient woman. But I know there will be readers who think they don't need any outside help, except perhaps for reading a self-help book such as this. And there will be readers who can point to widowed friends who fought their own battles through grief and emerged without a trace of a scar. It certainly can be done alone; it often is. If you have monitored your own responses and concluded that you really don't need help with anything except legal, financial and nitty-gritty details of your husband's death, so be it.

But there are a good many "recovered" widows who are stumbling through their lives without fully living. Maybe you know some of them. Some have severe sleep problems, gastro-intestinal problems, weight problems or alcohol problems. Others have become prematurely dependent on their children, or they have turned inward and eschew socializing, or they have developed agoraphobia and fear leaving home, or they have become crippled by suspicion and fear. And many others march bravely through the days, head high and smiling, but suffer silent agonies when alone at night.

Professional counseling can help avoid these kinds of lingering problems. In fact, almost all widows will profit by at least two sessions with a counselor. There is no guarantee that all their problems will be solved that easily, although for most that will be sufficient. A good counselor may spot an underlying problem, such as long-held anger or guilt, and recommend further treatment. For a few widows, their grief is just a spark that ignites a smoldering bonfire of long-term emotional problems. Those women may profit even more than the rest of us, by seeking professional counseling; they may become "whole" and "free" by getting rid of long-standing debilitating emotional roadblocks.

Most of us, however, just feel the natural effects of life's number one stress…loss of a spouse, and life's number one tragedy…loss of a love. We may feel we are going crazy, that we are losing our bearings, that we will never feel whole again and that we will never survive the awful pain of loss. Often we widows plod along as best we can, but hurting more than if we shared the load. The best "medicine," I repeat, is to seek at least two sessions with a trained counselor who has a sympathetic ear. Success with a counselor requires complete honesty, though, so make up your mind to go in with a "no holds barred" attitude. Cry on his or her shoulder, dig out those deep questions you have and ask them.

If you are disappointed after your first session, if you feel that you don't "click" together or that you don't trust his or her motives or abilities, cancel further appointments and try to find someone with whom you feel more rapport. Be wary of any psychotherapist or counselor who predicts after the one session that it will take years for him to help you, or one who immediately wants to hospitalize you (unless you are suicidal, drug dependent or out of touch with reality). Trust your instincts. If you don't feel this person is capable and concerned about your best interests, find someone who is. There are scoundrels in counseling as there are in most professions. But most are both ethical and effective.

I sought help only because I had promised my doctor friend that I would, thinking smugly that I had no real need for a counselor. As you read earlier, this counselor was able to help me with problems I didn't even know I had. I feel very lucky to have found, by referral from my internist, such a perceptive and sensitive helper.

When is the best time to get help? If you are just going to get a check-up on how you are doing in your grief work, think about it for a few days. Jot down all your concerns and all the questions you want answered. I made such a list at about nine months and determined to go in soon, although for the wrong reason. I wanted to get my money's worth and get as many questions answered as I could, but I wanted to go in while I was feeling totally "in control." I wanted him to say, "You don't need me. You are doing great!" Then I wanted to pick his brain for this book. He was very helpful and supportive about the book, but he detected my healthy case of denial lingering behind the mask of self-satisfaction. So he proved his worth and helped me much more than I had thought he could.

Dale didn't originally turn to professionals. At six months she joined a grief support group that had been together for about one year. "I eventually dropped out," she said, "and sought individual counseling, because the widows' group was 'a bit too clubby' for me." She had always avoided women's groups, such as sororities, bridge clubs, and country club groups. She found professional counseling more in keeping with her style. "I didn't want to discuss my problems with friends. I needed someone objective to talk with." Her counselor helped her sort out her responsibilities for the house, how to juggle her time between family, herself and the things she wanted to do for fun, "not what someone else wanted me to do or what I felt I should be doing."

Not everyone has the wherewithal (cash in the bank or comprehensive insurance) to take advantage of private counseling or group therapy with a professional practitioner. Pauli was quick to admit that she would have profited from sessions with a caring and perceptive counselor very early in her grief, but she couldn't afford the luxury. "He or she might have helped me work through my pain so I could move forward earlier. And I did seek help later on," she said, "when the children's needs overwhelmed me during their teenage years." In addition to the financial aspect, decades ago seeking help for emotional problems ranked right up there with accusing your boss of sexual harassment. It just wasn't done without mighty good reason, because the fact of it traveled with you forever as if it were a mark of sinful behavior.

Anna also mentioned that counseling for widows and their children was not available or acceptable in the sixties, when her young husband was killed in an auto accident. "Schools, too, gave no thought to my children's sorrow and loss," she said. "Becky, my seven-year-old, went through real trauma her first year without her Dad, and the schools gave us no help. My advice to any young widow with small children is to get counseling as soon as possible."

Especially in these days when we so appreciate the wisdom of "wellness" in our physical health, we should be able to see, as well, the good sense of maintaining wellness in our emotional health.

—OTHER SOURCES OF HELP—

If you agree in theory, but feel you cannot afford the hefty per hour rate of private counseling, or if you are convinced that your needs don't justify the expense, there are other options available. Most states have publicly funded mental health practitioners available for those who need it but can't afford to pay the full price. Look in your state's listings in your local phone book, or ask your physician where you might seek inexpensive help.

Many widows find solace by talking with their pastor, parish priest, rabbi or other spiritual counselor. If you feel squeamish about talking with your own pastor, and would rather speak with a more objective stranger, perhaps you can find a receptive spiritual leader from another congregation. A donation to defray expenses might be in order.

A couple of good friends of mine turned, in desperation, to some pretty far-out practitioners. They looked into witchcraft and palmistry. They contacted psychics and spiritualists; they attended séances in an effort to communicate with their dead husbands. One told me she went to a numerologist, who claims that everything in life is governed by numbers. She was advised to steer clear of a man she was currently dating (which was good advice), and when she found a NEW gentleman friend, she was told he was a "go" because of the numbers (which also was good advice). She and he married; it seems a good match.

Skeptic that I am, I suspect the "numerologist" was able to read her apparent concerns about the first man and her total trust and love with the second one. But what do I know? Some of what she was told reassured her, and she needed that reassurance. Unconventional as her sources seemed to be, they served the purpose of relieving her anxieties so she could move on in her life. If such alternative sources appeal to you, I would be foolish to put you down for it. The only thing I know for sure is that none of us knows anything for sure. Some formerly laughable ideas are now well accepted in the scientific community. Psychics, astrologers and numerologists may also become acceptable one day.

If you have access to a women's crisis center or a senior center, ask if they have counselors available or if they might provide a referral to some kind of grief counselor. Some communities offer information and referral centers for newcomers to the area, and some professional associations also provide the service free of charge. Most internists or family practitioners are too busy to spend the necessary time for extensive therapy, but they usually know what resources are available and at what price. I find they may be a bit too quick to prescribe medication instead of counseling, but you can reject that option if you are pretty sure you don't need drugs. If you do need a prescription, your own physician can choose the proper type and amount for you, and then monitor your progress with regular visits. Of course, warnings about mixing drugs and alcohol should be heeded. Don't risk complicating and exacerbating your weakened condition.

—GRIEF SUPPORT GROUPS—

Pauli sought help from her pastor and her family doctor when Will died and left her with three tiny kids. Unfortunately, decades ago few such people had formal training in grief counseling. "They were as helpful as they knew how to be at the time," she said. "And there were no grief support groups at that time, either. At least in my area." In 1968, after recovering her own sense of balance, she started a group for widows and widowers in Minneapolis, which became a model for several others around the country.

"About 15 years later," Pauli says, "I attended a meeting in Phoenix to discuss starting a widows group there. Imagine my surprise when I learned that it was to be patterned after MY Minneapolis group. I was shocked when I heard the leader talking about me and my efforts to start the original group."

Betty wholeheartedly embraced her grief support group. "The sharing of experiences made me realize that others are dealing with the same feelings and emotions, and we can all help one another through those feelings," she said.

Caroline read a newspaper article about a group for widows and widowers in the newspaper, but the article stayed by her chair for six months before she attended a meeting. She says, "The most important thing I learned from my group was, I am not crazy! Everyone there had the same feelings...and worse."

Regarding grief group dynamics, she said, "After a few years it was interesting to observe that the men usually found someone to marry and dropped out. The women were different. One poor soul, after 17 years of widowhood, was still talking as if her husband was alive. Another, after three years, was still describing in detail her husband's death. She was still in shock and disbelief." She told of another woman, whose husband had been dead for four years, who couldn't leave her home without someone with her. "She started talking in our group, and going out with us," Caroline said. "Now she has remarried and is happy. For most of us, the experience is all positive."

Several Milwaukee area widows who had participated in sessions for "Recently Widowed" run by Lutheran Social Services there, held a mock meeting for my benefit. It worked well. There was real free-wheeling, hair-down kind of sharing. On a questionnaire, I asked them each to what extent they felt they had been helped by their support group. The answers were universally enthusiastic. "Immensely," one said. "Helped me heal!" another said. "Very much," and "100 percent!" others said. One woman summed up what most women feel is the greatest benefit of grief support groups. "I think it helps to talk to others in the same boat, who truly understand."

These particular widows' groups, which start up periodically throughout the year, last for eight weeks. Some groups continue longer on their own, providing social benefits as well as support. They are, for the first eight weeks, led by trained facilitators, most of whom are widowed, and a trained professional serves as consultant in case she is needed. I think that should be one of your criteria when looking for a group. I am told unguided groups often deteriorate or become overwhelmed by a few dominating members. A good leader or facilitator will make sure everyone in the group feels free to contribute at each meeting. Guided groups with a specified duration also avoid the problem of ongoing groups, which must deal with new members appearing at every meeting. Having to introduce and give some background on each member at each meeting stymies the group's progress. When they all know the basics about each other, they are free to delve deeper into concerns and uncover problems.

After about two years, I attended an organizational meeting of widows and widowers near my home in Florida. It brought together an interesting collection of widowed people, but no one was sure what they wanted to get from a group. It was difficult in that most had been widowed for some time. Most of us had become too busy to get involved in the process of establishing a new club, and most were beyond the point where they needed to share fears and to confirm their odd behavior, which is so prevalent in the first year or so of widowhood. I believe some of them ended up forming a loosely knit lunch group of widowed people.

Different groups have different goals and different dynamics. They may concentrate on spiritual needs, on financial decision-making or on learning how to express feelings. Some concentrate on a different issue at each meeting. Sometimes their aims won't match up with your needs. Dale expressed unhappiness with the group she joined after it had been going for more than a year. The other members all knew each other well by then. "This group would get together for dinner, plays, political rallies, etc. Many were angry at their deceased husbands and said so. I wasn't angry, and I lost patience with their husband-bashing," she said. But, for those women, that group seemed to be meeting their needs. If your first experience with a group isn't right for you, try another.

Some widow support groups are organized through the auspices of national organizations, such as THEOS (the Greek word for God and an acronym for "They Help Each Other Spiritually"). According to their literature, a Pittsburgh widow and her minister started this group decades ago. Their focus is educational, emotional and psychological support rather than recreational, financial, legal or medical. The THEOS Foundation also sponsors seminars, workshops, conferences and publications for the widowed. Look also for The AfterLoss Group, Inc., which often works through funeral homes; Hospice, which works with the terminally ill; the YWCA., which offers various support programs; and AARP (American Association of Retired Persons), which helps communities provide widow support groups through their Widowed Persons Service. They also provide other services for widowed persons, such as outreach programs, referral information of local services and public education on the needs of the widowed and what services are available to them.

Churches, synagogues, hospice organizations and local community groups throughout the world offer programs to help new widows and widowers. They vary so widely—in what they attempt to accomplish and what they actually do accomplish—that there is no way to recommend or condemn any of them. Most groups don't scout out participants, but post their meeting time and place in community flyers, on local bulletin boards or in the newspaper. Before picking a group to join, think about what kinds of things you would hope to accomplish there.

- Are you interested in sharing concerns with people who will understand?

- Do you wish to meet other widows for social interaction?

- Would you like to help newer widows over the hurdles you have already crossed?

- Do you want to learn survival skills for living alone?

- Do you want spiritual help, or psychological support?

Larger cities probably have several different type groups from which to choose, and small towns may have one or two, but finding them may require some digging. Some are co-educational, which might appeal to you. Most women I spoke with said they were most helped by the free exchange of thoughts and ideas, and found that "widows only" groups were somewhat more conducive to that. Men and women, they say, either tend to intimidate each other, or fail to mesh because their needs and mental frameworks are so different.

Check your TV, radio or local newspaper's community calendar listings. Call larger area churches to see if they know of any support groups starting. Other possible sources are the local "welcome wagon," or comparable newcomer welcoming group, the YWCA, a women's center or a mental health clinic. *It is best to join a new group, and one with a limited lifespan.* Some begin every eight weeks, for example. Joining one where everyone already knows everyone else can be intimidating and require everyone to repeat their grief stories for you. The ones with limited terms often continue on in a social way after the initial guided exchange of thoughts.

Above all, *check the Internet.* If you don't have access or know how to do so, seek out someone who does. The local librarian can be extremely helpful. I just pulled up tons of information on my computer, by searching for "grief support groups." There is information on national groups and local ones. Go to a search site, type in your city or area, plus "widow support groups," and see what happens. If you wish specific help, use specific words (widow support anger, widowhood stages, new widow anxiety). Click on some of the national links that come up, and/or call the 800 numbers provided, asking if they have any local groups forming in your area. It is comforting to see how many sources are available to widows.

Try the following on your search engine: www.jewishbereavement.com; www.newhope-grief.org; www.coping.org; www.taps.org; www.fortnet.org/WidowNet (a worthwhile and comprehensive site); www.aarp.org/griefandloss/; www.GriefShare.org (Christ-centered support); www.theos.org (spiritual and emotional help); www.AmericanCatholic.org; www.widerhorizons.org; www.compassionatefriends.org. There are dozens of other sites.

If you decide a support group would be right for you, and you don't find anything currently operating in your area, talk with your spiritual leader, or someone at one of the organizations above about starting a new one. You may be surprised to find how many others in your area also are seeking help. If possible, try to get a qualified counselor/facilitator to guide the meetings.

—HELP FROM YOUR FRIENDS OR YOUR SELF—

If you aren't a group-joiner and you prefer to keep your concerns more private, don't be afraid to open up with a really good friend who also has known a wrenching personal trauma. It can be very healing for both of you to have one-on-one, soul-baring discussions with someone who has been there, so to speak. I have clung to some of those talks like they were life preservers and my ship had just sunk. I had always shared my deepest concerns with Bruce. But now, when I most needed a good, non-judgmental listener, a sounding board and a confidante, he was gone. So I relied on the offered shoulders of trusty friends, my caring children and other widows.

I opened up my wounds and dealt with festering problems in almost every stage of my grief. Sometimes your friend needn't even offer feedback, suggestions or opinions. She (or he or they) need only listen, so that you feel completely free to dig and deal with what you find. For the widow who prefers to bull her way through this test on her own, self-help resources abound. During most of our recovery period this is a viable option for the self-directed widow. Some of us learn better on our own. If you are specifically looking for help moving out into the world, university extension offices and local colleges often offer courses designed for "displaced homemakers." This includes all kinds of women who formerly were married and who operated the home plant, instead of developing careers in the marketplace. These courses also may be available as correspondence courses, off-campus.

It takes considerable self-discipline and effort to pursue self-help courses to the extent they can really help. Sometimes it takes more than we widows have. Especially early, our self-starting mechanisms and self-boosters are on the fritz and we are incapable of following through with exercises and readings on our own. If you find helping yourself isn't helping, consider that during those periods you might respond better to more structured help or to working with someone trained in grief therapy. You can return to self-help when your self is less helpless.

In addition to this book, there are other instructional or inspirational books and tapes of the self-help variety on the market, each meeting a different need and written from a different perspective. Many of them are several years old, but they still may be helpful. Hound your libraries and bookstores; ask widow friends, counselors or your pastor if they have any—or know of any—materials that would help you. Some of them stress legalities of widowhood, some stress finances; others are more general. AARP's Widowed Persons Service provides many self-help services and they publish a wide assortment of useful pamphlets and booklets, as do THEOS and others.

Journaling is a great way to discover your hidden thoughts, unleash angers, admit guilt feelings or clarify your thinking. Get yourself a blank book, spiral notebook or blue narrow-lined legal pad, whatever best spurs your creative juices. Set aside a time each day to write in it. I find it helpful to write in my journal right before I turn out the light to go to sleep. Having poured my thoughts out onto the paper, I am free of them and fall asleep more easily.

Whether you are self-directed and proud to find your way alone, or you choose to "get by with a little help from your friends," or you pop for some first-class therapy from the top professional you can afford, find whatever help you can to ease your struggle. Everyone needs help at one time or another and recent widowhood definitely qualifies as one of those times. So seek the type of help with which you feel most comfortable, and know that it isn't shameful to do so. Be proud of yourself for doing something constructive about healing.

ATTENTION: If you detect a serious problem developing, call your doctor or a counselor immediately! It doesn't matter if that happens two weeks, two months or two years after losing your husband, find help when you need it!

PART III
What Next?

Embarking on the Future

The world is round
and the place which may seem like the end
may also be the beginning.

—Ivy Baker Priest

15

How Can You Decide? Gaining Control of Your New Life

Will you, won't you, will you, won't you,
Will you join the dance?

—"Alice's Adventures in Wonderland"
Lewis Carroll

Annie's Journal (16 months)
My friends must think I'm about as decisive as a blob of protoplasm. I can't make the simplest decisions. Or, I should say, with all the decisions I have to make, I can't stand to make any I don't have to make. When someone asks whether I would rather eat at The Crab Trap or Harry T's, I shrug and shake my head. "I don't care," I say. And, believe me, I don't. It's hard enough to decide what to eat when we get there.

Congratulations! You get to make all your own decisions from now on...like it or not.

I always assumed decision-making would be simpler for a single person than for a married one. No need to "waffle" or "accommodate" to keep another person happy. With only one person, you only have to worry about one point of view, one ego, one set of values, etc. There would be no arguments, no resentment about decisions that were made in opposition to your views. You were going to win them all!

Well, chalk up another thing I was wrong about. Even though it may seem difficult for two people to reach a mutually acceptable decision, it is worse trying to reach one alone. You no longer have the benefit of a sounding board. And, you no longer have someone else to blame if the wrong decision is made. I find it intimidating to make decisions now that I know they are all final, rather than "suggestions to be considered." I had always been assertive about defending my position with regard to any decision we made jointly. I was not about to relinquish my right to be heard. I was usually completely sure of myself, right or wrong. Now all decisions are made by Me, Myself and I, and I don't trust any of us. The prospect is paralyzing. It must even be worse for women who always had willingly let their spouses make all the decisions.

Within hours of our husbands' deaths, we are required to make decisions and lots of them. As I mentioned in an earlier chapter, at first we are ensconced in a protective bubble, especially if the death was a shock. And, although we feel removed from reality, we seem to make fairly intelligent decisions at that point. The process becomes harder as reality sinks in and daily life descends on us with a vengeance.

I don't remember the exact occasion, but sometime within the second or third month I was called upon to make an instant decision regarding a major investment. I started to make it flippantly, thinking of the power I now held to determine my own financial future. But, I remember standing there, with my mouth hanging open, thinking, "Whoa Girl, you are going to have to live for a long time with the consequences of whatever decision you make right now." I felt as if I had just moved into the oval office. I suddenly knew what Harry Truman's desk plaque meant, "The buck stops here." It was chilling to realize that the buck stopped with me that day and forever onward.

At times I found the load of responsibility daunting, tiring, depressing. I got so that making every decision was like extracting an impacted tooth. Thank heavens all the "widow wisdom" says, "Don't make a major decision for at least one year. If possible, two." I clung to that adage like it was an impenetrable battle shield. At least I didn't have to deal with the big decisions for awhile! The little ones were bad enough. I got so sick of making even little ones by myself that sometimes I would just quit. I remember shaking my head one day and saying, "I will make no more decisions this week!"

As I gained strength and perspective, I realized that one-year cautious reminder wasn't intended to keep me from deciding which blouse to wear or what book to read. It was a reminder that we widows were likely to need some time before making earthshaking decisions, such as whether to sell the family home or to buy gold rights in Borneo with our insurance proceeds.

Gradually I realized there are various "grades" of decisions. For simplicity's sake, I label them "low," "medium" and "high."

—decisions, DECISIONS, *DECISIONS*—

Low-grade decisions might better be called "choices," so they will be easier to make. With "decisions" you need to go through a process, considering the consequences of each potential decision. With choices, you can just choose. This category includes any decisions for which there are no, or almost no, consequences. For example: whether you choose to wear your blue heels or your black flats probably will have no consequence unless you are the First Lady about to lunch with Mr. Blackstone, who produces the "Ten Best Dressed Ladies" list each year. Whether you choose to vacuum or dust first when cleaning your living room, probably doesn't matter unless you are about to be inspected by someone with a highly sensitive dust detector. And whether you choose to install your toilet paper roll so it rolls from the top or the bottom doesn't matter unless you have absolutely nothing else to worry about.

"Low," no consequence decisions such as these can be made arbitrarily. Pick a card, flip a coin, do whatever as fast as you can, and get rid of it as a problem. Then you can move on to the more challenging decisions.

"Medium" DECISIONS have some consequence, but they probably aren't important in the big scheme of life. It doesn't matter a great deal to your future, your safety, your happiness or the world in general whether you choose to order a super-duper hot fudge sundae or a single scoop of fat-free yogurt, unless you consistently make the same choice. Then it may have a number of consequences, affecting differently your pocketbook, your blood sugar level, your waistline and, possibly, your cholesterol level. Likewise, whether you choose to attend a business meeting or take a walk in the woods probably won't have any lasting significance for you or anyone else, although there may be short-term consequence with regard to how you feel about yourself and how others judge your dependability.

For these kinds of dilemmas, you can spend a minimum amount of time considering exactly what the consequences might be for each of the decision you could make. Depending on the complexity of the issue, you can run through these in your head while driving the car, or you can sit down and commit your thoughts to paper. You probably have employed this method frequently without even realizing it. It really is just a glorification of your mother's oft-given advice…"Stop and think!" she would say. Or, "Look before you leap!" It's good to remind yourself at this time, to exercise caution. While you might feel totally competent and stable, if you are within the first two years or so of widowhood, you are probably less stable than you think. Even knowing that, you can choose to be casual or flippant about these decisions, and then—to dig out another old cliché—you can be prepared to "Live and Learn." There were certainly situations where I lived and learned, but I wish my mother or a book like this had saved me from some of those unpleasant consequences.

Now, on to the biggies, those dreaded high-octane *DECISIONS.* Their outcome probably will make a difference in your life and/or someone else's, now and for some time to come. These are the ones that are likely to keep you tossing and turning and tangling the covers at night. Examples from other widows:

- Should I take a job now in a fast food restaurant at minimum wage, OR keep looking for a job that includes management training?

- Should I move to Hawaii with this chunk of insurance money, OR invest the proceeds for future income?

- Should I remarry this soon (three months) so I won't be alone, OR work through my grief alone for a year or so first?

- Should I spend this $200 on visits with a grief counselor, OR blow it on a fancy new dress and hope it makes me feel happier?

It seemed to me, when I had been a widow for just a year or so, that the answers to those questions were all easy. I would choose the conservative answer to each. But, time, age and experience taught me that there may be extenuating circumstances, which would make the opposite choices more reasonable. For example, in the first case, if you have young children and need the flexibility of an hourly position, it might be better to put off management ideas for the time being. In the second case, if you have inherited $2,000,000 and you have three kids and six grandkids in Hawaii, after a suitable period it certainly might make sense for you to move there. As for remarrying, you may have nursed your husband through a five-year illness, during which time he talked with you and his best friend about how pleased he would be if you two married soon after his death. In the last example, we would have to know whether this was your only disposable $200, how badly you needed counseling and when you last afforded yourself the luxury of a new dress. On that one, I'll have to admit that I almost certainly would vote for the counselor, for myself or for any other widow.

If the problem is critical, and there is no clear answer, how can you go about making the appropriate decision? If you were to try doing so before you were mentally stable enough to do so, you might attempt to use the method we suggested for "low" impact decisions. You could write down your three major problems, each of which needs a yes or no decision. For me that was, in my first months:

Should I sell my Wisconsin house and move to Florida full time? (Or vice versa?)

Should I feel free to "tap into my principle" to make ends meet until I start collecting Social Security in four years?

Should I proceed with remodeling plans for the cottage?

Should I buy a new car this year before this one starts costing me money, or drive this one until it dies a natural death?

Stop here, take out a pencil and paper and write down your three or four big dilemmas. Be sure to formulate the questions so they can be answered yes or no. When you have finished, read on.

Surprise! I am going to make all your decisions for you. #1—No; #2—Yes; #3—No; #4—Yes. Wasn't that easy? Easy, yes, but hardly scientific. And, believe me, you probably wouldn't want to spend the rest of your life with the consequences of such flip answers.

If, instead, you treated the questions like "medium" problems, you would think about the pros and cons for a minute or so and then decide. It might work out that you would be happy with the decisions you made that way, and you certainly would have saved yourself a lot of agony. But that is still pretty risky for decisions affecting your future health, wealth and happiness.

The only reasonable way to answer major lifestyle questions is the painstaking, analytical, time-consuming way of considering the options and possible results of those options. Until your emotions have stabilized, after a year or so, you might be incapable of doing the work necessary to arrive at the best possible decision. The reason every authority reminds us of the old wisdom of waiting is that there are times along that one or two-year road when we feel perfectly qualified to make an instant, intelligent decision. But experience has shown that those sometimes turn out badly. Later decisions, after a year or so for the new widow, generally are better.

Sometimes, not making a decision is making one. Sarah felt unable to make a decision right away, but her family made one for her. They moved her out of the family home and to a new state, near their home, within three months of her husband's death. She adapted there, but she often says that she regretted the quick move, and that the decision was made without her full and careful consideration.

Women with responsibility for children or dependent relatives, were least likely to move from the family home. Pauli waited six years to move away and to make an independent life for herself and her three children. She says that, if anything, she waited too long, being afraid her decision would upset her in-laws.

Although she thinks she "should" have asserted herself sooner, she knows that she did what she could when she could. Ginny waited until her youngest had graduated from high school (nearly eight years) to make a major move, so that her decision wouldn't be too traumatic for her boys. Their move seems to have been successful for all of them. But, that isn't to say that waiting eight years is right for every decision or every widow or every mother.

My mother-in-law was in the process of building her very first new home when her husband died in 1968. She was set to cancel the house deal immediately, but her kids insisted that she go ahead as planned. They showed her how she could do it easily on her income. She lived there, and enjoyed the house, for three decades before her death. My own mother had always wanted to retire to Florida, while my Dad wanted to stay in Wisconsin. After he died she waited the proverbial year or two before moving, to be sure she wasn't overreacting to his death. But, then, she moved with her sister to "Paradise." She swore that she felt better, that she was happier and healthier, there than when she was in Wisconsin. The Sunshine State agreed with her. She had more than a decade of pretty good years there before she died.

Looking through my notes and written survey responses, I found that quite a few widows chose to move to an entirely new location after about three years, as I did. They didn't rush into a move, but they made one as soon as they felt they could decide carefully to do so. Some, such as my sister Joan, moved closer to their children and/or grandchildren, and have enjoyed being a local Grandma. Having never had that option, I sometimes feel green with envy at their chance to live with their extended families nearby, as I did when I was growing up.

Nearly all the widows I know who moved, moved for well-considered reasons. Whatever the justification, they needed to make a new start in a new home in a new town, as if to provide a watershed event whereby to mark their own recovery. They knew they were capable of asserting their independence, and this uprooting experience of moving residences helped in two ways. Making the decision to move, choosing where and when, and following through successfully bolstered their egos. For many, it was their first experience with being in charge of a major lifestyle change. And, having moved to where they were now virtual strangers, most felt free to make innovative choices about how to live, what to do with their lives, whom to seek as friends, etc.

Some moved in spite of a haunting feeling that they were leaving their late husbands behind. They needed to make a break with those ties; moving did that for them. Several women told me they said tearful good-byes to their mates before leaving their long-time homes for the last time. It is possible they needed to feel their husbands weren't looking over their shoulders as they moved off into life as independent women. I do not mean to imply that moving is essential for all women. It certainly is not. But, with regard to decision-making, moving from the home shared with their late husbands, proved to be the most frequent major decision these women made. A change of domicile is usually a radical decision, requiring thoughtful consideration. There are others, though, which may have even more consequences.

Several years ago I watched a middle-aged widow almost leap feet-first into a second marriage within months of her first husband's death. She was like a starry-eyed teenager, madly in love with a widower friend. Thankfully, she postponed the decision long enough that they both realized their union would be a mistake. On the other hand, a young friend of my daughter's, whose husband died about the same time Bruce did, remarried soon after her first year. She is very happy, about her new marriage and their young children. The young adapt more easily.

—MAKING BIG DECISIONS—

Your first big decision to make about any big decision is: Do I really need to make a decision at this time on this subject? If not, and you would rather not, don't. Think about it, but set it aside for now. Decisions often find a way of making themselves, when the time is right. By relieving yourself from the pressure of deciding, your subconscious will be free to work on the problem quietly, while you go about your daily business. It may have the answer for you when you need it. Or the situation may change in such a way that there only can be one answer.

I firmly believe your subconscious is your best ally. But sometimes it isn't easy to trust the mystical powers that be. Recently I had to face the fact that several medium to major decisions would require my direct brain power. I had been waiting and waiting for outside interference, pondering and meditating and doing everything BUT systematically working through to a solution. For months I was convinced that any minute one phone call or one letter would arrive to make all my confusing plans fall into line. So why should I worry about it? But, no help came.

I was in my northern Florida home. I had contracted for a new villa to be built in Ft. Myers, a nine-hour drive to the south. I had made THAT decision fairly easily; and I had no trouble putting my current townhouse on the market. The new place would be done mid-summer. Meanwhile my Wisconsin home sat idle, waiting for me to open it for the summer, plant flowers and make it look lived in. But…questions about the logistics of this move were begging for answers. Some of these were more complicated by my having a dog.

Where do I go when I leave for the summer (Wisconsin or Ft. Myers)?
When do I go (before moving my stuff south or after)?
How do I get wherever I go (drive or fly)?
If I drive, do I go alone or with someone?
Do I move by myself (hauling a trailer or driving a U-Haul) or hire a mover (for such a small amount of stuff)?
If I do drive to Wisconsin, should I drive alone…or provide a one-way flight for my son to fly in from there and drive back with me?

These were not earthshaking decisions, but they were frustrating ones. And, I felt they "should" be making themselves. But, since they were not cooperating, I decided to approach them just like I would tell my readers to do. I wrote out the above questions, and then wrote down every option I could think of for each. I considered all the "what ifs" of each possible choice and finally arrived at what was a swell solution. My son Ric would fly in; we would rent a van and drive to Ft. Myers, where I could close on the new villa and we could move in my stuff. Then we would drive together to Wisconsin by July 1. Terrific! I called Ric, and everyone else concerned, and gave them our itinerary.

And THEN the phone rang! Woops, Ric had to be in Texas by mid-June for a new job. Oooookay. Time to shift to Plan B: I would pick up my Aunt Mary in Clearwater on my way to Ft. Myers and, after settling the new place, we would drive to Wisconsin. I would pay for her flight home after a visit. The phone rang AGAIN! The villa wouldn't be done until late July or early August. Good heavens! Before I could handle that development, the phone rang again! Buyers for my townhouse wanted to close and take occupancy by June 28.

Aha! That settled one thing. I had no place to live until late July. So, after all my time-consuming, rational, methodical decision-making, the darned decisions had ended up making themselves anyway. I would have to go to Wisconsin first. I have gone on far too long about these silly problems, but suffice it to say that it took more than one headachy, sleepless night to make a new set of decisions that would accommodate my new situation. In this case, I would have been better off not making any decisions until the situation clarified itself, but being an impatient type, I intervened and paid for it.

So, while it is true that decisions often end up making themselves, they don't always do so conveniently. When they don't, try to remain calm and approach the problem analytically rather than hysterically. Crying won't help; nor will getting furiously angry or sucking your thumb. I speak from experience. There is only one real lesson to be learned from my frustrations: *no matter how you make decisions, you must try to remain flexible about them. Things change. Learn to go with the flow.*

When it comes time for you to make one of your major decisions, there are several options. One of the best ways is to find a sounding board. Select someone whose judgment you trust, and ask them to help you make a decision. Sometimes vocalizing your options to another person is enough to help you see whether or not a choice is valid. Or that person may see drawbacks you don't, or advantages of a potential decision that you haven't recognized. Sometimes it is easier to make a difficult decision just knowing you have moral support while doing so.

Several widows said they approached decision-making with the help of their late husbands. They asked them, either aloud or silently, what decision they should make. Some got what they felt were answers, and marched through the process easily. Others found it more difficult and settled for working hard to figure out what decision their husbands would make if they were alive. If this works for you, fine. But your entire life has changed since your husband died. What might have been a good choice when he was alive, could be all wrong now. As difficult as it is, you probably will need to make the decision that is best for you and you alone, or you and any dependents. As I mentioned earlier, I generally try to make major decisions by careful analysis with pencil and paper. It doesn't always work, and it can seem like more work than counting the grains of sand on the beach. But, if you are up to it, it is your best shot at coming up with the right answer.

1. At the top of a sheet of paper state your problem as clearly as possible.

2. Label it as Low, Medium or High, with regard to the impact this decision will have on your future. (Presumably it will be fairly high if you are concerned about deciding.)

3. List all your options, the various ways you could solve the problem.

4. List the Pros and Cons of each option.

5. Play "What if…?" with each. What if this happens, or that?

Once a decision surfaces, ask yourself probing questions. "Is this really what I should do?" "Is this what I want to do?" "Is this what my family wants me to do?" (How important is that to you?) "How might I regret this decision?" Finally, ask yourself, "What is the worst thing that could happen if I make this decision?" If that happened, what would you do?

If this exercise doesn't point clearly to a decision that satisfies you, put it away for a time. Your subconscious now has all the information it needs and can work on it without you. If possible, leave yourself an escape hatch with truly big decisions. Rent out your home for a year while you try living in Jamaica, for example. Then, if the island has snared you, sell your home and buy a hut. Move in with your eager widower friend for one year, keeping separate checking accounts, before trotting off to a judge. Whether you call it trial marriage or living in sin, it usually is better than racing into a lifelong commitment when your judgment is likely to be impaired.

If you are still actively grieving, these flip ideas may sound completely off the wall. But, consider them fair warning. Many widows have made rash decisions and lived to regret them. If you are tempted to make a big change, or do something really exciting, it's best to slow down and go through the agonizing exercise above. Give your plan a rigorous barrage of "What ifs." It is ever so much easier to do this before diving in, than after you hit bottom and come up gasping for air.

On the other hand, I was often paralyzed by decisions big and small as a new widow. I was so afraid of making a wrong one that I couldn't make any. If all these cautions intimidate you to the point that you become immobilized, you may be better off listening to the advice of Genevieve Ginsburg, M.S., author of *When You've Become a Widow.* She says that once you have considered the consequences and arrived at a decision, "Just do it!" You can drive yourself crazy trying to make the perfect decision. Try not to do that. At some point, just make a decision—any decision—and go with it. You might feel better if you plan an escape hatch, as I mentioned. How could you get out of the mess, if that's what it turns out to be? Then go ahead, and treat it as a learning experience. If you have never had the opportunity to make decisions and abide by them, diving in might be the only way you will ever learn to swim.

Keep in mind, that most decisions are not cast in stone. It one turns out to be truly wrong for you, after a time, make a better one. Trial and error will eventually work. If you do cast a decision in stone, such as selling the family estate, concentrate on the advantages of that decision and don't let yourself look back in regret. It is only a house, after all. Your life would not be as happy as it had been before, anyway. Move forward, and don't look back. Learn to "Bloom where you are planted."

Decision-making ranks right up there next to loneliness as one of the worst aspects of widowhood, according to many I talked with…and that's seconded by me. I hated it those first months and years. That part has gotten easier as time goes on, though. I guess I have made thousands of decisions alone now; most of which have been at least satisfactory. With experience I have gotten better at it. I usually know when to stop and think, when to jump in blindly. I know pretty much which ones might come back and bite me, which ones can only broaden my experience.

Learning how to make good decisions is a bit like learning to ride a bike. You'll be afraid at first; you might skin your knees a few times, but eventually you will make them easily and automatically. Like riding a bike, though, no matter how adept you become at making decisions, you must remember to pay attention, to watch out for potholes and oncoming traffic.

16

Designing Your New Life: Good Choices Can Help You Heal

Life is the art of drawing sufficient conclusions
from insufficient premises.

—Samuel Butler

Annie's Journal (23 months)
It seems like I just got settled into Door County and I already have to plan my trip back south. It wasn't so bad when there were two of us, but I don't know how much longer I can take this disruptive life alone. Open the house, plant flowers, get the yard trimmed, get the house cleaned inside and out, reacquaint myself with neighbors and friends. Then close it all up, pack the car and move to the other house, open it up, plant flowers, get the house cleaned.... Help!

[If you are too recently widowed even to think about major changes to your life, give yourself a hug and turn to another chapter. A time may come when you will wish to return here for help in making your new life more manageable.]

As a University of Wisconsin journalism major in the '50s, I had to take News-Writing 101, where we all learned the rudiments of writing news stories. "The lead (usually first paragraph) should include answers to the 5 W's and sometimes an H: Who? What? Where? When? Why? And sometimes, How?" Having had that drilled into my head when I was 19 years old, and having continued to write news stories and news releases for most of my adult life, I find myself adhering to this rule in all aspects of my life. This has served me well in many ways, including designing a new life for myself as a single woman.

You can elaborate on these questions as best suits your needs. Just for example, at about two years I formulated these questions to start my quest for a new life.

- **Who?** *(Or whom?) Whom do I want to associate with and cultivate as friends?*

- **What?** *What do I want to do with the rest of my life?*

- **Where?** *Where do I want to live, full-time or part-time?*

- **When?** *When do I want to make a change, if I do?*

- **Why?** *Why do I feel the need for a change? Is this a good reason?*

- **How?** *How can I make a major change (financially, physically and socially) when the time is right?*

My answers changed drastically as I healed. For about two years, inertia locked me into a life very much like I had lived with Bruce, except that I was so terribly alone. When I thought about moving or changing my lifestyle, I usually thought I should stay year-round in Wisconsin. I would dabble in writing and art and concentrate on my wonderful friends. To ease financial burdens, and my feelings of always being displaced, I would sell my Florida place.

Then my fibromyalgia would kick in and remind me that I suffered far less pain and felt more flexible in a warmer climate, so I would flip-flop over to the idea of living all year in the Florida panhandle. I had a great circle of friends and lots to do there. It wasn't until my third summer alone that I worked through my plan and began turning it into reality. I surprised myself, as well as most of my family and friends, by purchasing a new townhouse in Ft. Myers, Florida. It was another two years before I decided WHOM I wanted to cultivate as friends and WHAT I wanted to do with my new life.

I didn't make my decisions in the same order I learned them in school, and you probably won't either. There is no right or wrong order to these factors. Individual circumstances will dictate which, if any, changes you make in your life and when you make them. For lack of any good reason for changing the order, I present them here as learned.

—WHOM DO YOU WISH TO KNOW?—

It may seem quite odd to think about whom you wish to have as friends. Most of us have really stumbled into our friends over the years. We became friends because we "hit it off" when spending time together. We went to school together, lived in the same neighborhood, went to the same church, worked together, served together on committees, played bridge together, worked out at the same gym, or met in any number of ways. In some cases we became friends with women whose husbands worked, or bowled, or went to school with our husbands. We probably didn't think much about it. We had become acquaintances and then friends, when we developed a special rapport with each other.

Why might you want to think about it now? If you still have plenty of friends, who include you as always after you are widowed, and you don't intend to move away from them, you may not need to think about it at all. Just count your blessings. But very often widows find their pool of pals shrinking after they are alone. Couples generally stick with couples, not because they no longer like women who have become widowed, but because they have more in common with other couples than they do with widows. Likewise, you may find that you feel closer to other widows and divorcees, because of the trauma you have shared, than you do to most married women. I'm not suggesting that you begin excluding married women from your life, for heaven's sake, but that you recognize how your circle of acquaintances may change some during your adjustment to being single.

Whether you need to consider whom you want as friends also might be a factor of how you answer the other questions. If you decide to move to a new neighborhood, new city, state or country, you will have an opportunity to influence the makeup of your circle of friends. You may decide to just let it happen naturally, much as it always has. That's fine. It is certainly true that you can't force friendships. But it is also true that your friends will likely evolve from those people who share a locality, an activity or an interest with you. By choosing your locality, activities and interests with that in mind, you will subtly influence your circle of acquaintances…and thus, your friends. It's easy to see that the five Ws and H are often closely aligned.

While licking my wounds from the breakup of a poorly chosen relationship, I spent about six weeks nursing my favorite aunt through her losing battle with breast cancer. This period began on the day of my fifth anniversary of becoming a widow. It was that day that I walked out on a man, who shall remain nameless. Suffice it to say I had almost married my first date as a grown-up, and had almost thrown away everything I had wanted of my new life! This recovery period was trying and sad for me, but the interlude provided me with more free time than I had had for years. Having learned the hard way that big decisions shouldn't be made casually, I knew I needed to spend this time making deliberate decisions about the Who, What, and How of my future.

I had already decided *Where* to live (Ft. Myers), *When* to move (two years before), and *Why* (because I wanted to live in a dependably warm climate, and in a town with greater opportunities). I had selected a townhouse in a golf club community, not necessarily the best decision made for the best reason. I actually told people I wanted to live in a golfing community, just in case I might meet a man and get married. "I want to be sure he'll be gone a lot," I chuckled. I had been partly serious, and that's a pretty lousy reason for picking where to live, but I was pretty happy with my location.

I had learned how to play golf in my early teens, and had played a mediocre game off and on for more than four decades. I thought I might enjoy taking it up seriously, as a way to meet people and become involved. My new neighbors were almost all golfers; many were obsessed with it. I am sure that if I had met a man from there, he would have been gone a lot. But I found, when I started my period of self examination, that 1) my golf game was no better than ever and 2) I wasn't enjoying it. I wasn't even enjoying the walk. Walking 18 holes of golf once or twice a week was far less satisfying to me than walking four miles a day through the woods or on the beach had been in previous neighborhoods. I also realized that I had tired of golf being the only subject of conversation at neighborhood gatherings. I needed more mental stimulation; I needed to feel more useful, and I needed to expand my circle of acquaintances. I wondered how I might salvage my life by making some other changes. What did I want to do? Whom did I want to know? How could I make it happen?

I knew I wanted to write, whatever else I did, but I didn't want to become a hermit writer. That's a real danger for writers. I need people. If I didn't, and I was willing to stay locked away alone in my musty garret, I might be a better and more productive writer. But writing alone is not enough for me. I knew I needed first to determine what kind of people I wanted to get to know. I thought about that a lot, and I suggest you do the same if you will be in a position to make such changes. Even if you stay in your hometown, in your same home, you can—if you wish—influence the make-up of your circle of friends.

The one positive that can come out of widowhood is a new awareness of one's self as a whole person, with special talents, special likes and dislikes, special beliefs and special needs. If this awareness is new to you, it may seem like a wake-up call to change your whole life and everything in it. You may decide to enroll full-time in college or apply for your first real career position or put on your jeans and start marching for peace with others of the same mind. That's fine, but if you aren't totally sure of what you want, it might be better to start with smaller changes. If you sense something missing, you can make a single change in your life that will widen your associations and experiences. For example, if you have gotten into a bridge-playing mode, and you tire of seeing the same people over and over, you might wish for something new. What if you signed up for a computer class at the local college, or went to work part-time at the hospital, or joined an activist group to save the local wetlands? The trick is to know your real self well enough to become involved with people who are more like you.

I'm a liberal, always have been. Can't help it; it's genetic and pervasive. I had a fight with my boyfriend in the fourth grade because I was for Roosevelt and he was for Dewey! (Talk about dating oneself!) As an adult, however, I had become active in politics only during the last month or so before presidential or congressional elections. My self-analysis in 1996 happened to coincide with that presidential election year, so it followed quite naturally that I would volunteer to work with the Democratic Party "for the duration." That single decision set in motion a spiral of activities that still keep my calendar full and keep me in touch with a whole busload of like-minded people, many of whom I now consider friends.

Several of those friends attend the Unitarian Church, which happened to be near my home. Bruce and I had attended a Unitarian Church when our children were in elementary and middle school, but I didn't realize until I began attending services regularly, that it was the perfect religion for me. Unitarians thrive on social activism, which was right up my alley, and members of the congregation are bound only by the credo that people of all faiths, or lack thereof, are worthy of respect. To this day, most of my energy has been directed toward these two institutions, the Democratic Party and the Unitarian Church. The overwhelming majority of my friends belong to one or both groups. I like that. When I feel enraged by what I consider an unfair election, or by gross mistreatment of local minorities, I can vent my pain with nearly all my friends (most of my relatives, too) and know they understand and share those feelings. This sharing of basic values provides a terrific base for lasting friendships. I can guarantee you that conservative Republicans who share their basic values have that same comfortable feeling with each other. It's a terrific tie. If you are by nature political, consider becoming an activist as a way of meeting those with whom you share gut-level issues.

My choices are good for me, because of who I am. *Your* choices should reflect who *you* are. Consider many factors that could help you find compatible friends. Is your faith important to you? Do you find intellectual discussion stimulating? Do you enjoy quiet times? Are you a political animal? Are you most comfortable with people of your own ethnic/national background? Are you happier when working hard or relaxing? Is your job your life? Do you thrive on time spent with children? Do you have a cause that inspires you? What is it that you share with each of your current friends? How easily do you make new friends, if it becomes necessary or desirable to do so?

—WHAT WILL YOU DO?—

What you choose to do with the rest of your life will be influenced by many factors, some beyond your control. Your current and future economic prospects, for example, may make your decision urgent and immediate. Your age and physical health will determine what limitations you must consider. Where you live and what opportunities are available will make a difference. Do you have responsibilities you have to consider, such as dependent children or ailing parents? Your education level or job training might make your decision easier. Do you have a secret ambition you've never talked about? Do you regret never having completed your high school, college undergraduate or graduate degree?

All these, and other factors, must be considered. If you are locked into a career but feel you need something more, consider developing a totally new extracurricular interest. Enroll in a class, learn something new. Help someone who needs help. Work on your physical fitness. Join a group to stop smoking. Go to a lecture series or panel discussions at your local college. Volunteer to work on props for a local playhouse. Try to remember that your choice, whether to try new directions, or to stay on your current course, will partially determine whom you know as well as how you spend your time.

Ask yourself probing questions to help determine which path is suited to the real you:

- *What traits do you most admire in others?* (Loving nature? Personal ambition? Exercise of talent? Generosity? Tireless energy? Concern for others? Ability to lead? Tolerance? Education?)

- *What is your favorite way to spend a few hours?* (Reading a best seller? Digging in the garden? Volunteering at the hospital? Writing poetry? Pumping iron? Playing tennis? Walking? Baby-sitting?)

- *What subject would you like to be an expert in?* (Middle East affairs? Playing the guitar? Rocks and minerals? Designing web pages? Crocheting? Chinese cooking? Learning disabilities? Impressionist artists?)

- *What makes you angry enough to join with others to do something about it?* (Threats to the environment? Cruelty to animals? Poverty? Large class sizes? Drivers who run red lights? Excessive personal wealth? Prejudice? War? Abortion?)

- *What can you do better than anyone you know?* Bake bread? Yodel? Play bridge? Pen calligraphy? Recite Shakespeare? Stitch quilts? Raise money for AIDS treatment? Kayak?

- *What would you want said about you in a newspaper story?* That you have funded a university "chair"? That you helped influence a new law protecting the elderly? That you are the best teacher in your county? That you volunteer as the "reading lady" at the local library? That you made a dent in racism in your community (as I did)? That you helped start new political clubs in your area (as I also did)? Or that you published a heartfelt book on widowhood (as I would have done sooner except for these other interests)?

During my first years as a widow, I didn't have to think about what I wanted to do. I had a mission. I wanted to write and sell this book. Easy enough, right? Wrong. I spent years "almost selling it" to New York editors, but I finally took a hiatus from the book to try living as a woman, rather than just a widowed writer. When I hit the wall with that idea, I leaped headfirst into social activism. I over-did it and hit that wall with a real thud. I have survived, but not without some major setbacks that might have been avoided with more careful planning.

Why do I tell you this? To let you know that life has a way of grabbing your "decisions" and running with them. Be careful making them. Know your limits ahead of time, and try to keep a reasonable rein on your dreams. Try not to let your social conscience or your pig-headedness get you into trouble. Although, when all is said and done, I have to admit that I probably wouldn't change very much. My memories, newspaper articles about me, my self-growth, and my extensive network of diverse friends are rich rewards for my long hours of hard work. With a little hindsight, I guess I only would have paced myself more care-fully and taken better care of my physical health along the way.

It's good to step back once in awhile, and look objectively at yourself and your life. Right now, the process may be especially painful, but as time passes you will notice changes, improvements in your "self." Your life might not be exactly what you had in mind, but are you content with yourself? Are you doing worthwhile things? Are you associating with good people? Are you growing as a person?

—WHERE WILL YOU LIVE?—

When I was noodling my various options of where to live, after two years or so alone, I often felt overwhelmed with guilt. "What an ingrate I must seem, to complain about my split life," I would think. Those who knew I lived in Florida for the winter and in Door County, Wisconsin, for the summer, usually said the same thing. "Wow! You have the best of two worlds." Well, yes, weather-wise I guess I did. But for every such blessing, one must pay a price. On the one hand I felt guilty for feeling restless dissatisfaction; on the other hand I knew I needed to make some decisions that would both inspire my life and ease my pocketbook.

After much analysis, I finally figured out why I was not deliriously happy with my double life. By dividing myself between two communities, I never became an integral part of either. I was not quite a tourist, but neither was I a "full-timer." I was one of the "summer people" in Door County and a "snow bird" in Florida. I missed out on so much social interaction when I was gone that I often felt like an intruder when I returned. In addition, neither house felt like "home." Both places were small and located in popular seasonal resort areas, so they felt more like vacation cottages. These problems never bothered me when Bruce was around to share the load and the life. Maybe they still wouldn't have bothered me, if I were a willing retiree, as so many of my acquaintances were in both places. But I am by nature a very busy person, and probably always will be. I finally realized that I wouldn't be happy until I felt an integral part of a community. Sometime near the end of my second year alone, my nagging thoughts about selling both places and buying one real home took hold. I didn't like feeling like a poor uprooted seedling. I needed to sink my roots somewhere, so I could flourish and grow. At first I worried myself into a stew about which place I should live. The result was never productive, just upsetting. Finally, I sat myself down and gave myself a good lecture.

"Relax," I said to myself. "You have no deadline, and if you are careful with your finances you can hang on another year, if necessary. Just go with the flow." I thought that was a nice sensible lecture, and I hoped my theory that "most decisions have a way of making themselves" would prove true in this case. Although I relaxed as much as I could about it, memories of blizzards, ice storms and slippery roads soon joined with my fibromyalgia to crowd Door County out of the picture as a full-time place to live alone. Florida was nudging itself into first place, but my life's puzzle was still missing a few pieces.

Sometimes I was jealous of my widowed friends who lived in their "hometowns." It seemed to me that being surrounded by familiarity would not only be easier, it would be extremely comforting. However, my parents were no longer living, my four siblings and three children were scattered. In addition, because of having the two homes, we had kept community and church attachments to a minimum. I felt more a woman without a country, than one with two countries. Although I knew I could decide to stay in one or the other of my little homes, and make a concerted effort to build more and better attachments to that community, I wasn't comfortable with that answer. I felt I needed something new, a fresh start, but exactly what that might be eluded me for some time.

There is no way I can actually help you make your decisions. I know that and you know that. But I've found that reading other people's thoughts and questions helps me form my own. The following questions are for just that purpose. Some, or maybe most, may not apply to you in any way. But another might just jiggle loose something that will help.

The hardest part probably will be deciding whether or not to move at all. Or maybe your decision will be whether or not to buy a second home somewhere.

WHETHER TO STAY PUT OR CONSIDER A MOVE

- *Can you afford to stay in your current location? Can you afford to move if you wish?* Like it or not, we each need to be guided in our lifestyle choices by our ability to pay. If money is an issue, respect that and set appropriate guidelines for yourself.

- *Do you have a job you cannot leave? Could you get a similar job, or a better one, where you want to live? Could you improve on the job you have without moving?* Read newspapers from your proposed new hometown; get a feel for the job situation. Could you ask others for recommendations and letters of reference to carry with you?

- *Is your current house or apartment satisfactory? Could it be adapted to better suit you? Can you afford to remodel it to your liking?* If you want to stay in your current home, a few minor changes might make it seem new and more pleasant for you.

- *Is your home just a place to live, or does the family consider it "the family home"? Do you?* It can be tough, for you and the rest of the family, breaking up a long-time family home. It's fine to be sensitive to your family's nostalgia, but if you feel you would profit by a move, and the home isn't meeting your current needs, don't be afraid to assert yourself. If the home provides you with a feeling of security and belonging, and you want to stay, try to stay.

- *Is your current home's location convenient, now that you live alone?* Do you need to move from the country to the city for convenience? Do you need to be within walking distance of shopping and doctors? Would you feel more comfortable living closer to others, in an apartment building, a mobile home park or a condo, than alone in a house?

- *Do you feel safe where you live? How might you feel safer?* Is your neighborhood unsafe, or do you just feel vulnerable because you live alone? Ask someone to help you make the home more secure, if it otherwise meets your needs.

A good many of the widows I know stayed right where they were after their husbands died. They loved their homes and they were surrounded by all they needed to lead the satisfying life they envisioned for themselves. Many of them lived in small towns with extensive and priceless support systems in place. For some, this included extended family, their parents, siblings and/or children and their families. For many, their social lives also were full because they were ensconced in community activities and/or an integral part of a church family. Jeanne, Ginny, Irene, Thelma and others come to mind as widows who thrived on continuing involvement in their community, and healed in the hands of a caring network of friends. A few years ago an exhaustive survey found the one factor most likely to produce longevity was not heredity, exercise, clean air, healthy eating, or climate, but having that strong small-town or neighborhood support network. Knowing that someone cares about you apparently enhances your ability to live a longer, healthier life. That can probably be doubly important to widows.

However, if your decision is to move, you will probably need to consider several issues. What general geographical location might be best for you? What kind of setting might you prefer (urban/rural, neighborhood or complex) for your home? And, finally, what type of domicile would be best (single-family? townhouse? high-rise/low-rise apartment or condo? mobile home?) Even if you already know exactly what you want to do, read on. You may surprise yourself.

CHOOSING A GEOGRAPHICAL LOCATION:

- *Is weather/climate important to where you settle?* Are you physically or emotionally burdened by your current climate/weather? If all else is right about your home, how might you make adjustments to ease that concern?

- *Is it important for you to live near your family? (Parents, siblings or children?) How near?* At first you may think you can't make it in your home alone, or that you just have to get away, or that you must move in with family. If physically and financially possible, let yourself adjust to widowhood before making any major move. As you heal you may find living alone is what you really want.

- *Do you have physical conditions, such as allergies, arthritis, fibromyalgia, etc., which might be helped by moving to a different location?* If you aren't sure, ask your doctor. Some places are thought to be better for some kinds of allergies, but they may encourage other ones. Certain kinds of arthritis and other ailments respond better to certain climates.

- *Do you feel healthier in warm weather or cold weather? Dry or damp?* What are the financial costs related to making a home comfortable for you in various climates?

- *Did you, alone or as a couple, ever dream of living someplace else? Why?* Is that an option for you now?

CHOOSING A SETTING OR NEIGHBORHOOD:

- *Would you prefer to live in a bustling city, small town or out in the country?* If you decide to move to an entirely different location, it might be best to do a test run. Try visiting friends, or renting a place for a few weeks, before making a major commitment.

- *Do you prefer to be in walking distance of shopping, activities, etc.?* If you are willing and able to drive a distance, make note of that. Would you be satisfied having bus or taxi service available?

- *Need you be concerned with the quality and convenience of schools?* This will be a primary consideration if you have children who are now, or soon will be, of school age.

- *Do you wish to live in an area with cultural and/or intellectual stimulation?* If you answer yes, think about how often you might (or do) take advantage of these activities? Can you afford to participate regularly in these activities? Are they an essential part of your life?

- *Do you wish to live near a specific church, synagogue or other place of worship?* It's good to weigh carefully the merits of being near your place of worship. Would you participate more if you were close? Would that be good? What might you be willing to/have to give up for that convenience?

- *How important is it that you live near current friends? Do you make new friends easily?* It's hard to move away from the known, especially friends you have known for years. But if all else indicates a move, don't be afraid to meet new people. Think about ways to meet new friends. You'll find helpful suggestions in chapter 13, "Maintaining Relationships."

CHOOSING A SPECIFIC DOMICILE:

- *Do you thrive on sounds of busyness, or do you feel more comfortable with peace and quiet?* We all have different tolerance levels for noise. Some are stimulated by sound; others are wearied by it. Know your own needs. Can you adjust your home in some way to make the sound level agreeable to you?

- *Do you live alone? Are you physically able to live alone at this time?* Unless you are alone and know you shouldn't be, don't rush into a new situation involving other residents. The grinding pain of living alone as a new widow will ease as you heal, and you may heal more quickly by living alone.

- *If you have others living with you (such as children or aging parents), what kind of home might best meet their needs?* Make lists of your specific needs, conveniences and desires, along with those of each of your dependents. Try to find a compromise solution that meets as many as possible of all those needs. Don't be too selfish, but if you are in charge now, be prepared to be the one that must make this decision.

- *Do you need to move to a complex that can provide progressive care as you may require it?* If there is any chance you will need physical care in the near future, this might be a good time to consider it in your plans. Ask your family for advice on this one, unless you are certain of your needs.

The answer to just one of these questions may be so defining that it will determine exactly where you will live. That will be the end of your dilemma. If it isn't quite that easy, I hope the many questions will prod you toward making a decision that is right for you at this time. Try to remember that very few decisions are cast in stone. They usually can be changed, almost immediately or after some time. However, if you are considering a move that requires a major outlay of funds or a considerable investment of time and effort, do plenty of research and toss the idea around with someone you trust before signing any papers. It can be pretty messy and costly to try to re-sell a home you just bought. If you aren't sure what to do, sleep on it…for a month, six months or more. On the other hand, if all indications are for you to make a move, but you are just fearful to take the first step, consider this question: Might your recovery be helped by the move? Very often it is. A new home, new location, new friends, and a fresh start can boost your spirits and build your self-confidence. If your answers lead you to stay put, however, your recovery may be eased by having less stress to deal with and having the comfort of the known around you.

If I had had this book available as my guide when I was deciding to move, I might have avoided a poor decision. I mentioned earlier that I had chosen my new home and location for the wrong reasons. I did so because at about three years, while I was visiting friends in Ft. Myers, I had—as yet undiagnosed—hyperthyroidism. (Your thyroid is your organ regulator.) With it out of whack, totally hyper as mine was, I became a walking, talking whirling dervish. Thinking, like everything else, was on super-fast speed. My friends still laugh about the day Annie bought a new house in the morning and all the furniture that afternoon. I didn't do too badly, considering, but I'm embarrassed that I didn't think things through better.

—WHEN WILL YOU MAKE A CHANGE?—

It bears repeating that you should not rush into any major changes as a new widow. Unless you have extraordinary reasons, it is recommended that you not consider a move for at least one year, preferably two. Dire financial straits are not uncommon for new widows, though. If such is the case, you will need a wise financial advisor to suggest your best options. If there is a way to postpone a major decision, it is best to do so. Most of us are less than dependable the first several months. We can be impulsive one moment, thinking ourselves more competent than we are (especially if we are suffering from hyperthyroidism). Another day we can be dull-witted, from medication, grief, lack of sleep, shock, etc. For some time, we may be unable to reason or work with numbers. We can't be depended on to make reliable decisions.

Once you have decided to move, it might be tempting to rush right out and put your home on the market to see if it will sell. Let me tell you, that would be a mistake. I know of several friends, mostly couples, who did that and had a firm offer to purchase within hours. Some of those offers included clauses requiring the owners to move out within a few weeks, before they had even decided for certain they wanted to move. Don't "test the waters." Wait until you are certain and then proceed. Ask a realtor for a list of comparable homes sold in your neighborhood to get a ballpark figure. Unless you have a knowledgeable friend or relative to help, I would recommend against selling your home yourself if/when the time comes. A professional realtor can be worth his or her commission to a recent widow. It doesn't hurt to have your own advisor to help when you and the realtor are setting the price and negotiating terms. But, a professional real estate firm can help in myriad ways. Your broker probably would advise you, for example, how to ready your house properly before putting it on the market. They can tell you whether to paint, fix, or replace items before showing it. They can help you settle on the best price. They can advise you in many ways, one probably being that you should be ready to accept the first good offer, or you might never get another.

That having been said, I have had my troubles with realtors. If you aren't careful, they may set an unreasonably low price. They like to sell properties fast, and a low price can do that. When I sold my Door County house, I sent letters to three Door County realtors I liked and respected, and asked them to tell me what price they thought my cottage should be listed for. One of the three suggested a price more than 50 percent higher than the other two did, and much higher than any comparable house in my neighborhood had sold for. She explained why. She could see that waterfront property was suddenly at a premium, and that my place had a particularly appealing shoreline.

I was leery of what to do, but I went with her because I had a hunch she was right. The house sold for the full price within a few weeks. I would be the first to tell you there was an awful lot of luck in that. The person who wanted it didn't have to quibble about price. But I cite the story to show why you shouldn't just accept at face value the first price one realtor suggests. On the other hand, there are realtors who will suggest a higher price just to get the listing, and then expect you to drop it considerably if it doesn't sell right away. It's a tricky business, knowing who to trust and when to trust them. Unless you are pretty sure of yourself, a knowledgeable friend can be a great asset when putting a home on the market.

The "when" of a major decision depends on your specific set of circumstances, of course, but these questions may help you select the best time for you.

- *Do you have school-age children to consider?* It is always best to move children to a new location in the summer, giving them time to adjust and get acquainted before going to a new school. Most children are quite resilient, and can—if they must—adjust to a change in mid-year, but that might be asking too much of a child who has recently lost his or her father. If you must move sooner than you'd like, seek help for your child or children in making the change.

- *Can you wait for winter weather to end?* Moving even a short distance in the winter can be uncomfortable, with bad roads or blustery winds to contend with. Even more difficult can be moving into a strange home alone in the winter. You don't want to find out your furnace needs replacing when it's 10 degrees below zero, and you are in a new area where you don't know a soul nearby.

- *Has it been less than one year? Have you asked others for advice?* Even if you must move quickly, you should rely on help from stable friends or advisors to help make these major decisions.

- *Have you given this decision your full attention and made it carefully?*

- *Does your financial situation dictate that you must make this change now?*

—WHY MAKE A CHANGE?—

For some women a move is critical. One Florida widow told me she felt uncomfortable in her own home, in her town and her social group, after her husband died. She felt it had been HIS home, HIS town; their friends were HIS friends. She was wise enough to see that she would never feel accepted, happy, and content as long as she stayed in that home. After three years she moved just two hours away, but it was enough. She didn't have to try to maintain relationships she was insecure with. She relaxed and made a new life, a new home, with new friends and new organizations. It was only then that her progress in healing became apparent. She is now happily sharing life with a new man.

Each widow will have her own set of concerns, but here is a list of questions, which surfaced in a support group, to help you ferret out your answer:

- Do you feel you need to move away from your husband's "ghost," so you can heal completely?

- Do you feel the need to make a fresh start in a new location, with new friends?

- Is this move designed to alleviate allergies or a painful ailment?

- Have you always wanted to do what you are about to do?

- Will you feel more financially secure in your new setting?

- Do you think your chances of meeting a new man will be better in the new location?

- Will you feel safer in your new location?

Above all, read and answer the following question as honestly as you can:

- *Are you making a decision to change because of this author's influence?* If the answer to that question is even a "Maybe," **STOP!** That is *not* a good reason. I know nothing of your situation, and I am not qualified to tell anyone that they should or should not change their life. Make sure your WHY is honest and sound. Some widows profit by moving; others profit by remaining in their familiar homes. Try very hard to figure out which would be better for you.

After making your decision, take some time before putting it into action. Give it time to either gel or fade away. If you do, after careful reconsideration, decide to make a major change, all 12 million widows in this country wish you well and hope you never regret it.

With regard to where I'd live and homes I would choose, I made pretty good decisions. They have passed many tests in these intervening years. I have never been sorry, even about some real clunkers of ideas. But please remember that I changed, and my plans changed, over a period of several years. Don't be in too big a hurry to uproot yourself from what may be a wonderful, warm and comfortable position. Let life help in your decision-making. My advice is to think about these things, analyze your feelings about each aspect of your life and hang loose.

Slowly but surely my decisions sort of made themselves, fitting my jigsaw puzzle life together piece by piece. I will tell you more about that puzzle in the Epilogue.

17

Men: "Can't live with them" or "Can't live without them"?

To fear love is to fear life,
and those who fear life are already three parts dead.

—Bertrand Russell

Annie's Journal (8 weeks)
For 56 years I believed that one cannot separate sex from love or love from marriage. "You can't have one without the other" as the old song goes. But, I am told now that my grade school "larnin'" has a lot of catching up to do. Seasoned widows advise that the rules have changed. Not only are we likely to find love without marriage, we may be expected to enjoy sex without love OR marriage. That's a lot to consider, when I feel like a 56-year-old born-again virgin.

Men get a chapter all their own, because: 1) I like men; 2) they make up nearly half the world's population, and 3) they often play important roles in our real and fantasy lives. Our decisions about whether to include men as anything "more than friends" in our new lives, are probably more individual and personal than any other choices we make as widows. This chapter is more a compendium of widows' thoughts and experiences than a study of widows and men. It concludes with tips and cautions for the woman interested in dating.

In my written survey and personal interviews of widows of all ages and stages, I found their answers to questions about how they felt about men bewildering. I tried to establish patterns from them, with little success. Answers from those widows who had become involved with new men were especially hard to categorize. They were in different kinds of relationships, they had been widowed anywhere from a few months to 50 years, and they reported vastly different levels of happiness.

Initially I was surprised that so many widows who were alone either seemed indifferent to the subject of men or stated emphatically that they had absolutely no interest in including men in their new lives. It's important to recognize that the majority of these respondents were middle-aged or older, and about half were first or second year widows. Overall, their answers fell into one of the following generalities; the majority of those aged 50 and over fell into category 1 or 2:

- "I simply have no interest in having a man; my life is full without one."

- "I would like having dinner and conversation with a man occasionally."

- "I might enjoy a relationship someday, maybe even living with a man, but no marriage."

- "I hope to fall in love and get married (and have kids), just like in the movies."

What can we assume from these findings? Nothing, I'm afraid. The size of the group was too small, and the survey was conducted without reliable statistical methods. The original written survey was sent to widows on my holiday greeting list, and to widows in my neighborhood or church. Other surveys were distributed at widow support groups and at several For Widows Only! seminars my friend Pauli and I conducted in the mid-90s. At best I could conclude only that these women vary widely in their experiences and in their attitudes regarding men, but that a seemingly disproportionate number of middle age and older widows make it clear they are not in the market for a new man. They aren't shopping because they have little interest in buying.

Could this be because they know they can't find anyone to measure up to the "absolute saints" they remember as their late husbands? That is certainly possible. Others recall with clarity their late spouses' shortcomings and failures, which makes them gun-shy. There is an undeniable correlation between our ages (and prior experience) and our "prerequisites." We widows generally become increasingly picky in our old age. Most of us probably wouldn't settle for a pretty face or for sexual attraction, as we may have the first time around. As soon as I could even contemplate the idea of allowing another man into my life (at age 60), I drew up a list of required attributes that included all of Bruce's finer qualities and all of his many talents but none of his shortcomings. In short, I was probably speaking for the majority of women my age, when I said, "I want a perfect man or none at all."

That being the case, we all had better snuggle up to the idea of a long single life. Even imperfect men are in short supply, and perfect ones exist only in the simplest romance novels. Women know they limit their chances of finding another mate by drawing such unreasonable criteria, but they don't seem to care. In spite of almost universal agreement that they had happy first (or second) marriages, the majority of widows said they were not the slightest bit interested in remarriage. Exceptions to the rule were young widows and gals who had been widowed young and then lived alone for decades.

"So far, I have met almost no single men," Dale said, "but I have made no effort to do so. I am just not that interested. It would be nice to have someone to go to a movie or dinner with on the weekend. Nothing more at this point." She was 70 when widowed and had been alone for three and a half years. Thelma, widowed at the age of 57, said, "I really like men. I miss the sounds of their voices and hearing 'man talk.' I would love to have someone to go out to dinner with and just be friends—and I really miss having someone to dance with." Their comments were typical of many of the women I interviewed who were widowed after having been married for decades.

That was all I wanted, too, for the first four years or so. I had an occasional teary New Year's Eve or birthday before that, when I really longed to be part of a couple. But as one of those women for whom widowhood provided the first experience of living alone, I knew I needed time to prove myself, to grow up if you will. Even though I found living alone difficult those first painful years, I continually amazed myself as I healed and found that I was capable of dealing with most problems by myself. I was in no rush to give that up, and I knew I wouldn't give it up for just any guy.

Betty said, "I would enjoy having lunch or dinner with a man, mainly for a man and woman conversation for a change. I miss male companionship." But when asked about entering a more serious relationship or remarriage, she said, "I am not interested in getting accustomed to someone else's habits. I have become quite independent." "Living alone is not my choice," Jeanne said, "but I say quite honestly, living with anyone other than my husband would be out of the question for me. I loved my husband with all my heart, and a replacement, for me, would be unacceptable." Joan recalls her 35-year marriage in glowing terms, but she has no interest in finding another man with whom to share time or interests.

Listen carefully to what we are hearing: "My marriage was so wonderful that I never want to do that again." Isn't that curious? Don't we usually want to repeat our successes, take a second whirl on the merry-go-round if the first was fun? Believe me, I do not intend to be critical of these widows who shun the idea of remarriage; I hear myself saying almost the same thing. I am simply trying to understand what we really mean when we say it.

One important factor is that our concept of marriage as a social institution in America has taken a radical turn. Let's return to one of my favorite source books, *The Day America Told the Truth,* an exhaustive study of Americans' *real* beliefs during the 1990s by James Patterson and Peter Kim, highly respected writers at J. Walter Thompson Agency in New York. They say:

- *Nearly half of us truly believed there was no reason to ever get married.*

- *The majority of both married men and married women weren't sure why they had gotten married in the first place, and they did not know whether they had done the right thing by getting married.*

- *When asked in absolute confidentiality, only one in three Americans gave love as their primary reason for marrying.*

- *Forty-four percent agreed that most marriages would end in divorce.*

The most common reasons given for the dissolution of a marriage are the same as always. Men and women always have had difficulty communicating with each other; they've had different standards of morality; they have argued about money, the division of household labor, child-rearing, etc.; verbal and physical abuse are not new to this decade, century or millennium.

One big difference now is our attitude about the necessity of marriage between two people who wish to live together. Marriage used to be required, or at least expected, of couples who lived together. It no longer is. The concept of living "happily ever after," once the minister says, "I now pronounce you husband and wife," is still a goal for many couples. Others feel that for various reasons they don't wish to take the altar trip again. Several women who tried both living together and being married, said they think that marriage can put an additional strain on a relationship. Before they were locked in by law, they claim that they treated each other more respectfully and lovingly. Not all agree with that assessment, of course. After her first year of marriage, following decades of widowhood, Pauli said, "Being married is wonderful!...every widow or widower should remarry!"

I am quite sure Anna, who also was widowed for 28 years before her second marriage, would support her view. I confess that I have had to chuckle at both Pauli and Anna, as each struggled to make the adjustment back to wife from independent woman. Decades of independence can't just be ignored. Anna told of accepting a spontaneous invitation to go shopping and have lunch with a friend during the early weeks of her new marriage. When she got home she found several urgent phone messages on her recorder from her new husband, and he called again soon after she walked in. "Where have you been," he asked urgently. As she was telling me about this, her eyes became huge with amazement. She told me, "I just frowned and asked, 'Why?'" After 28 years of not having to "report in," she was completely confused by his concern. To be fair, her husband's first wife, of the same age, had died just months before, and he probably was terrified about losing Anna, too.

Pauli says, "Being married *is* wonderful, but I had a lot of adjustments: moving to a different state; leaving my children and only grandchild; relinquishing my position as head of household. But, probably the most bothersome was remembering to consult Joel regarding the social calendar. Another major step was combining checking accounts! When I did that, I knew I was here to stay." She continued, "My wish for every widow—especially you, Ann—is that at the right time you will meet the right man again, and live happily ever after." To her that meant marriage.

As nearly as I could determine, the less time a woman had been married before being widowed, the more eager she was to remarry. And, the more recently the widow had remarried, the more enthusiastic she was about having done so. In general, these younger widows were far more pro-marriage. What can we deduce from this? We can't prove anything, of course, but we can stir up some trouble by trying to guess at some differences.

- Is it safe to say that the first and second decades of marriage may be remembered more fondly than the third, fourth and fifth decades? That's a definite "maybe," but many who had been married for half a century or more said they had very happy marriages. They just did not want to do it again.

- Do you think younger women want another chance because they feel cheated by having so few years with their mates? That seems reasonable.

- Is it possible younger widows' finances are so limited that they subconsciously long to have a provider again? And older widows, most of whom are more financially secure, don't need help? That might be a contributing factor.

- Do you think young women's sexual needs are more prevalent than those of older widows? That is debatable, and few respondents discussed it, so I won't.

Each woman is different, but each may find tidbits of truth scattered among those suggestions as well as the following. I attribute much of the difference in attitude toward remarriage between (most) younger and (most) older women, to the changes that have occurred within marriage itself. For example:

- Generally speaking, today's younger widows are likely to have entered their marriages on more equal footing with their husbands, because most couples marry later now, and have gained a sense of independence before marriage.

- Especially if both spouses work outside the home, housework and childcare usually are more equitably shared now than they were decades ago. If you doubt that, check out all the dads and kids at playgrounds and grocery stores on Saturday mornings.

- Because of the awareness of divorce statistics and causes in recent years, potential hazards may have been anticipated and bargained about before the couple took the "I do" leap.

- In most of the more recent "enlightened" marriages, a man seldom "lays down the law" to his wife, where that was common years ago. Now the man risks his more independent wife walking out under such circumstances.

- Fewer of today's young women feel they must be subservient to their husbands. Some say this independence raises the divorce rate; others say it prevents the gnawing resentment so common among older wives.

- A lot of couples who married before the rise of feminism had a rough time adjusting to new roles in the 60s and 70s. That was a tough stretch for Bruce and me, although we grew from the challenge and worked it out. For some the battle scars were deep and never quite healed.

Please don't call to argue with me about these assumptions. I have no proof of any, but I do think they are ideas worth considering. For one thing you might get some hints about issues to be resolved ahead of time if you ever do meet a man and want to consider marriage.

Most women seem to like talking with men, laughing with them, being around them. Many just don't want to adapt to one man's needs. And, they don't want to wait on one. It is much more trying, especially for a mature woman, to live with a man than it is to live alone. A friend told me, "With a man, it is constantly necessary to compromise, give in, lose arguments, consider his wishes, keep the peace. After doing that for so many years, some of us just like not having to do it anymore." A recent widow told me, "I like eating what, when and wherever I wish. And I like being able to turn the TV and stereo off or on. My choice." Another said on a survey, "I love being in control of the thermostat and whether the windows are open or closed." As one lady told her support group, "I just like not having the stress of trying to keep two such different people happy." Another one said, "I really like being right all the time." A widow of about 70 said, "I just couldn't give up control of the TV remote, not anymore." Another woman, in her sixties, said, "I am just too old and tired to do it again."

I enjoyed some of those "privileges" of living alone right from day one. However, for brief periods during my first two years I also became obsessed with the idea of getting together with another man. This ran the gamut from just looking differently at male friends to becoming obsessed with the idea that I was destined to marry one particular widower. In retrospect that situation turned out to be humorous, but at the time, there was nothing funny about it. I only reveal my silliness because I suspect this kind of fantasizing may be common to widows. And, this kind of inconsistent thinking is common with widows during their early years alone.

—THE MARRIAGE/HAPPINESS FACTOR—

A major study from three decades ago, which seems to have held up under more recent scrutiny by Susan Faludi and other social critics, is called "the marriage/happiness factor." This exhaustive study concluded that the happiest people in America were married men. Second happiest were *un*married women. Then came *un*married men and, finally, least happy were married women. This finding still causes quite a stir, as I suspect it will here. About the time the study was published, a lot of married women were heard staunchly defending their stay-at-home status and insisting that they were happy with things just as they were. But, the study's findings seem to have been confirmed as time has moved on, by increasing numbers of wives pursuing careers and by an escalating divorce rate.

It's possible that once women realized they could support themselves, they also realized (or admitted) they weren't all that happy with hubby after all. It's also possible that husbands didn't adjust well to the loss of their wives' full-time attention. But, I think this new phenomenon should be good news for newer and future marriages. If women know before marriage that they can earn a decent living and manage their lives alone, their marriages won't be so heavily based on dependence, as they often were in past generations. Probably more will be based on mutual respect and shared interests. And, with today's more egalitarian views, the division of labor on the home front may be more equitable than in years past. That, alone, should ease a lot of marital strife.

Wait a minute; we have a strange dichotomy here. Married women, as a group, are apparently the least happy population sector, but the overwhelming majority of widows said they had been happily married. How can that be? If the study is correct, it must be that most marriages are happier *after the fact*. Otherwise, we could only conclude that men from happy marriages die in greater numbers than men from unhappy marriages do. Actually, just the reverse seems to be true. The Social Security Administration actuarial studies haven't quantified happiness, but they have shown mortality rates for unmarried men greatly exceed those for married men.

Some anti-marriage sentiment among older widows may be due to 1) acceptance of the fact that remarriage is unlikely because of sheer numbers; 2) the realization that they are, for perhaps the first time, in control of their own lives; and/or 3) finding they appreciate the reprieve from constant homemaking. While a widower's home life suddenly becomes far more complicated and overwhelming, a widow's home life often becomes more simple and controllable. Homemaking for one is easier than homemaking for two. It may not be as satisfying but, unless your husband carried a good share of the load, it usually is easier and less time-consuming. Without realizing it, I think this factor played a role in my own hesitancy to rush into another relationship. I liked my reduced workload.

—WHY WIDOWERS REMARRY QUICKLY—

While it is true that many widows, especially those over 50, shun remarriage, widowers don't. Most of them, of all ages, remarry—and fast. Some widows like to think it is because women are stronger, more able to grieve properly and to live alone. A few bitter women said men need someone to do their housework, cooking and laundry AND to keep their beds warm. Fair or not, most women do agree with the old maxim that "women grieve, men replace."

I talked with six widowers, and each assured me they had grieved just as hard or harder than women. Mortality statistics bear this out. Widowers internalize their anguish even more than widows do, and suffer dangerous physical consequences. "It seemed to me," one guy said, "that it would be in my best interests in all ways to find someone with whom I could share the rest of my life. Why suffer if you don't have to?" Another said, "I don't do 'alone' very well. I needed someone to share my pain." And one man admitted that suddenly being faced with all the housework almost did him in. "Just living in our house became a daily ordeal. I never realized how much she did every day. I just couldn't do it all."

I have tried to imagine being a widower, having just lost the woman I loved *and* the person who took care of cooking, shopping, laundry, cleaning and myriad household tasks for me every day. If I was a widower, and I knew that I could choose between learning how to do all the housework alone, or finding another helpmate to love, I would opt for the helpmate. Wouldn't you? There are other reasons that most widowers remarry within a short time. Some have been "window-shopping," which almost all men do. A few others have had new wives selected for them, by their dying wives, which sounds a lot worse than it actually is. I only know of two such cases, both of which have been wildly successful matches. Wives may make wiser choices than bereaved husbands. This must be the ultimate gift of love from a dying spouse.

In widow support groups I often heard discussion of the "casserole brigade" or "pantry parade." This is where the poor, grieving widower receives a continuous supply of home-cooked meals, delivered by women of all ages, each of whom just happened to have gotten her hair done that afternoon. It's like one long line of willing applicants for the job opening. Widowers can apparently just sit back and take their pick from the passing parade. "But, before you put on your marching boots," one salty widow said, "keep in mind that, according to statistics, most 60-year-old men prefer looking at shapely 40-year-old majorettes than portly 60-year-old tuba players, whether we can toss a mean tuna casserole or not." When others nodded, she said, "Be prepared. It's a tough playing field out there."

—REALITY: BITTER PILL, OR FANTASY COME TRUE?—

To all these negative issues, add that most of us quickly discover we are not as captivating as we thought we were. I am reminded of a Milwaukee friend, who was divorced in California and traveled back home with her two young boys by train. "During that long trip home," she said, "I entertained myself by imagining how many and which of my old boyfriends would meet my train, having heard of my recent availability." Not one did. Months later she was still reeling from the continuing silence. Not even a phone call.

Let's be honest. Who among us has not imagined that, if we were suddenly alone, we would be whisked off into the sunset by our secret teenage love, our boss, our tender obstetrician, or that gorgeous hunk driving the UPS truck? I could make a lengthy list of my "fantasy suitors" over the years, especially in my younger years, couldn't you? If yours were like mine, they were no more than fleeting fairy tale princes conjured up to revive a temporarily sagging self image, but they combined to present an image of us always being loved by someone…no matter what happened. That's the way it is in the movies we see, in the books we read. Why wouldn't we expect it to be that way in real life?

Of course, some of you may have such a Cinderella experience. It happens. I know several widows who were suddenly whisked off by their princes. Widows of all ages reestablished youthful relationships at class reunions. I've heard of couples reconnecting through the Internet's people searches. Many of these couples were fairly young, but it happens to seniors, too.

- Some close friends introduced a widow in her 50s to a recent widower of the same age. The two sat up and talked all night long, and decided by morning to get married. And, it worked.

- Another widow, at the age of 78, answered her doorbell to find a man she had known in high school. He was soon a part of her household and, the last I heard, they were having a great time together.

- A good friend of mine was widowed for more than a decade before she summoned up the courage to call the man she had loved before she married, and for whom she had carried a torch ever since. They fell in love all over again.

- In the 1950s, parents split apart a young couple because of religious differences. After both were widowed in the 1990s, they reconnected at a reunion and were joyously married.

Although the majority of single women will not see their daydreams of being rescued come true, some will. And, although most middle-aged or older widows will not remarry, many will. Others will date casually, form attachments, find soul mates, enter into serious relationships, and/or live together as if married. If you are interested in having a man in your life, don't be too cowed by the statistics. The numbers would be formidable indeed, if all single women were actively seeking single men. But, keep in mind that many—if not most—divorced and widowed women say they have little or no interest in attracting men. That leaves all the more men for those who want them.

We each are sculpted by the times in which we've lived, by our family's values, by our religious beliefs, etc. The same situation might have a different effect on each of us. But, it might prove helpful to refresh our memories about some basic differences between men and women, especially in their attitudes about each other.

Probably the most important factor to keep in mind is that men often have a hidden agenda when dealing with women. Several sociological studies say that from puberty on *most* guys think about sex much more often than *most* women do. Men were engineered that way to ensure the continuation of the species, they say. I guess overpopulation hasn't been around long enough for evolution to reflect the lower "need" for sex in men's minds. I've been told that whether they are young, old, married or single, most straight men look at women, and think about having sex with them. They fantasize, they flirt, and with the slightest hint of encouragement, they may assume you want them to pursue you. Another factor to keep in mind is that a lot of men see nothing wrong with promiscuity or infidelity. And, like the "fast" boys of our youth, high-testosterone men of our adulthood often profess eternal love to get short-term sex.

These aren't the only difference between the sexes, of course, but they are the ones most likely to cause headaches for the woman who is suddenly thrust back into the single world. Statistics on these issue vary, but I suggest that you read the words "most men" to mean "the majority of men," which could be as little as 50.1 percent, not necessarily 99.9 percent. Don't let the numbers overwhelm you. But, do be advised.

Why do we need to know this about "most men"? Because, knowledge is power. Keeping these differences in mind, we widows can arm ourselves with a little extra caution around men and possibly avoid ending up in a heap of trouble, if indeed we wish to avoid trouble. I think it is safe to guess that most women would rather avoid unsavory liaisons. I met a few who made no secret of their wishes to participate in casual sex after they had finished grieving. But, most widows "of an age" indicated that they preferred to wait for the whole package, love and faithfulness included, or nothing at all. The danger lies in our vulnerability. In our craving for human touch and emotional connection with another man, we are easy targets for men with other things on their minds. Several widows said they had been seduced into arrangements they later regretted. I am living testimony to that reality. I hope you will profit from my concern.

One long-time widow smiled when she read my earlier declaration against encouraging married men. "Let me know how you feel about that issue in a few years," she said. I laughed, and later repeated her comment to another widowed friend at a party. We laughed together about it, too. But then the subject turned more serious, as we bemoaned the fact that so many of "the good men" are married. It's a fact that becomes blatantly obvious to widows who are interested in finding a man.

Think about your new status regarding married and single men, especially if you have noticed any discomfort around them. Awareness of potential pitfalls can be helpful. But try not to let these experiences negatively affect your relationships with good, honest male friends. To the extent you can, remain relaxed but vigilant. Soon you will recover and feel more at ease with guys, and they will relax and accept you as yourself. The one thing I noticed from my surveys was that when the right man came along, even those widows most determined to live alone, easily made the switch to "coupledom."

—IF YOUR FEELINGS FOR MEN REVIVE—

After several months—or years—of being uncomfortable with the idea of being with another man, many widows recover their primal senses and begin to consider what it might be like to date, to have sex again, to live with or be married to another man. The speed with which this phenomenon occurs depends on our basic personalities, our previous sexual experiences, our marriage relationships, our self images, our reactions to aloneness and our chronological ages, among other things. Sometimes it is triggered by our response to a particular man.

At about eight months into my own grief, a very good friend of Bruce's asked if I was ready to think about dating. He had a recent widower he wanted me to meet. I knew I should feel flattered, but all I felt at first was revulsion. Just the word "date" made my skin crawl. It transported me back to my mostly miserable high school days. The concept of "dating" held mostly fear and trepidation for me when I was young, and it held even less appeal to me as a newly single older woman. This must be a fairly common response. Hugh O'Neill, who writes a column called "Modern Love" for *AARP*, the magazine, suggests in the March/April 2003 issue, that we might calm our nerves by not thinking of it as dating. "You're only looking to see where being around each other leads," he says. I think this is good advice. The word "date" can put us under undue stress.

Several months later I agreed to meet this man briefly, when I stopped in Milwaukee on my way back to Florida. I tried not to think of this as a date. We were just meeting and having dinner with our mutual friends. He turned out to be good-looking, sweet, sensitive and bright, a real "catch." But I knew I wasn't ready for anything more than friendship even then, and he was obviously eager to remarry. Before we could meet again, he got his wish. He was married. He read parts of this book's earliest chapters and commented from a widower's point of view. He made the comment that he felt I jumped too fast to a discussion of remarriage. "What about dating and getting acquainted," he asked. I think he was right about that, but so many widows answered questions about men with their views of remarriage, that it continues to be a problem. It is as if, for many women, their only options are remarriage or remaining alone. They see a date as just the first step.

Only time will tell whether any of us will remarry, of course. I no longer say that I never will, but I "seriously doubt" that I will. As I have mentioned, most widows told me they had no interest in remarriage, which might be called a happy accident. The odds against remarriage seem to be overwhelming, especially for more mature widows. One study states that among adults who are in their 20s and 30s, there are more single men than single women. This is explained by the fact that women generally marry men who are older. On its web site, SOLO for Singles says, "If you want a man in your life at any time, there are some pretty practical reasons for finding this man when you are younger."

They say this phenomenon levels off at about age 40, and from then on, women begin outnumbering men by a greater margin each year. According to the Administration on Aging, in the year 2000, there were 143 women over the age of 60 for every 100 men the same age. For persons 85 and older, the ratio was 245 to 100. They also state that in the year 2000 there were "over four times as many widows (8.5 million) as widowers (2 million)." I have seen these figures repeated in several articles, although the Census Bureau has confirmed that there are 12 million widows, as I have mentioned earlier. It is possible the census counts all living women who have ever been widowed, while other groups count only those who have not remarried. *By definition, widowhood ends with remarriage.*

Those interested in pursuing a relationship, may find that the lack of men is not their major problem. For some it will be the culture shock. A lot has changed since we participated in the mating ritual as teenagers.

—THE TIMES AREN'T WHAT THEY USED TO BE—

It's not just that individual men have changed, or that we women have, although our age and experience certainly have changed us all. The biggest change may have been in what we call "the times." Except within orthodox or fundamentalist religions and cultures, rules and mores are looser now for everyone. How much looser these seem now, than when you were a young woman, depends on how long that has been for you. If you are a 30-year-old widow, you will not be as stunned by social changes as if you are nearly 60, as I was when I first began dating again.

Expectations for a relationship simply aren't what they used to be for most of us. Of course, one might say they never have been. Our parents and grandparents probably scoffed at what we may have thought were "strict guidelines" for setting up liaisons with boys and men years ago. The rules have gradually loosened ever since the Victorian era, but it seems they have become especially lenient in the past two decades. In part, I expect we can blame, or thank, our explosion of technology, which brings television and Internet programming into our homes with all kinds of provocative subject matter.

Younger widows will find it somewhat easier to adjust, having a shorter span of change to deal with since their first dating memories. But, those of us who were reared in the "one foot on the floor" forties and fifties may struggle with our stricter upbringing. Do the old rules <u>ever</u> apply in today's battle of the sexes? Sure they do, if a woman insists on them and finds a reasonable partner willing to go along with them. A recently widowed man, who was faithfully married for decades, may feel just as alienated by the new freer attitudes as widows of the same age. So it's best not to assume that all single men are in tune with these sexually liberated times.

Some of the old rules no longer seem to make sense for fully mature adults. And we will have to admit that some of them didn't work all that well even when we were young. You may remember some of these rules, and not be surprised by what today's singles say are the updated versions.

- Never call a boy on the telephone. *Women are as likely to initiate a call now as are men.*

- Never be forward; wait for him to approach you. *Women often are as forward as men are these days. Many men claim they like knowing of their interest, instead of having to guess.*

- Never kiss a boy on the first date. *Kissing, and more, may be expected on a first date.*

- Never make love until you are married. *Most people now agree that marriage need not be a prerequisite for enjoying sex, although there is a wide range of what's acceptable and when.*

- Never live with a man until you are married. *Many middle aged and older couples opt for enjoying love while rejecting marriage, to avoid complications to their estates, etc.*

Many of you may be unwilling to give up your new independence for just any man. "If it happens, it happens," you say, but you are not pushing it. Some women isolate themselves, and go out of their way to avoid even a remote possibility. It seems they are not even willing to take the chance of being swept off their feet, only to regret it later. In reality, some are simply afraid and feel too far removed from the days of courtship to try again. And, there are other considerations. One older lady, married for several years to her second husband, warned me, "Be careful about remarriage," she said. "I thought I was getting another Prince Charming. But all I really got was another old man to take care of." I almost cried for her, and filed the note in my mental computer.

At one time it was probably thought that marrying any man at all was better than spending the rest of your life alone. Now I think most women find they can lead comfortable, interesting, even exciting lives as single women, provided they are financially secure. They no longer need a man to verify their worth. This is not to say that most of us wouldn't trade in our independence for that absolutely right match. We probably would, especially if we had a reasonably successful marriage before.

At four-and-a-half years I confided in my journal:

It's clear that I probably will spend the rest of my life alone. So, I am going to set some interesting personal goals and try to make my life as exciting and rewarding as possible. If, someday, my Prince Charming strolls by (with his walker?) I might be susceptible to his seduction. But, at least I will have had an independent and satisfying hiatus, done many of the things I've dreamed of doing, rather than just filling in the space between two relationships with man-hunting.

Immediately thereafter, my social life changed drastically. Just one man, one profession of love, and I was consumed with needing to be part of a couple again. When that ended in six months, I dated semi-regularly for a year or more. Then, I got tired of it. I proclaimed to my good friend Bob that I had had it with dating. I was simply not interested in finding a man anymore. "It is too frustrating and too time consuming. I have more important things to do with my life," I said.

I can't remember exactly what those "things" were now, because suddenly Bob and I became a couple, and within weeks we were partners, and house-hunting together. (Yes, living again with someone you love is quite wonderful.)

From my experience and my research I have to tell you, that even if what you really want is to be living with or married to a man, I have always been a firm believer in a maxim by Nathaniel Hawthorne:

> *Happiness is a butterfly, which when pursued is just beyond your grasp…*
> *but, if you will sit down quietly, may alight upon you.*

If that seems a bit too cerebral, how about "*Qué sera, sera*"…"*What will be, will be?*" In retrospect, I believe this helps women avoid disappointment. But, I also can see that women who develop full and interesting lives are, frankly, more appealing to men. So, whether you want a man in your life or not, it would probably be in your best interests to concentrate on making an interesting life for yourself.

—REALISTIC DATING FEARS—

There are more serious concerns about dating than whether you can find a man or whether this man will like you or you will like him. Many mature widows look only for platonic companionship with a man, and many are able to keep that companionship from getting more serious. However, if you are considering dating at all, it is wise to think about some very real concerns present in the dating scene of today that were not as prevalent when you "went out with boys."

DATE RAPE:

With today's more lenient sexual mores, many single men prefer to skip the previews and get right to the main attraction. When they encounter resistance, some become more physically aggressive about their needs, just as they did years ago. Others, however, may resort to date rape drugs, making women more vulnerable to rape than ever before. Sexual predators can secretly add a dose of Rohypnol, or another date rape drug, to a woman's drink, making her a helpless victim. Rape can be committed while the woman is in a drunken haze, sometimes oblivious to the fact she has even had sex. Although younger women probably are most vulnerable to date rape, all single women interested in dating should read the following precautions and be alert to this modern-day danger.

- At parties or in bars, don't accept open drinks of any kind (alcoholic or not) from anyone you don't know well or trust.

- In bars always get your drink directly from the bartender, and watch him carefully.

- Hang onto your drink. Never leave your drink unattended or turn your back on it.

- Limit alcoholic intake, so you can keep your wits about you.

- Avoid party drinks from open punch bowls, pitchers or tubs.

- If you overhear talk of date rape drugs, or if anyone present seems too drunk for what they have consumed, leave the gathering immediately.

HIV/AIDS AND STDs:

My biggest fear in 1995, when I considered serious dating, was the chance of contracting the HIV/AIDS virus. As a faithful, long-married woman, I had felt completely safe; the only "if" being whether my husband had remained faithful to me for 35 years. I had no reason to believe he had not. But, when we re-enter the dating market in this new millennium, we are faced with much uncertainty about our partners. Who has he been with? What precautions has he taken? Has he been tested? Would he be honest with me?

If your date happens to be a recent widower, and he says he was a faithful husband for a decade or more, one might presume he would be a safe sexual partner. But, that is a big and uncertain IF. Authors James Patterson and Peter Kim tell us in *The Day America Told the Truth*, "One in three AIDS carriers we talked to have not told their spouses or lovers." That is scary.

Betsy, a good friend and fellow-widow who works passionately as an AIDS educator/activist in Ft. Myers, says there is only one solution. "Just tell him, 'No condom, no sex.'" She suggests you keep a foil wrapped condom in your purse for such a moment, to avoid the excuse of his not having one. "If his intentions are honorable he should not refuse...and if she offers to help him put it on, there is no better foreplay. A sense of humor always helps," she says. Betsy, who also blows up condoms like balloons during her talks about AIDS, is 79 years old and still as sharp as when she taught high school math.

There is good reason to be concerned about HIV/AIDS, but don't let the scare mongers keep you from enjoying love again. Do your homework and do what you can to protect yourself. Insist on the use of a condom; insist on seeing recent HIV test results. The Internet has tons of information, too much really, but it can be trimmed down to reasonable size. If you aren't accustomed to searching the Internet, get some pointers at your local library. Librarians are usually well-trained to help. For this purpose, you really do not need to know how AIDS is killing millions of men, women and children in Africa. That is an utterly horrendous situation, but save that information for when you are seeking to become involved with a critical social action project.

While you are there, look up information on STDs (sexually transmitted diseases). The consequences may not be fatal, but they often are quite painful and devastating. Find out how to prevent them, recognize symptoms and where to seek treatment.

VIOLENCE:

Life is probably nowhere nearly as dangerous as the news and movies make you believe, but it is probably not as safe as it used to be, either. Women have to be much more careful about being picked up in a bar or at a party, for example. Violence is more commonplace than it was when last we batted our eyelashes. Large cities seem rife with danger; but small towns have it lurking around the corner. I discussed self-protection in an earlier chapter, but dating warrants extra precautions. Some hints:

- Don't go out alone with anyone you have just met, unless someone you trust can vouch for him.

- Insist on public dates during daylight hours, until you are better acquainted.

- Let him know your rules for getting acquainted ahead of time and stick to them.

- At the slightest sign of uncontrollable anger, write him off as a potential suitor.

- Don't give out personal information, such as phone number or address, until you are comfortable.As you may recall, the chapter on safety ended with this warning. It's also appropriate here:

"Don't be scared; be prepared."

FEAR OF PHYSICAL INTIMACY:

In a couple of widow support groups I visited, the subject of sex prompted lively discussion. One woman said, "Just be sure you keep this anonymous, because my children think they were the result of immaculate conceptions." Another said, "My kids are in their late teens, and they think they invented sex. I just let them think so; what does it hurt?" "My kids are nearly 30," another widow said. "I am sure they accept my sexuality intellectually. But they don't want to hear about it or see any evidence of it." Middle-aged women may be aware of changing mores within society and of wider acceptance of what is "natural behavior," but they can't necessarily force such great changes within their own lives. With that in mind, here are two hints that emerged from a good support group of widows in Milwaukee.

- Don't feel you must scrap your own moral code just because so much of society has. Act within your own set of values or those of your embraced religion. To do otherwise may cause you immeasurable guilt and loss of self-esteem.

- On the other hand, don't feel compelled to stand by the rules you followed as a teenager if they no longer seem viable to you. Times and mores have changed, you have changed, and your life has changed.

Some widows fear intimacy simply because they are embarrassed about their mature bodies. Most women (and men) of any age feel uneasy with new sexual encounters. Sex seems very natural with a familiar partner, but it can seem awkward and frightening with a new one. There is no cure for this, but presumably your strong feelings for the man, and his gentle understanding, will nurse you through the awkward period when the time is right.

CON MEN:

Although it seems like a subject for a bedroom farce or an old-fashioned melodrama, there really are con men that prey on the vulnerabilities of widows for their money. In chameleon-like ways, they pose as lawyers, bankers, investment counselors, etc. Their scams are legion. And while reading about them can be amusing, the effects these scams have on their victims can be tragic.

My lawyer-friend, Casey, gave me a strange piece of advice within two weeks of Bruce's death. He knew this was too soon, but because we didn't see each other often, he felt he had better say it while he could. "If you ever become seriously interested in a man," he said, "you check him out and make sure his assets are at least as much as your own." He explained that my estate, while it is not very large from the perspective of living off its income, could sound large to a man who needed money. I have not made a hard and fast rule of only dating men who have more assets than I have, although I think I would be pretty suspicious if a guy began pressuring me to get more serious in a hurry, or sign papers.

I won't name names, but I personally know of two middle-aged divorced men who admitted to me they intentionally moved to Florida for one purpose, "...to find a rich widow to marry." The last I knew, neither had succeeded, and they both seemed to be with women they were helping to support. I only mention that to let you know this isn't just the stuff of Hollywood plots.

I have not had any problems along that line so far, but I have talked with other widows who relate horror stories of losing part or all of their life savings to charming men they "fell in love with." One divorced friend lost every asset she had to a man who professed love and rushed her into marriage. Within three months he had cleaned out her savings to pay his bills. She has not recovered either financially or emotionally from this betrayal by a man she thought she loved.

My favorite motto: "Be Alert; the world needs more Lerts."

—SPECIAL PROBLEMS FOR YOUNG WIDOWS/SINGLE MOMS—

In a discussion of dating, as with other facets of widowhood, the youngest of us experience special problems. There were, at the time of the 2000 census, 425,000 widows under the age of 45. This seemed like a lot to me, considering their youth, but actually their problems are magnified by the fact that there are so few of them. They lack good peer support systems. We older widows tend to forget how terrifying it might have been if we had lost our husbands during our early years of marriage.

Young widows actually may be more interested in dating, and sooner, than older widows, but they face significant barriers. In the earlier stages of grief they feel little rapport with divorced or always single men of their own age. And there are only 166,000 widowers under 45 years of age in the entire country. The likelihood of finding compatible partners who "have been there," who truly empathize with their trauma, is extremely slim. Grief for the young also may be heightened by their lack of financial and emotional preparation for widowhood.

In their desperation to make sense of their hellish situation, it is not uncommon for frantic young widows to slip into brief but passionate sexual encounters while still in the throes of numbing grief. Sex, like crying or screaming, provides brief relief from the intolerable physical tension of early widowhood, but this brief escape often compounds their problems of grief in the long run. Grief counselors and psychologists warn against the hazards of such sexual encounters. But, for those who have gone this route, we want you to know it isn't all that unusual.

If these young widows have children, as so many do, their crazy lives become even more complicated. They may feel so entirely responsible for their children's well being, and feel such concern for their children's grief, that they simply forego their own personal pleasures and their own grief work. Most widows I met who had been widowed when their kids were young said they devoted their lives to their kids and pretty much avoided men until the children were well on their own.

With very careful budgeting, Pauli was able to stay at home the first six years, although she believes now that she and the kids might have been better off if she had worked at least part-time. "I think we all might have been happier," she said.

"I would have had more money for the family, more contact with involved adults, and a stronger self-image." But, as an ultimate solution to the problems of young widowed mothers, she sent along the following message: "Remarry immediately!" Of course, she was saying this in jest, as she admits it took her 28 years before remarrying.

Some very young widows did marry quickly, and soon regretted their decision. One said in her survey, "I can see that I made a bad choice in my hurry to remarry. I did this for the children, but he was nowhere nearly as good a father as their own father had been. I felt stuck in an unpleasant situation for decades."

Often young widowed mothers must work full-time just to make ends meet. By the time they get home, make dinner and do some housework, they can barely find quality time to spend with their kids. They have little or no true leisure time, much less enough energy to go dancing or to the movies with a date. Add to all that, the cost and difficulty of finding baby-sitters. Some of these widows face the complication of having children old enough to balk at being left with a sitter, but still too young to be left alone. Parents Without Partners, and other such groups, schedule events for parents and their children to alleviate some of these problems. This can be a way to meet someone with whom you share a great deal.

The threat of pregnancy is reserved for the young, too, just to further complicate their dating. This may help explain why so many young widows simply forego dating until their children are grown. Having a baby with your husband might have been a major cause for celebration. But conceiving out of wedlock at any age can be devastating. To a young grieving widow, this could add a horrendous burden to her already crushing load. I'm not in the business of advising birth control methods, so I recommend you discuss this with your doctor. Only total abstinence provides 100 percent protection from pregnancy, of course, but your doctor will know how you can best protect yourself so that you can feel more free to date and enter a serious relationship when you are ready.

Children of any age are concerned about their newly single mom seeing a new man. And mom is concerned about how this will affect the kids. If you are a young mother with kids at home, you may agonize for weeks or months about introducing them to a new man in your life. Young widows told me they badgered themselves with questions.

- "Is this relationship serious enough to involve the kids?"

- "How soon do I introduce them?"

- "How do I bring them together?"

- "Would it be better at home or at an event?"

- "Should I have a long talk with them first?"

- "Should I have them talk to him on the phone first?"

- "Should I let them know how nervous I am about them meeting?"

- "How will the kids handle it if things don't work out and another man disappears from their lives?"

These young widows didn't provide answers to all these questions, but one told me, "I considered this a major problem and became physically ill over it." She finally went to a bookstore and read whatever she could get her hands on about this subject. Another young gal, whose husband was killed in a bike accident when she was 24, said, "Sometimes I used the Internet to find answers about dating…and to some of my kid problems, too." She had the best luck with a chat room made up of single parents.

The Internet can be a gold mine, once you learn to search it efficiently. If you have trouble searching, look for "search tips" on your search engine's home page. An even better idea may be to ask your child how to do a good search, if they are as computer savvy as most are these days. Looking together for answers to your questions and theirs may turn out to be a great conversation stimulator. And, if the child is really helping with the search, he or she will feel more involved, more grown up and trusted by you.

—A BRIEF PRIMER ON SEEKING A MAN IN TODAY'S WORLD—

If you're interested in finding a man, go for it. Don't let yourself be influenced by statistics or by what others think or by some of the humor circulating on e-mail. I received one recently, titled "*Understanding Men: (from a woman's perspective)*," a part of which follows.

1. *The nice men are ugly.*

2. *The handsome men are not nice.*

3. *The handsome and nice men are gay.*

4. *The handsome, nice and heterosexual men are married.*

5. *The men who are not so handsome, but are nice men, have no money.*

6. *The men who are not so handsome, but are nice men with money think we are only after their money…. Etc., etc.*

Cute, but not really helpful. If you have decided that the time is right, and you want to meet a nice guy you can talk with, have dinner with, and maybe etc., there are several different ways to proceed. You can be passive, active or aggressive in your search, depending on your nature and your determination. I rely heavily here on contributions by my long-single editor son Eric, who met a fine woman at an organized Singles Party. I also rely on advice from a widowed friend, who met her new husband through a dating service. I call my Eric "Ric," and my friends will be known as "The Smiths."

THE FATE WAIT:

In our fantasies, encouraged by popular magazine articles, we often imagine running into Mr. Right in the most mundane places. Maybe it will be in the organic vegetables section of the supermarket, or while we're strolling the beach at sunset. Maybe we'll be rescued from a deluge by Mr. Right and his big umbrella, or find him reading our favorite book in an easy chair at Barnes and Noble. I used to imagine being seated with "him" for a long airplane flight. This is certainly the method that demands the least effort, and it makes for wonderful daydreams, but finding the right man usually takes a great deal of serious thought and a willingness to spend a lot of time meeting a lot of men.

THE FAMILY/FRIENDS FIX-UP:

I always thought this was the easiest, safest, most popular and most successful way to meet reliable single men. People who care about you would never knowingly introduce you to someone of questionable character. I would have given this method an AAA rating, except for some negative press from my contributors and from one bad personal experience.

The Smiths say, "Don't expect your friends to set you up—they won't. And, if they do, you may wish they hadn't." My own experience was mixed. Several friends tried half-hearted matchmaking attempts when I felt it was too early. When I was ready, three years later, no one had any ideas for me. Later I had one set-up by casual acquaintances, and I nearly made the worst mistake of my life. They were looking for someone who would be good for him, not for me. So, it's a crap shoot, but it's still worth a try. Just use your own good sense; don't put too much stock in other people's choices.

If you decide to go this route, ask if they know of anyone interesting with whom you might have dinner occasionally. That way they won't think they have to choose a lifelong mate for you. If you have any "hot buttons," or absolute requirements, such as smoking, religion or politics, let them know.

PARTICIPATION IN GROUP ACTIVITIES:

Continue participating in any mixed groups you can. Try to keep up your contact with couples, because people who are coupled seem to think everyone should be. Sign up for church or neighborhood-arranged social activities; continue (or begin) singing in the mixed choir or community chorus; offer to stand by as a substitute for mixed softball or bowling leagues, or for mixed doubles bridge. Many activities require equal numbers of men and women, and your offer to fill in when needed should be well received.

The Smiths say, "One must be willing to take a chance and get out into the world, meet a variety of people and enjoy the experience. Some, of course, will not be your 'type' but enjoy them for what and who they are. The effort involves joining ski clubs, golf leagues, tennis clubs, health clubs, bridge groups, alumnae clubs, attending class reunions, going to church, joining church social groups or putting an ad in *Single Life Magazine*. Or you can take a more active role and sign up with a service."

SINGLES SERVICE SIGN-UPS:

According to SOLO for Singles, on the Internet, "In matchmaking services, matchmakers do the choosing. In dating services, members do the choosing." They say matchmaking works more often because a good matchmaker gets feedback and is privy to information most singles don't have. Ric says there are several on the web, such as www.Matchmaker.com. "Here you submit a profile and an optional photo. Then you can search their files using various criteria. This saves a lot of time by pointing out red flags up front—religion, age, children, etc. It is completely anonymous for as long as you like—all e-mail goes through the site until you decide you would like to give out personal information." He warns that some are scams, so do your research. "And, be careful early on," he adds, "about giving out personal information (phone, address), of course."

Matchmakers use feedback from people who have been matched by them to build and fine-tune members' profiles. SOLO say matchmakers can't accept everyone into their pool of candidates, but they try very hard to match up their members. They add the caveat that not all matchmaking services are reliable. "Like everything else, you have to use good judgment."

If you decide you would prefer to make your own choices by going with a dating service, be aware that you will only know ahead of time what the other person wants you to know. In addition, SOLO says dating services always have a few singles, up to 10 percent, who are "hot," and get asked out by everyone. I have a very attractive friend like that. Whenever we go places together, she is like a magnet to men, and I feel like wallpaper. You know the type; they don't even need a service. "There is nothing wrong with that," SOLO says, "…but the rest of us neat people may be overlooked in the 'feeding frenzy' to grab those 10 percent."

The Smiths, who met through a dating service, said, "Dating can be a lot of fun, but it is time consuming." They added that one should be wary of these agencies, as they are costly and may try to levy extra charges that are unnecessary. "And if you are overweight, forget a dating service; most men want women on the slender side. Age can be a disadvantage, so keep a young appearance and outlook and keep your age a secret," they added.

The following hints may help in selecting a reliable service.

- *Up Front Methods:* If they won't tell you prices over the phone, be suspicious. Research shows these firms usually use very aggressive sales tactics and are the most expensive.

- *Reasonable Fees:* If they insist it is important to pay $2,000 for their service, because "you get what you pay for," don't sign the contract. Size of the fee is seldom assurance of service.

- *Reasonable Questions:* Are their profiles designed to help you find a mate or to help get you to sign up? If they make you feel desperate, that this is your "last chance," be wary.

SOLO concludes, "The right matchmaker can help you find someone who is a good fit for you. A dating service can provide you a way to contact a lot of people who are looking for someone to date. *Not doing either leaves you exactly where you are."*

USING THE INTERNET AND WWW:

"A friend met his wife in an Internet chat room," Ric said, but noted downsides. "Most chat rooms quickly degenerate as immature jerks discover them and take over." He says his friends connected quickly enough that, when the chat room went bad, they continued via e-mail. He cautions, "Chat rooms also are notorious for posers—middle-aged men posing as teen girls, etc. Many of the Internet horror stories about abductions and such seem to start in chat rooms. Very risky."

Ric mentioned a few other search methods, such as "personal ads," both print and electronic. "They provide very limited information," he said. "And the writer tells you only what he or she wants to tell you, then usually in such vague terms or clichés as to be useless. (Does anyone *not* like walking on the beach?)" He has not heard of any success stories.

ATTENDING SINGLES EVENTS/CLUBS:

Another popular method for meeting singles is "Singles Parties," sometimes organized via the Internet. "Everyone is there because they are looking for a partner," Ric said. "The one we went to was 'Super Singles,'" (which holds such parties in various cities throughout the country). "It is very structured, with many activities and a strict method of indicating interest. Obviously, this is my favorite method." Nothing succeeds like success. At this particular group's parties, equal numbers of men and women are included. At some others, invitations are open and can result in wide differences. An older friend told me of one singles' dance in Clearwater, Florida, which resulted in something like 1100 women and 15 men.

I met some of the neatest people I have ever known in our church singles group. This resulted in several pleasant dates for me as well. A few singles joined the group from outside the church, but primarily we all shared liberal leanings (religious, political and social). This common ground encouraged deep friendships, and sometimes, more.

Bob and I met here. Enough said? [More in the Epilogue about Bob.] Because Bob was divorced and single for 20 years before I met him, he belonged to several singles groups. He also was a founding member of the Sailing Singles Club in this area, which mixes boating activities with social events for singles. Search your classified ads for singles groups looking for members. Or, get together with a couple of friends and start one that would bring together singles who share your interest. You could start a book discussion group, a "doubles tennis for singles" group, a singles rock-climbing group, a singles gourmet cooking class, or a singles anything else that catches your fancy. Joe, a good friend from four decades ago, became active in a singles golf league in Southwest Florida, which attracted a large group during the warm and wonderful "winter" season there. What would be just right for your interests, for the area where you live, for balanced participation between men and women? Use your imagination. If you don't try, you'll never know.

It is good to try a variety of means, as some work some times and others work at other times. What absolutely will *not* work? Watching TV, reading novels or doing needlepoint at home alone.

The Smiths provided some very good hints for widows looking for partners.

- Do remember that one is quite vulnerable the first couple of years; don't move too quickly into a relationship.

- If you meet someone you enjoy, keep your relationship on a platonic level until you know each other well.

- If you can see that your relationship is getting serious, you will need to know if you are physically comfortable with each other. The strict moral codes of our youth no longer apply and we have much more freedom today.

- Today it is considered perfectly acceptable for an unmarried couple to travel together. A weekend together occasionally is a means of finding out how well you relate to each other on a 24-hour basis.

They sent along a list of attributes to consider when you might become interested in a long-term partnership or marriage, along with some good advice.

- Choose someone with whom you have common ground—level of education, prior happy marriage, social standing, life experiences. Marriage is easier if you don't have to adjust to someone radically different from yourself.

- You and your partner should have similar goals and attitudes. Know the background of, and as much as possible about, your future mate.

- Rule of 60—very important! If you are approaching 60 years of age, do <u>not</u> marry until after you turn 60. If you do, you forfeit all of your deceased spouse's social security benefits.

- Visit your lawyer and have a pre-marital agreement drawn up. This avoids a lot of problems should there ever be a divorce or when one of you dies. It is a way to avoid losing your assets and heirlooms to your spouse's children.

- Don't expect stepchildren to accept you right away, especially if they are young and still dependent on their parent.

- Make an effort to enjoy each other's friends and extended families.

I must add my two cents worth to the Smiths' advice about going slowly. From personal experience I can tell you, it's awfully easy to think you are falling in love, when you have been alone and unhappy for some time. Try to stay away from that L-word, and what it implies, until you are really sure this man is right for you. Living alone can be a lot healthier, more enjoyable and more rewarding than living with the wrong man. Take your time and do your homework.

To end this chapter with a chuckle, I leave you with the poem that ended the humorous e-mail from which I quoted earlier:

> *Men are like a fine wine.*
> *They all start out like grapes,*
> *and it's a woman's job to stomp on them*
> *and keep them in the dark*
> *until they mature into something*
> *you'd like to have dinner with.*

Epilogue: There Is Life after Grief...Even for Widows

Happiness is beneficial for the body,
but it is grief that develops the powers of the mind.

—Marcel Proust

Annie's Journal (21 months and counting)
When someone first suggested that my grief might take as long as two years, I knew they were kidding. On the one hand I thought no one could live through two years of such agony, and on the other hand I doubted it would ever end. At this point, the hole in my life is still so gaping that everything else perches on the edge around it. But, I admit that I can see more sunshine pouring into this hole every day, so it doesn't seem quite so deep and scary. And, I have found all kinds of little compensations for being alone, each of which helps to fill up a bit of the cavernous void.

Update from Annie (Thompson) Estlund:

I mentioned several times that in some ways, for some widows, life might be better after widowhood than it was before. Has it been better for me than it was before?

Well, yes, in some ways it has. But that requires a quick explanation. Life has been better for me, because I am better than I was before. I am more confident; I feel more competent; I have developed several latent talents; I have done important work for my community; I appreciate life more; I appreciate people more; I know myself better and I like myself better. I also know without a single doubt that few, if any, of these changes would have come to pass, to the extent they have, without my going through the pain and struggle of widowhood. Like many women of my era I am more self-actualized because of having gone through the trials of trauma and grief.

If I had known I would experience this dramatic spurt of self-growth, would I have been willing to pay the price? No, I would not...not in a million years. I not only would wish for Bruce to be alive, I also would never willingly put myself through such an ordeal. But, since it turns out that I'm here and he isn't, I think it is quite appropriate to recognize this benefit that has spun off from what was otherwise pure tragedy.

For some widows it may be as simple as gaining a healthy measure of self-respect for having dealt with the rigors of grief and surviving. Others may simply gain a new perspective on life itself, giving their life more focus. Others may take the opportunity to dramatically change their lifestyles, either to more fully use their skills and talents or to more fully enjoy their remaining years. Is that disrespectful? Does that mean your husband was guilty of holding you back? Does it mean you will always be happier alone? No, no and no. It just means that you are alive…alone, but alive! It means you are a capable person; you can make good decisions and you can appreciate positive results.

Rather than nurturing guilt feelings about your new life, it would be better to consider the wisdom of Ralph Waldo Emerson. "Every sweet has its sour; every evil its good," he said. Even from something as horrible as death of a spouse, some good can arise. And the more willing you are to build yourself a better life, the more good will come of it. For those of us who married before establishing ourselves as mature adults, self growth can be easier when we don't have to consider how it will affect our marriage.

I don't know about you, but there were plenty of times during my early grief, that I couldn't imagine I would even survive another day or week, much less months or years! I was pretty sure that I was weaker than the millions of other widows and that I would never be able to summon up the strength, courage and energy it would take to recover. I don't know where that strength, courage and energy came from, but come they did.

I'm also stunned that my life became so full after the first few years that I couldn't find time to finish this book and get it published until now! I had worked very hard on the initial writing of most chapters, so they would be written while my grief was fresh and raw. I reviewed and polished them over the first four years or so. Then I sent those chapters off, with a proposal for the entire book, to a wonderful agent in New York, and I kept myself busy while he saw that it made the rounds.

Meanwhile, at his suggestion, Pauli and I tried to build a nationwide organization called *For Widows Only!* in the mid-90s, to "build a platform" for the book to rest on. We offered a pretty darned good newsletter, workshops and a variety of other services. We helped quite a few widows, but at a big price. Our finances finally yelled, "Uncle!" and we had to fold that ambitious operation. We didn't mind not making a profit, but neither of us could afford to bet our future food bills on its success, and we weren't savvy enough to attract outside funding. Oh, for deeper pockets!

To make a very long, sad story into a very short, sad story, my agent, who believed in this project, tried for two years to sell it. He finally returned my proposal with the following note. "Annie, I have never had a project that came so close so often and didn't sell! Maybe you should try an agent with a fresh approach." Sort of good news-bad news. Actually, the best news is that this book is better now than it would have been then. I've matured as a writer, but more pertinent is that I learned so much about myself and about widowhood in those intervening years. I think you'll profit by that increased knowledge.

Meanwhile, something unforeseen had happened to me, and the book was no longer my entire focus. For a few months I had a new man and a new life. Both projects took a great deal of my time and energy, and I nearly killed myself trying to keep all my balls in the air. My unfinished book simply had to follow the path of the organization of the same name. It had to take a break, so that I could. I had developed Graves Disease, and my hyper-active thyroid had me spinning like a "whirling dervish," to use an old-fashioned term.

Solo again and semi-recovered by January 1997, I accepted a "job." I became a full-time (60-80 hours/week) unpaid Coordinator of Lee County Pulling Together. Members of our church had started this group to fight against our county's designation as "the most segregated metropolitan area in the South," by a population study at the University of Michigan. We (especially I) worked very hard, and although we didn't solve the 300-year-old problem, we did make some differences in Lee County, Florida. By conducting 8 to 10-person study circles throughout the area, we eventually educated more than 2,000 citizens about the problem. We helped in bringing about several policy changes, and we initiated actions that helped to make a difference. Racism is somewhat less prevalent and so is segregated housing. As one member of our Board of Directors assured me, "You're a dent-maker, Annie. You made a dent in a big problem. You should be proud."

I grew exponentially in this job, learning and growing on the run. But after two years, lack of funds and depleted energy took their toll. Once again, I had given more than I had; my zeal had outstripped my wherewithal. I had to leave the organization so I could recover from a recurrence of my Graves Disease. If you just want to get a lot done in a hurry, hyperthyroidism can be very effective.

If you treasure your health, though, it is a killer. I will always have my "bulging eyes," and the glaucoma that apparently resulted from the treatment, to remind myself of that.

But please don't weep for me. Both are under control now, and I feel wonderfully blessed for all I learned about myself, for the incredible and diverse friendships I made, and for what good work we accomplished for the Ft. Myers area.

A bit of my energy during those years was spent enjoying our church's singles' group. We had pool parties, Sunday brunches, a book club, a "pajama party," tourist trips in the area and lots of gab sessions. It was there I became acquainted with Bob. As I tell people now, tongue in cheek, "We *used* to be friends." After about 20 months, that friendship took a dramatic turn. Because I had quit golf, and he had given up blue water cruising, our paths were more nearly parallel. We decided to "try dating." We talked about the possible ramifications of that for several days before we actually went out on a date, but on our second real date, we went house-hunting. We weren't quite as nuts as it sounds. Actually, we did that more as an exercise in getting to know each other than to find a home to buy. But, five months later, we felt we had learned enough about each other and our mutual needs, that we sold our two small homes and bought a larger house together. We still live there.

Our house is on a canal, with direct access to the Caloosahatchee River and the Gulf of Mexico, which is nice since Bob arrived with a big sailboat. We have added a few other vessels now; nothing fancy, but we travel that way when we can. We have been to the Keys, to the Bahamas and, most recently, we completed the Great Circle Route. This is a 5,000-mile trip, mostly on inland waters, from Florida up the East Coast's Intra-Coastal Waterway to New York, up the Hudson River to the Erie Canal, where we ended the first summer's travels. The second year's trip wound up into Canada and through the Trent-Severn Canal, Georgian Bay and the North Channel to Lakes Huron and Michigan, then down various rivers from Chicago to Mobile Bay. After a few days on the Florida Panhandle Intracoastal Waterway, I had to jump ship and come home, so I could nurse this book through to publication. Bob and a friend brought Dutch Treat across the Gulf of Mexico and back to Ft. Myers.

The trip was sometimes wonderful, sometimes boring, sometimes terrifying, sometimes blissful, sometimes aggravating, sometimes delightful. We saw amazing terrain and met wonderful people. I can't say that I had another tremendous spurt of personal growth from this adventure. But I am proud that I have evolved from a total wimp, who got seasick on my first day sail on Bob's boat with the singles club, to a pretty seaworthy first mate, all for the love of my silver-haired captain. I did a lot of the steering, and except for landing us on a rock in a Canadian lake and almost driving us into a stumpy swamp in Mississippi, I did really well.

Sometimes it's hard for me to fully recall my other life, which was lovely and happy, but more sheltered and home-oriented. I guess time marches, or sails, on. Bob and I are busy and happy. My three kids and their families, and Bob's two and their families, are well, busy and happy. Life is good again.

I have tried to tailor this book's message to this maxim: "Pain may be mandatory, but suffering is optional." I first saw that in a *Parade Magazine* interview with actor Nick Nolte in 1992. I have recently seen the maxim attributed to actor Craig T. Nelson and to M. Kathleen Casey. Regardless of who lays claim to it, it strikes me as a terrific attitude when you hurt. I taped it to my refrigerator in 1992 and left it there until *it* fell apart, and I knew that *I* wasn't going to.

But perhaps some explanation is in order. I had always known that most traumas were beyond our control. This became particularly clear while we sat in our family room and watched two glistening skyscrapers, filled with innocent victims, turn to a mound of rubble on September 11, 2001. We were all traumatized; most of us became quite depressed, although quite removed from the actual event. However, even in this very special case, I believe that these surviving spouses, mostly young brides and mothers, probably could recover more quickly once they could exercise some control over their reaction to their trauma. A sense of personal control helps us all in these seemingly helpless situations.

In the loss of a husband to death, *I could never say that you could avoid pain or even that you could avoid suffering.* But I believe each of us can decide whether we will (1) deal with our grief and then prepare to get on with our new life, or (2) choose to make suffering itself our new way of life.

Although some days it seems that our suffering will never end, most of us in this book have chosen path one. We hope you will, too.

Our message to you: *Don't be afraid to grieve; but as time goes on, don't be afraid to live.*

◆   ◆   ◆

"Quilt of My Life"
by Annie Estlund

It took 55 years
to design, piece and stitch
the quilt of my life into
an intricate "Wedding Ring" design.

Then one morning, in only seconds,
the quilt fell apart in my hands,
leaving only frayed bits of fabric
and broken threads.

I now toil 'round the clock
to fashion a new quilt,
working pieces both old and new
into a "Lone Star" design.

It won't look the same,
its strength is untested,
but it comforts me as I carry on
with the second half of my life.

◆   ◆   ◆

I promised Pauli that I would help her construct an update of her life for you. You may feel you know my good friend well by now, as she has been with us for the entire journey. She has played a big role in this project from day one, and she continues to be an inspiration to me.

Pauli (Shelden) Jensen Friedmann:

Pauli and I became fast friends while attending Cottey College in Nevada, Missouri. After graduation from this two-year women's college in 1955, I went back to Wisconsin, attended journalism school in Madison, met and married Bruce, and we had three kids by early 1960.

Pauli, the more independent one of us, flew off to become a glamorous airline stewardess for Pan Am. I was so jealous, but she apparently also was a little jealous of what I had. She came to visit us just before our third child was born. While she was there, she asked me what to do about a date for the weekend after she was to fly back to Minneapolis. Before arriving in Wisconsin, she had met a great guy there and had accepted a date with him for the weekend. But she already had a standing date with Joel, a young man she had been dating for some time.

The ultimate romantic, I suggested she go out with the new guy, Will. "You can always go out with Joel another time," I said. She took my advice, dated Will, married him the next year and they had three kids. Unfortunately, her story took a devastating turn. She and her precious Will learned that he was dying of cancer just days before their youngest child, Erik, was born. It was during her difficult recovery that we first began planning to write a widowhood book together. After 28 very difficult years alone, Pauli reconnected with Joel. They were happily married for a decade before the ultimate horror. Joel died suddenly of a heart attack, in much the same way my Bruce died. Pauli was a widow again.

After about one year into her new grief, I asked her to jot down random thoughts about her second widowhood. How was it different; how was it the same? What has helped her the most? Did she have any regrets about remarrying? Here are some of her thoughts.

"My kids finally had the dad they had always longed for. Erik, 38, cried when I called to tell him the horrible news of Joel's heart attack and death. 'Mom, Joel is the only daddy I've ever known,' he said. My three loved Joel and often sought his advice. They even helped him give a huge birthday party for my 60th birthday. My grandson and granddaughter also loved 'Grandpa Joel.' We were a real family again, and our family now included Joel's two adult children, their spouses and now, 5 little grandsons.

"Joel died 8 days after our 10th wedding anniversary. At some point during our marriage I made him promise me that I could die first; because I knew I couldn't go through this grieving process again. Well, we don't always make those decisions. I do know for sure that we are given the strength to do what we have to do. I learned that from my first experience. What has gotten me through it all, more than anything, is this little prayer. It has helped me so many, many times these many years.

> *Oh, do not pray for easier lives*
> *Pray to be stronger (wo)men.*
> *Do not pray for tasks equal to your powers,*
> *Pray for powers equal to your tasks.*
> *Then the doing of your work shall be no miracle,*
> *But you shall be the miracle.*
> *Every day you shall wonder at yourself,*
> *At the richness of the life that has come to you*
> *By the grace of God.*

"I THINK this emotional roller coaster is slowing…and some days I think I have a firm grip on everything. And then other days I think I've crashed and burned! How could I have survived this past year without the tremendous support from my family, synagogue family, physician, close friends and neighbors? Because none of my immediate family lives here, I have welcomed these many kindnesses. Also regular long distance phone calls from family and long-time friends have helped tremendously (including you, Ann!).

"Soon after Joel's death my physician, at my request, referred me to a counselor. I really didn't think I needed help, but my common sense told me it was a good idea. It was! Having someone to talk with who was not emotionally involved really helped me.

"And I've followed through on one of my favorite suggestions to new widows: Never decline an invitation to lunch, a movie or dinner. If you do you may not get a second invite. If you must say no for a reason other than not 'feeling like going,' make a date right then and write it on your calendar. Thus, I've had lots of breaks from the tedious job of going through a lifetime of Joel's papers, pictures and assorted treasures.

"I plan to remain in this college town we liked so much, in the comfortable home we made together. We enjoyed every opportunity to entertain friends for a Fourth of July barbecue, Passover Seder, or a last minute potluck. Not having family here has advantages. I have places to visit—Hawaii, Phoenix, or the San Joaquin Valley in California. I will continue my volunteer involvement and perhaps add a few more projects. I love to garden, enjoy my book club, and I have even considered doing some oil painting again."

Pauli is a survivor, as are most of the women I talked with for this book.

Following are several fragments, left over from my reworked "Quilt of Life," you might say. They all pertain to life beyond widowhood and are meant to serve as a glimpse into the future, to help make the present more tolerable.

An anonymous father of two, business executive, as quoted in *The Day America Told the Truth*, by James Patterson and Peter Kim, 1991

"...my mother didn't go to college; she didn't go to high school. She was one-dimensional, raised the kids....the night my father died, I stayed up until five o'clock in the morning with our two friends, drinking beer with my mother, which I had never done in my life. And I found out that here was a woman that was incredibly talented, an incredible brain. I thought of her as Mommy. Then, all of a sudden, she's telling me she listens to Itzhak Perlman and all these things when my father wasn't in the house, because he felt threatened that she liked something he didn't understand completely. And I think that was very typical of that generation....what a damn shame...."

MISCELLANEOUS QUOTES FROM RECOVERED WIDOWS

- **"What I am most proud of myself for is that I have come through the test of time without overwhelming debt."**

- "I would rather have my husband still here, but death is final, so second best is independence."

- **"The best part of my new life is that I became an independent woman."**

- "I have come to feel an intrinsic part of creation with infinite connections to the past, an intensified appreciation of the moment. And frequently I laugh at myself for my greediness in soaking it all in."

- **"I'm very proud of the new life I've created. I have wonderful children, grandchildren and friends. I work a little, write poetry, quilt, travel, and I have a good life."**

- I've traveled to Australia, New Zealand, The Netherlands, France, Scotland, England, Ireland, and to many places in the US. I know I would not have done that had my old life remained as it was.

- **"I was widowed with four young children, but I was able to make a living and invest wisely. They all graduated from college—that was a weight lifted! And I was so proud."**

- "The experience of those years has done much to enhance me."

- **"When I look in the mirror I see a woman who is older, wiser, somehow more lovely than before I was widowed."**

- "Of course I've become much more independent. I find myself traveling quite a lot. I surprise me!!!"

- **"I have to wonder whether my husband would still love me if I had become as independent as I am now while he was with me. I would hope so."**

- "I'm certainly not happier, but I am more content than I was. I think it's because I know myself really well now, and I only have to please one person now…me.

AND FROM A FEW OF THEIR FRIENDS...

- "There is a depth to her character that wasn't there before. It makes her far more interesting."

- **"She became a stronger person, a more self identified person, with the death of her spouse."**

- "The significant characteristic I've noticed in her and in you, as well as others who are dealing with grief, is the return of optimism. I don't know how it arrives...but, just like spring, it does!"

- **"And now I see that she moves well, and smiles and laughs often. She seems relaxed and confident."**

- "She has big bundles to manage and she handles it all...She's a jewel."

- **"In my view, she is like she was forty-five years ago...funny, optimistic and loving. It's great to see her blooming!"**

- "I tend to forget all she has been through. But, unfortunately, I doubt she would ever have become the self-sufficient lady she is without that trauma."

- **"I hate to say this about my good friend, but she was a shrinking violet when he was alive. Now she seems to know no limits. She's a marvel."**

**"From inside a dark cocoon,
It's hard to believe you'll ever be a butterfly."**

—Annie

A POEM BY KAREN, OF HER MANY LOSSES

so what is grief you asked
and i
having just received a certificate
in having grieved
had nothing to say
how strange
for me
well
my friend
it's hard to put to words
but grief can be
a gift, a teacher, some tears
it comes with many masks
the mother
of sorrow or relief
and I have paid my dues
and maybe yours and theirs
my parents, my friend,
my child, my husband,
my sister's child
a slice of life
and some would say my heart
but wait
there is a happy ending
no kidding
for grief has softened my edge
absorbed my tears
and given me something
to write about
a focus for my heart
and a new beginning

0-595-29110-4